CORPORATISM
and
COMPARATIVE
POLITICS

■ Comparative Politics Series

Gregory S. Mahler, Editor

COMPARATIVE
POLITICS
SERIES

CORPORATISM
and
COMPARATIVE
POLITICS

The Other Great "Ism"

Howard J. Wiarda

M.E. Sharpe

Armonk, New York
London, England

Library of Congress Cataloging-in-Publication Data

Wiarda, Howard J., 1939–
Corporatism and comparative politics : the other
great "ism" / by Howard J. Wiarda.
p. cm. — (Comparative politics)
Includes bibliographical references and index.
ISBN 1-56324-715-1 (cloth : alk. paper). — ISBN 1-56324-716-X
(pbk. : alk. paper)
1. Corporate state. 2. Comparative government. I. Title.
II. Series: Comparative politics (Armonk, N.Y.)
JC478.W53 1996
320.1—dc20 96-21990
CIP
Printed in the United States of America

The paper used in this publication meets the minimum requirements of
American National Standard for Information Sciences—
Permanence of Paper for Printed Library Materials,
ANSI Z 39.48-1984.

BM (c) 10 9 8 7 6 5 4 3 2 1
BM (p) 10 9 8 7 6 5 4 3 2 1

Contents

Preface

From time to time, entire disciplines and fields of study are challenged—turned topsy-turvy, forced to rethink and reexamine all their earlier assumptions and ways of approaching their subject matter—by the impact of a single concept or a new approach. We call such approaches *conceptual models* or *paradigms;* when a fundamental change occurs in how we understand or conceptualize a particular subject matter or approach to the discipline, we call that a *paradigm shift.*[1] In this book the disciplines and fields of study we are talking about where this shift has occurred are political science, political sociology, and political economy, particularly the subfields within these disciplines of comparative politics (Latin America, Western Europe), comparative development, and comparative public policy studies. And the concept or paradigm that has forced this rethinking, this reconceptualization, this paradigm shift, is corporatism.

Since the late 1960s, corporatism, or the corporative approach, has emerged as one of the leading approaches in these fields. Corporatism has taken its place alongside liberal-pluralism and Marxism (both explained in chapter 1) as one of the three main approaches in these several fields. For this reason, we call corporatism "the other great 'ism'" because it now stands next to these other two as the third great paradigm—though far less known than the other two—in the social sciences. The emergence of this new approach has sparked great controversy as well as a vast outpouring of case studies and new theoretical writing designed to test and explain the corporatist paradigm.

While we have an abundance of literature on liberal-pluralism and its relations to the comparative politics approach to the developing nations, known as developmentalism; and while the literature on Marxism and its relations to dependency theory and political economy is similarly extensive; we lack a single, clear, readable exposition of the corporatist approach. Corporatism has been the subject of a large number of case studies in various parts of the world, and there is some theoretical writing on the subject, mainly from political economists and Western European specialists, that dates to over twenty years ago; but there is no one, single volume that pulls all these case studies together into a comprehensive whole, examines corporatism from a comparative and dynamic perspective, and at the same time seeks to update and provide new perspectives on the large theoretical and political-sociological issues involved.

This book seeks to accomplish these purposes—and more. It summarizes the vast but largely case-study-oriented corporatism literature, explores the theory and intellectual history of this concept and its complex dimensions, and provides an overview of the corporatist approach and its contributions to the several scholarly fields where its impact has been the greatest. In the course of the book, we explore the reasons for corporatism's resurgence as a concept and a frame of reference. We are also interested in the sociology of corporatism, its distinct forms in different areas, corporatist political economy, and the dynamics of change within the corporatist framework. Nevertheless, even with all these subject areas, what is presented here is not a complete analysis of corporatism in all its manifestations but an interpretive overview of it.

Make no mistake about it, corporatism is a controversial subject, and there is a lot of misunderstanding surrounding it. Many identify corporatism with fascism from an earlier era; others confuse it with the modern business corporation; still others try to dismiss corporatism or wish it away, preferring to hang on to the earlier approaches even though they may no longer represent accurate or complete pictures of social and political reality. But the corporatism phenomenon cannot be so easily dismissed, and certainly the societies and political institutions organized on a corporatist basis or exhibiting corporatist characteristics are not about to disappear simply because some writers wish they would. Corporatism is here to stay!

It is important to acknowledge up front, especially to an American audience, the political sensitivity associated with drawing attention to corporatism and elevating it to the status of a viable political alternative. The topic is sensitive because the individualistic and liberal-pluralist ethos and ideology are so strongly ingrained in the American political consciousness. Americans are often reluctant to admit the power of certain groups in our society to control the economic and political system. But powerful interest groups tied into a strong state are precisely what corporatism is all about. Moreover, that seems to be the direction—despite recent talk about privatization, downsizing, and the like—in which we and other modern as well as developing nations are heading. This book helps get the corporatism phenomenon out of the closet and onto the table for examination and discussion.

At the same time, there remains great confusion about corporatism: Is it an ideology like Marxism or liberalism? Is it a form of social and political organization found in various countries? Is it a new and important social science approach? Or is it, somehow, all of these? This book seeks to sort through the controversies and confusion surrounding corporatism in order to arrive at some careful, balanced conclusions about this new (but also very old) concept.

Let us here define corporatism provisionally as a system of social and political organization in which major societal groups or interests (labor, business, farmers, military, ethnic, clan or patronage groups, religious bodies) are integrated into the governmental system, often on a monopolistic basis or under state guidance, tutelage, and control, to achieve coordinated national development. Even using this preliminary definition (we discuss these matters fully in chapter 1) we can see that a country or regime based on corporatism is going to be quite different from one based on liberal-pluralism (where interest groups are free and independent from the state) and from Marxism as well, because corporatism likes to claim that it is based on group and class harmony rather than on the Marxist concept of class conflict.

But corporatism can also take many different forms: quasi-medieval, as in some parts of Latin America; ethnic- or clan-communal, as in many areas of Africa or the Middle East; Confucian-communal, as in Asia; or the modern, participatory, social-welfare forms, as in Western Europe. Corporatism may take statist or authoritarian forms, or it may take more liberal and democratic forms; it can be present in one form in developing nations and another form in developed ones. Corporatism is thus present in many types of societies and regimes, and it may well be growing (*creeping corporatism*) in the United States. But if corporatism exists in so many forms and in so many different societies, what is its usefulness as an explanatory device for the social sciences? This book provides answers to these questions by examining the complex, multifaceted dimensions of corporatism worldwide and its impact on and gradual acceptance in the fields of comparative politics, Latin American studies, European studies, political sociology, and the developing nations.

This book seeks to fill a vacuum in these fields and on this important subject by providing a brief, readable, comprehensive overview of corporatism and the corporatist approach. In successive chapters we examine the phenomenon of corporatism in its several dimensions: the history and political theory of corporatism, the varieties and sociology of corporatism, corporatism's presence in developing and developed nations, its growing importance in the United States, the criticisms that have been leveled against corporatism both as an ideology and as a social science research concept, and at the same time the persistence and even resurgence of corporatism and neo-corporatism in a variety of regimes and policy arenas. Among the provocative questions we wrestle with is whether corporatism can help the developing nations bridge the transition from traditional institutions to modern ones; another challenging issue is whether corporatism in its newer ("neo") forms is almost inherently present in the large-scale, bureaucratic, and statist social-welfare-oriented political systems (including those in the United States, Western Europe, and Japan) of the advanced industrialized nations.

This book has been written for the use of students in undergraduate and graduate comparative politics courses; courses on political development; on Western Europe, Latin America, and other developing nations; and courses in political sociology, political economy, and public policy. Political theorists might also find it of interest, since it deals with one of the major ideologies and theoretical constructs of the twentieth century; as would students of American politics, who can use this book to place the United States' experience in a broader comparative perspective. Scholars as well as general readers interested in the political sociology of modern society may also find intriguing themes and ideas in the book.

Research for this and related studies was undertaken with the aid of grants from the American Philosophical Society, the National Endowment for the Humanities, the Fulbright Program, and the Faculty Research Council of the University of Massachusetts. Institutional support came from Harvard University's Center for International Affairs, the Political Science Department at the University of Massachusetts, the National Defense University in Washington, DC, and the

Center for Strategic and International Studies. Catherine Fisk, Michael J. Kryzanek, Larman Wilson, Ieeda Siquera Wiarda, and Gregory Mahler have read and commented on all or parts of the manuscript. Patricia Kolb has been a particularly good editor, and Doris Holden, as always, a superb typist. It is the author alone, however, who is responsible for both the analysis and the occasional barbs directed at other corporatism scholars that may follow.

Howard J. Wiarda

Note

1. Thomas Kuhn, *The Structure of Scientific Revolutions* (Chicago: University of Chicago Press, 1971).

CORPORATISM
and
COMPARATIVE
POLITICS

1

Corporatism and Comparative Politics

During the past fifty years—ever since World War II—there have been two great, rival, alternative approaches in the field of comparative politics, and in development studies and the social sciences more generally. These two approaches, or paradigms, are: (1) liberal-pluralism and (2) Marxism. Liberal-pluralism was largely found in the Western, democratic nations (the United States and Western Europe), and in these approaches scholars in these countries used to study comparative politics; while Marxism, otherwise known as *scientific socialism,* although not entirely absent in the Western tradition, remained a distinctly minority strain there and was concentrated more in the Soviet Union, the Eastern bloc countries, and a number of developing nations—for example, China, Cuba, Vietnam, North Korea. It is obvious even from these opening comments that not only did liberal-pluralism and Marxism serve as the two major competing approaches in the social sciences for many decades, but also that these two *intellectual paradigms* were products of, bound up with, and a part of the Cold War, superpower rivalry of the last half-century.

To these two major, more familiar approaches has now been added a third major approach: corporatism. The recent resurgence of corporatist approaches to studying comparative politics, the politics of developing nations, public policymaking in advanced industrial societies, and a variety of issues relating to social change, labor relations, social welfare policies, and other topics had their origins in the 1960s and 1970s when a number of pioneering scholars suggested that neither the liberal-pluralist nor the Marxian approaches were fully adequate to treat the new phenomena they were observing in their studies. These new phenomena included the incorporation of interest groups *into* the decision-making machinery of the modern state; social pacts to guarantee labor peace, involving unions, management, and government regulators; industrial policies undertaken by various governments that involved obligatory participation by business and labor; and public policy in the areas of social security, welfare reform, education, and social and economic change more generally in which the state, or government, specified which groups had to be brought in and consulted both in the making of the policy and its implementation. In none of these issues and policy areas did the traditional liberal-pluralist approach, or the Marxian one, prove adequate or provide the intellectual framework to fully comprehend the processes involved. Either these approaches were silent on the topics or they furnished inadequate categories for coming to grips with and understanding them. It is in this context that the corporatist approach arose, because it did seem to offer the intellectual framework that was either lacking or incomplete in the other main approaches.

Here, then, is the contribution and the attraction that the corporatist approach provided: it offered us a handle, a method, an approach for understanding some new social, economic, and political phenomena (the role of the state, the formal incorporation of interest groups into government decision making, new areas of public policymaking, and so on) that the other approaches failed to provide. The corporatist approach was and is primarily an honest attempt by scholars to understand some new phenomena in modern societies (for example, the increasing rationalization and bureaucratization of society, the changing structure of labor and industrial relations, the involvement of interest groups in actual policymaking and implementation), to respond to new socioeconomic and political phenomena that the liberal-pluralist and Marxist models were not especially helpful in providing. In this sense the corporatist approach should be seen as going beyond the earlier approaches and providing students of comparative politics (as well as policymakers) with a set of conceptual tools for understanding modern politics.

But at the same time, the corporatist approach should be seen, in my view, not as entirely supplanting these other earlier approaches but as complementing them in various ways and helping to provide answers to questions for which the other paradigms proved inadequate. Meanwhile (and this is the fun and often controversial part), the study of corporatism and even the term itself became caught up in many of the ideological, political, and intellectual battles that surrounded and came to characterize the liberal-pluralism and Marxism approaches, often confusing or complicating the issues and causing great controversy. Let us try to explain.

Liberal-Pluralism, Marxism, and Corporatism: The Three Great "Isms" of the Modern World

Liberal-pluralism, Marxism, and corporatism have for a long time offered competing perspectives on society, governance, and state–society relations. But they have also, at different times in history, presented competing ideological visions as well. In the next chapter we will focus on the history of corporatism as an idea and ideological movement; here, we try only to explain the basic structural or institutional differences among liberal-pluralism, Marxism, and corporatism. In all three concepts the focus is on the relations between society as represented by interest groups and the state or government, and hence on the dynamics of what are called state–society relations.

In liberal-pluralism, which is often considered to be the dominant reality as well as the main political ideology and approach to studying politics in the United States and Western Europe, interest groups are free, unfettered, and completely independent from the state. Interest groups can organize on any issue; in the modern liberal state there are few if any restrictions on interest-group activities. As a result, there are thousands of interest groups in the United States, at the local, state, and national levels, all competing in the political arena. Such free and vigorous interest-group activity, and the overlapping webs of associations to which most Americans belong (churches and synagogues, unions and business associations, PTAs and grassroots associations, lodges and clubs), have long been considered among the glories of American democracy. Moreover, it is out of the competing interest-group struggle, a long and rich literature in the liberal-pluralist tradition approach suggests, that good and effective public policy emerges. For the plethora of competing groups serves not only to advance a great variety of policy positions but also forces everyone to compromise, to accommodate and reach a democratic solution. And in this intense competition among interest groups, according to liberal-pluralist theory, the state (executive, legislative, judicial branches) plays a relatively minor role. It umpires and referees the group struggle but does not try to control it; the state, in this theory, serves as a transmission belt and filter for interest-group activities, but it does not dominate the process or seek to impose its own purposes on it. In liberal-pluralism, the interest groups and their activities are the main focus of the political system.

Under Marxism and especially in its Leninist form, the opposite characteristics apply: the state is powerful ("the *dictatorship* of the proletariat," as Marx put it), while interest groups are subordinated. Of course we all understand that there are also democratic and parliamentary versions of Marxism (such as in Scandinavia and other Western European countries) in which interest groups are also free, but here we are talking about the totalitarian version of Marxism as it was long practiced in the Soviet Union, Eastern Europe, and other Marxist-Leninist states. The word "totalitarian" itself implies total control: no groups or associations are allowed to exist freely or apart from the state. Under totalitarian Marxism (and fascism too, as practiced in Nazi Germany) the state may create its own, *official* interest groups, but such groups have no independence or autonomy apart from the totalitarian behemoth. Quite unlike liberal-pluralism, under totalitarianism it is the state that makes all the important decisions, while the "interest groups" serve as window-dressing to the regime in power, at times also helping to implement the state's policies. It is one of the hallmarks of such totalitarianism that there is no grassroots participation from below in decision making (through public opinion, elections, interest groups, or in any other way), only top-down authority (from the state or all-powerful government).

Corporatism occupies an intermediary position between liberal-pluralism and Marxian-totalitarianism or fascism. Corporatism's advocates like to say that they represent "the third way," an alternative route to modernization that avoids the disadvantages of the other two. On the one hand, corporatism advocates a strong, guiding, directing state but not one that is totalitarian. On the other, corporatism is usually characterized by state-structured and regulated interest groups, but not by total control as in Marxism-Leninism nor the completely unfettered interest-group struggle (which corporatists argue produces chaos and often paralysis) of liberal-pluralism. At the same time, corporatism advocates class and interest-group harmony over conflict and seeks to accomplish this by incorporating interest groups representing all sectors of society into the decision-making structure of the state. So under

Table 1.1

A Spectrum of Regimes

Liberal-Pluralism	Corporatism	Marxism-Leninism or Fascism
Weak state	Strong, directing state	Total state
Strong interest groups	Structured, limited pluralism of interest groups	Weak, totally controlled interest groups

corporatism we have (1) a strong but not totalitarian state, (2) structured (neither totally controlled nor fully free) interest groups that are usually limited in number and functions, and (3) interest groups that are part of the state—as distinct from completely independent, as found under liberal-pluralism. Whenever we see government control, structuring, or licensing of interest groups, we are likely to see corporatism.

Hence, in picturing the differences between liberal-pluralism, Marxian or fascist totalitarianism, and corporatism, we need to think of a spectrum rather than either-or choices (see Table 1.1). At one end of the spectrum (liberal-pluralism) we have a weak state and, usually, strong interest groups. At the other, Marxist-Leninist or fascist, end of the spectrum we have a totalitarian state and weak, totally controlled interest groups. In between, where corporatism lies, we have a strong (but not total) state and structured interest groups (partly free, partly controlled) that are limited in number. Different regimes may be strung out at various points on this spectrum, including some that may involve varying degrees or combinations of these features.

A considerable variation in types of regimes may be found within the corporatism category. Some corporatist systems (such as those in Scandinavia) allow relatively free interest groups, permit widespread public participation, and have a limited state; this is usually referred to as "societal corporatism," "open corporatism," "democratic corporatism," or "corporatism of free associability." This version of corporatism is often based on a constitution or contract or series of contracts negotiated between the state and its component corporate units (business, labor, agriculture, religious groups, military, etc.) that spell-out the rights and responsibilities of all parties—giving corporatism a legal, constitutional, and democratic character. Other corporatist systems (such as Franco's Spain or Salazar's Portugal) had a strong state and strict controls over interest-group activity; these regimes can verge on dictatorship, authoritarianism, even fascism. We must remember, therefore, that there are "hard" as well as "soft" versions of corporatism, secular as well as religiously based corporatism (more on this in chapter 2), open as well as closed systems of corporatism, participatory versus exclusionary corporatism, democratic versus authoritarian versions of corporatism.

While considerable variation exists among corporatist regimes, the distinguishing characteristics seem to be (1) a strong, directing state—stronger than most Americans with our freewheeling pluralism and freedom would be willing to allow, (2) restrictions on interest-group freedom and activity, and (3) incorporation of interest groups into and as part of the state system, responsible both for representing their members' interests in and to the state *and* for helping the state to administer and carry out public policies. In other words, under corporatism, interest groups often become part of the state, incorporated into it; they are agencies that are no longer just private but that have taken on *public* responsibilities. We need to keep these criteria in mind as we consider in chapter 6 the growth of corporatism in the United States.

Furthermore, some corporatist systems have mixes of, for example, corporately represented bodies whose members are chosen by functions (military, religion, agriculture, commerce, industry, etc.) and democratically elected chambers whose members are chosen on the basis of one person, one vote. So, just as corporatism in its "open" or "societal" varieties can verge toward liberal-pluralism on one end of our spectrum of regimes and toward dictatorship and totalitarianism (Mussolini's Italy) on the other, there can also be—as we see in greater detail in chapter 4—liberal-pluralist systems that begin verging toward corporatism (the United States at present) as well as Marxian-socialist regimes (the People's Republic of China, for example) that may have various corporatist features. The discovery, or rediscovery, of corporatism shows that, if nothing else, we need to open our minds to a wide range of regime possibilities and variations that go considerably beyond earlier methods of classifying regimes (dictatorship versus democracy, for example, or liberalism versus fascism).

Overall, what bears emphasis is:

1. Corporatism's emergence as a social science and regime-type alternative to liberal-pluralism and totalitarian Marxism-Leninism or fascism
2. The distinctions in terms of interest groups' freedom versus control and the role of the state in these three types
3. The considerable variety of regimes that can fall under the corporatist category

The Corporatism Phenomenon: How Widespread?

Corporatism may be said to be present when the following conditions apply:

1. Society is organized, in whole or in part, not on an individualistic basis (as in the case, historically, of the United States), but in terms of the functional, societal, or "corporate" units (family, clan, region, ethnic group, military organization, religious body, labor or business unit, interest groups, etc.) that make up the nation.
2. The state seeks to structure, limit, organize, or license these groups as a way of controlling them—limited pluralism.
3. The state tries to incorporate these groups into the state system, converting them into what are often called "private-sector governments"; while the groups themselves seek both to take advantage in terms of programs and benefits for their members from such incorporation, and at the same time preserving some, usually contractually defined (as in a constitution or basic law) autonomy or independence *from* the state.

The countries and regions where these conditions apply, we are now discovering, are far more widespread than anyone had earlier imagined. Moreover, there is little evidence—again, contrary to earlier theorizing—that these countries and regions characterized in whole or in part as corporatist are moving inevitably or universally toward individualism and liberal-pluralism on the U.S. model. Corporatism is not only widespread but also ubiquitous and present not only in a great variety of regimes but also expanding even in countries (like the United States or Western Europe) previously thought to be strongly in the liberal-pluralist mode.

A partial listing of these regimes (a complete discussion is in chapter 4, "The Varieties of Corporatism") will serve not only to show how widespread corporatism is and its considerable varieties but also to give a clearer picture of what is meant by and encompassed in the term "corporatism":

- In the communalist, organic, Confucian, group-oriented, non-individualist, clan, family, tribal, and local community-oriented societies of East and Southeast Asia, one can find the germs of corporatist society—the forerunners of the modern corporatism of Japan and other countries.*
- Latin America is primarily Western in its culture, religion, politics, and society; but it is also a colonial offshoot of sixteenth-century Spanish and Portuguese Europe and organized historically on a group, communal, clan, family, and organic basis.
- Africa is also organized in part on a clan, ethnic, or tribal basis ("precorporatism"), which many scholars are now seeing as more important than the often artificial national boundaries imposed by the colonial powers.
- In the cultural and social traditions of India and South Asia, there are similar organic, communal, group-oriented social organizations—such as the caste associations—that can also be seen as providing a "natural corporatist" or "precorporatist" basis to society.
- Similarly, Islamic society contains roots that are strongly clan, tribe, and community-oriented—not all that different from the other corporate or community-based societies listed here.
- Western Europe practices an advanced or social-welfare form of corporatism, where major societal interests are often formally represented inside the state and help carry out social and economic programs on a sectorial (often called "neo-corporatist") basis.
- The United States has long been considered a predominantly lib-

---

*The author's earliest writings on corporatism were concentrated on Latin America and Southern Europe. But—and this is one of the pleasures of writing in a public forum—as a result of these writings, the author received numerous communications from Asia and other areas saying, "Oh, your model applies in my country [India, Thailand, South Africa, South Korea, Saudi Arabia, Egypt, Tanzania, Japan, the Philippines] as well."

eral and individualistic country, but as we see in chapter 6, this is now changing as the United States too moves toward a more sectorally and functionally based society.

- Russia, the Commonwealth of Independent States, and Eastern Europe (the former Soviet Union and its empire) evidence considerable corporatist influence from their past histories; even under communism there was a sectoral (workers, peasants, military, intelligentsia) organization of society. Now in the wake of the Cold War and the breakup of communism, some of these historic communalist traits are being resurrected or reorganized; but in many of the former communist states there is still great confusion as to which form of society (liberal-pluralist, corporatist, authoritarian, revived communism, various mixed forms) will prevail.

This brief survey illustrates two major theses of the book: (1) how widespread corporatism is in different regions and countries of the world; and (2) the different forms that corporatism may take, ranging from "natural" or "historical-cultural" corporatism in its tribal, ethnic, regional, or social group-oriented forms, to the modern welfare-state forms of postindustrial European and North American society.

We will have more to say on these different regional kinds of corporatism, the several varieties of corporatism, and the dynamic factors that help account for the changes from one form of corporatism to another later in the book.

The Corporatism Phenomenon: Why So Controversial?

It is clear not only that has corporatism had a profound effect on the social sciences, offering a third and alternative social science model to liberal-pluralism and Marxism, but also that it is widespread, characteristic of a wide variety of regimes and movements in both the Third World of developing nations and the First World of modern industrial states. For a long time (about forty years) corporatism was largely neglected by social scientists and students of comparative politics who saw it as a throwback to the 1930s and World War II. But in recent years corporatism has reemerged—although not without great controversy. As we go through the following list of reasons as to why corporatism is so controversial, we will see that this concept, like many concepts in the social sciences, is loaded with political, ideological, and emotional baggage. But this is even more so in the case of corporatism.

In this section we merely introduce the reasons for the controversy surrounding corporatism. Later in the book we discuss these issues in more detail.

1. In the popular mind, corporatism is, or was, often associated with fascism and therefore carries highly emotional connotations. That is because in the 1920s and 1930s such fascists and semifascists as Mussolini in Italy, Hitler in Germany, Franco in Spain, and Salazar in Portugal used, in part, a corporatist system of organizing their economies and political systems. But in fact, corporatism can take many forms, left and center as well as right, Christian as well as secular, socialist as well as fascist.*

2. A second, related reason for the controversy is that corporatism is often assumed by historians to be a product of the period between World Wars I and II, a thing of the past now superseded. But in fact, not only is corporatism now reemerging in various regimes and forms, but we are also discovering that many supposedly liberal and pluralist regimes have been practicing a disguised form of corporatism for many years.

3. In the past corporatism was often denounced by its opponents as a "smokescreen" for authoritarianism or as a "confidence trick" played on workers. In some regimes and in some circumstances, corporatism may have been or done these things. But corporatism has also had many other and often more positive usages: as a way of organizing diverse and fragmented societies; as a means of filling a void in a nation's associational or organizational life; as a way of centralizing and concentrating political power; as a system of organizing and implementing social programs; as a way of integrating both business and working-class elements into political society or, alternatively, of controlling and regulating their participation; and as an alternative model

---

*The association of corporatism with fascism was brought vividly home to the author when he lectured on corporatism in the Netherlands. An elderly member of the audience came up afterward and told the author that he had fought against corporatism, the German occupation, and fascism during World War II while trying to liberate his country from the Germans, and therefore that it was difficult for him to accept either the resurgence of corporatism or that it could be used as a neutral, social science term.

of society that seeks to preserve unity, class harmony, and a sense of community as modern mass society begins to emerge.

4. A connection has been discovered between corporatism and capitalism and between corporatism and big bureaucratic states. Indeed some analysts have gone so far as to argue that some form of corporatism is virtually inevitable in all large, advanced, industrial societies where there are strong currents of national economic planning and modern social-welfare programs, and hence the need to rationalize and organize societal interest groups to provide input into and to help implement these programs. Could it be, in other words, that all big, advanced, bureaucratic societies evolve toward a system of corporatist organization?

5. Corporatism is often accused of being a right-wing, conservative, and elite-directed way of dealing with the great pressures brought on by industrialization and modernization, and indeed corporatism has often provided a basis for conservative and/or authoritarian politics. But we know now that corporatism can also take liberal, pluralist, populist, social-democratic, socialist, and even communist directions; after all, Joseph Stalin, the communist dictator of the USSR, once accused his one-time partner and later foe Leon Trotsky of being a corporatist.

6. In the study of corporatism, some intense personal, scholarly, national, and regional rivalries and jealousies are involved. Corporatism began as a European phenomenon, then was revived in the area of Latin American studies, from whence it spread back to Europe once again. But the Europeanists seldom acknowledge the Latin Americanists' contributions to the literature; Latin Americanists are seldom aware of what the Europeanists are researching; and meanwhile other areas (Africa, Asia) have come up with their own versions of corporatism that are seldom known to the other two.

7. Corporatism, in some of its manifestations, has not been very acceptable to reformers. For corporatism is not just a set of political, economic, and social institutions; in some societies the corporate, organic, group-oriented way of thinking and acting is so deeply embedded in the society that it has become part of the political culture. If corporatism is so entrenched, then it will likely require two or three generations to change, not just some revision in the legislation. And that kind of cultural continuity as well as the long time span are often unacceptable to those who wish a more a rapid reform.

8. Recently, corporatism has begun to be popular again as an ideology, in ways that have not been the case since the 1930s. Because of the lingering connotations of fascism, it is seldom explicitly called corporatism; instead the terms used are communalism, solidarism, cooperatism, or even ethnic pride. All of these terms refer to the renewed longing for a sense of community, togetherness, and belonging that seem to have been eroded under the pressures of modern, impersonal, bureaucratic, mass society. But it was precisely the attempts to maintain or recapture the communalist community ties and values that helped give rise (see chapter 2) to corporatism in the first place.

9. Finally, and most importantly for the purposes of this book, corporatism is controversial because it serves as an alternative social science/comparative politics approach to the other great "isms" of the modern world: Marxism and liberal-pluralism. Particularly in its more religious and Christian-democratic manifestations, corporatism has long been strongly opposed to Marxism and Marxism-Leninism; and now with the collapse of the Soviet Union and the disintegration and discrediting of Marxist-Leninist regimes virtually everywhere, the Marxist approach is in strong disrepute. But corporatism often also stands in contrast to the dominant liberal-pluralist approach of American and European social sciences and presents an alternative approach and model. This has earned corporatism the antipathy of those who *truly believe* in liberal-pluralism; more than that, the corporatist approach has challenged the currently dominant liberal-pluralist orientation of American foreign policy to refashion governments abroad—especially in the Third World, where many of them are founded on corporatist principles—in the American liberal-individualist mold as wrongheaded, ethnocentric, and destructive of local institutions and ways of doing things. So the debate over corporatism not only has important comparative politics and social science implications but also is crucial in thinking about American foreign policy as well.

Over the past three decades, these issues and themes have stimulated an enormous amount of interest in the corporatism phenomenon. Moreover these are important and very controversial themes. They get at the heart of many of the key issues of national and cross-national social and political development and public policy, and they importantly affect the way we perceive, grapple with, and seek to understand not just foreign societies (where corporatism has long and often been strong) but also that of the United States (where corporatism is growing). At the same time, corporatism and its attendant implications touch some raw political and ideological nerves. The corporatism issue has received so much attention precisely because it relates to and impacts the most important issues of our day.

The Four Forms of Corporatism

Corporatism tends to emerge in societies that emphasize group or community interests over individual interests. The strong individualism of the United States, for example, helps explain why, until recently, corporatism seldom found a receptive breeding ground in America (more on this in chapter 6). Earlier, we had provided some preliminary guideposts to help us identify where and when corporatism was present: (1) a strong but not a totalitarian state; (2) interest groups that are usually limited in number; and (3) interest groups that are part of the state, usually existing in some form of contractually defined relation to the state, rather than complete independence from it as in liberal-pluralism. Whenever we see government control, structuring, or licensing of interest groups, we said, we are likely to find corporatism present.

Corporatism exists in a number of forms, cultures, and time periods, which makes it difficult to offer a single definition that covers all its forms. For now, let us keep in mind our "guideposts" rather than try to formulate a final definition, because in many respects corporatism represents a mood, a way of thinking (functionalist, statist, communalist), an approach that defies hard-and-fast rules. Here we try to explain what corporatism is, to try to understand it; later we offer a formal definition.

In this study we identify four forms of corporatism. These four forms have existed in different time periods, but there is often a progression or evolution from one form to the next. Moreover, as would naturally occur during an evolution, there can be various mixed forms, thus accounting for the considerable diversity of corporatisms that we find. In addition, because there is a progression from one form to the next, we posit that there are dynamic factors—explainable using the corporatist model—that help account for the changes. In this introductory chapter we present these four forms of corporatism and offer brief comments on the dynamics of change from one to another; later in the discussion, we elaborate on these themes in greater detail. The four forms of corporatism are: (1) historical or "natural" corporatism; (2) ideological corporatism; (3) manifest corporatism; and (4) modern neo-corporatism. In addition to these four forms of corporatism, we also offer at the end of this discussion some preliminary considerations concerning a general model of corporatism.

1. Historical or "Natural" Corporatism

Historical or "natural" corporatism can be found in a great variety of premodern societies, especially those founded on traditions that emphasize solidarity, group identity, and community. Such societies tend to value group solidarity over individualism, which is what makes it hard for many U.S. foreign assistance programs—based naturally on the American tradition of individual initiative—to operate successfully in these societies, a theme to which we shall return later. By historical or natural corporatism we have in mind the ethnic, clan, and tribal basis of much of African politics; the emphasis on group and community that ties together many of the Confucian-based societies of East Asia; the similarly group-, clan-, and caste-based societies of South Asia; and the solidarist conceptions that tie together ruler and ruled into mutually supportive roles in those societies based in part on the Koran. Even in the West, by which we mean Western Europe (before the onslaught of the Renaissance, the Enlightenment, and the Industrial Revolution), there were many natural-corporatist institutions: the extended family, the neighborhood, the community, the parish, regional and ethnic loyalties (now often being reasserted), military orders, guilds, the Roman Catholic Church and its orders, and the aristocracy or nobility. These are all *historic* corporatist institutions; they tend to have been there almost from time immemorial, to have grown *naturally* in the society.

Historical or natural corporatism is often the glue, the cement, that holds together societies in their early premodern stages. It emphasizes the seemingly natural, timeless, and basic institutions of society. It often predates the formation of the modern nation-state. It is frequently a part of the historical political culture of the society; hence the emphasis in the analyses of some writers on the connections between culture and corporatism. Rulers of the emerging or new states may try to use these historic and natural corporatist institutions as a basis for their own power, as a way of holding society together during the early, difficult stages of modernization and nationhood, or as a way to emphasize local or nativist values and institutions to keep out intruding foreign ones. At the same time, the historic corporate groups may try to keep the ruler or the emerging nation-state at arms length as a way of retaining their own identity. Usually in the first stages of modernization a tug-of-war goes on between the central state trying to establish, consolidate, or augment its power, versus the corporate groups that want to keep autonomy and a contractually defined independence from the central state. Where the central state completely snuffs out these autonomous corporate units, tyranny, absolute despotism, and dictatorship usually result; but where the corporate bodies continue to exist in some mutually satisfactory and legally defined relationship to the central state, that is usually called "constitutionalism," even "democracy," in the emerging nations. But note how different that is from American-style constitutionalism.

Very often these historic, "natural," and precorporatist groups continue to exist after the formation of the nation-state and in some, often uneasy relations with it. Witness the continuing importance of ethnic institutions in Africa, caste associations in India, tribal rights in states based on the Koran, and the Roman Catholic Church and the armed forces (heirs to the tradition of autonomous military orders) in Latin America. In Asia too, it is clear that group, community, and solidarist features persist into the modern age, standing in marked contrast to American-style individualism, often making it difficult for Westerners to understand these countries where Confucianism still holds considerable sway. The central government must then negotiate with these groups or snuff them out, which is becoming less acceptable; the result is a type of corporatism that often looks considerably different from the Western or European type.

2. Ideological Corporatism

The emphasis on the individual and on individual rights accelerated in the West during the eighteenth-century Enlightenment; in the course of the French Revolution beginning in 1789, and subsequently throughout most of the rest of Europe, group rights (of the Roman Catholic Church, the guilds, and other groups) were extinguished. Thereafter, at least in the West, the atomistic individual ruled supreme, while the older system of historic or natural corporatism was snuffed out.

But many, especially Catholics and conservatives, rejected what they saw as an excessive emphasis on the individual and longed for the solidarity, organized society, and group rights of the *ancien régime*. At first their message was entirely reactionary, an attempt to turn the clock back to a bygone *status quo ante*. However, beginning in the mid-nineteenth century, as we see in more detail in the following chapter, a number of writers, intellectuals, and religious figures began to formulate a more positive response to the alienation and anomie of the modern, industrial age. They called their new ideology *corporatism,* and throughout the remainder of the nineteenth century and the early decades of the twentieth their philosophy and recommendations gained many adherents. Corporatism became the "other great ism," alongside liberalism and Marxism, of the twentieth century.

Under corporatism, society was to be organized not on an individualistic or liberal basis but in terms of society's component groups: the family, the parish, the neighborhood, organized labor, fishermen, peasants, business, industry, religion, armed forces, university students, professional associations. These groups would help decide economic and social policy; they, along with the state, would regulate their own members. Rather than on an individual, one person, one vote basis, representation in government bodies under corporatism would be on a group basis: seven seats for the military, eight for business, and so on. A number of "corporations," representing both labor and management, would be created to help regulate wages, prices, and production in specific industries. In this way, group interests and solidarity would become stronger than the individual ones as represented in liberalism; similarly, the class-conflict model of Marxism would be replaced by the presumedly class harmony model of corporatism.

The corporatist ideology proved to be very attractive early in the twentieth century in societies where liberalism and individualism seemed to be producing near-anarchism (Spain, Portugal), where class conflict was feared to be getting out of hand or producing conditions for a Bolshevik-like revolution (Germany, Italy), and/or where the state or government needed to get a handle on the national economy in the face of depression or completely unbridled capitalism and its accompanying social ills (virtually all countries). In fact, throughout Europe as well as Latin America, corporatism was extremely popular as an ideology during the 1920s, 1930s, and early 1940s (before the end of World War II). Hundreds and even thousands of books, articles, and

news stories were written about it. Corporatism was becoming so popular that a Romanian political philosopher wrote a book in French that
became a best-seller throughout Europe in which he proclaimed that
the twentieth century would be the century of corporatism just as the
nineteenth had been the century of liberalism.[1]

It should be noted that there were several different forms of corporatism at this time. Some were authoritarian, some more democratic. Some
were religiously based, grounded for example on the Catholic encyclicals *Quadregessimo Anno* and *Rerum Novarum*, while others were secular in orientation. Some provided only for group representation, while
others combined this with geographic or individualistic representation.
The unifying feature in all these regimes, however, was the emphasis on
group rights and representation over that of individualism. In the hey-
day of corporatism between World Wars I and II, Austria, Belgium,
France, Germany, Greece, Holland, Hungary, Italy, Norway, Poland,
Romania, Portugal, Spain, Sweden, and Switzerland all were attracted
to or experimented with various forms of corporatism.

It was only in the West (Europe and, by extension, Latin America)
that historical or natural forms of corporatism turned eventually into a
full-fledged ideology of corporatism. Other areas—Africa, Asia, areas
under Islamic sway—often continued to practice their historic forms of
corporatism, group solidarity, and communitarianism but without developing ideological corporatism. One suspects the reason for this lack
of a corporatist ideology is that these non-Western societies were never
inundated—until recently—by the West's emphasis (exaggerated,
some would say) on individualism. So these societies continued to
practice their historic and natural forms of corporatism on into the
modern era. Only when they too began to be impacted by the onslaught
of Western-style individualism and capitalism in the late-twentieth
century did these areas also begin to fashion a corporatist philosophy
both to manage the processes of modernization and to help preserve
their traditional, group-oriented ways (more on this in chapter 3).

3. Manifest Corporatism

Corporatism sounded nice on paper, in theory, perhaps even as an
ideology (solidarity, community, class harmony), but in actual practice
corporatism did not work out very well—at least in the short term and
in terms of the kinds of corporatist regimes that actually came to

power. Fascist Italy, Nazi Germany, Vichy France, Franco's Spain, Salazar's Portugal, Metaxas's Greece, Dolfuss's Austria, Vargas's Brazil, Perón's Argentina—none of these were exactly happy, friendly, admirable regimes. All of these began—or turned rather quickly, once in power—to authoritarian or totalitarian forms of rule. Their human rights records were often atrocious at best. Rather than presiding over a system of class harmony, these corporatist regimes frequently used dictatorial means to suppress *all* interest groups—especially organized labor. So it is not surprising that with the defeat of Germany and Italy in World War II, the ideology and system of government associated with them should be thoroughly discredited—even though in some countries (Argentina, Brazil, Portugal, Spain) authoritarianism continued to linger on although now de-emphasizing their discredited and manifestly corporatist aspects.

The corporatist regimes of the interwar period faced numerous similar problems, which help account for the failure of these forms of manifest corporatism. First, the storm clouds of war were already hovering over Europe in the 1930s, making the kind of social engineering envisioned by the corporatist writers and intellectuals difficult at best. Second, the global depression of the 1930s meant that there were inadequate financial resources available for the corporatist restructuring. Third, all these regimes came quickly to realize that they needed big business to keep their governments afloat economically, which meant the business sector of the economy was often able to escape thoroughgoing corporatization. Fourth and related, the control and licensing mechanisms of the corporate state came down heaviest on organized labor, which—in an era ripe with the possibility of Bolshevik revolution—was seen as the greatest threat to the regime in power and a source of potential revolutionary upheaval. Hence the corporatist idea of class harmony became instead one in which the trade unions were suppressed, often viciously so.

Because of the general discrediting, corporatism went into eclipse after World War II. For the next thirty years the term "corporatism" was seldom mentioned. Even in those regimes that continued as corporatist hangovers from the earlier epoch—Franco's Spain and Salazar's Portugal—corporatism was either forgotten or redefined as a system to deliver social welfare. Interestingly, however, in a number of developing nations (Argentina, Brazil, Chile, Egypt, Indonesia, Peru, South Korea, Taiwan, Tanzania, and others) that in the 1960s and 1970s began to experience development problems and crises parallel to those experienced by the European nations in the 1920s and 1930s—rising labor unrest and thus the need for social harmony, a level of pluralism that was producing chaos, the drive to better manage and control national economies requiring closer tightening and coordination—a corporatist system of social organization looked very attractive. But because of the earlier discrediting of corporatism, these newly emerging countries usually preferred to avoid that label and call it something else: "new democracy," "communitarianism," "guided democracy," "tutelary democracy," or something similar. However, if one scratched below the labels, it was often a form of corporatism that one found in these developing nations, aimed at maintaining order in the face of change and at keeping control on increasingly pluralist societies. Corporatism thus continued to be practiced, but it was done in new areas of the world outside of Western Europe and under new guises.

4. Modern Neo-Corporatism

Modern neo-corporatism is very much different from the kind of authoritarian, top-down, and statist corporatism that was characteristic of Europe in the interwar period and of many developing nations in the 1960s and 1970s. Neo-corporatism, which is often called "societal" or "open" corporatism, is characteristically present not in developing nations but in already modern, industrial, social-welfare-oriented countries. Neo-corporatism incorporates societal or interest groups directly into the decision-making machinery of the modern state on such issues as industrial policy, social welfare, pensions, and economic planning. Usually the groups involved in such incorporation are economic: unions, employers, and farmer groups—though, depending on the policy issue, cultural, social, and professional groups may also be involved. Neo-corporatism implies formalized consultation between the state and its major societal interests, with the main difference from U.S.-style pluralism being the incorporation of these groups usually under state auspices *directly* into the decision-making process and their (usually) formal representation and vote (which often implies veto power) on the vast regulatory and planning apparatus of the modern state. Neo-corporatism thus stands in contrast to the historically laissez faire quality and independence from the state of most U.S. interest groups. And, instead of the often authoritarian corporatism of the past, neo-corporatism is clearly compatible with parliamentary democracy, with a form of pluralism, and with modern social welfarism.

Neo-corporatism is mainly present in the advanced European countries where business, labor, and the state have often reached a tripartite agreement, or what is often called a "social pact." Usually such social pacts, carried out under government tutelage and direction, involve labor's giving up its right to strike in return for employers granting wage increases and expanded benefits. Cooperation, consultation, negotiations, and compromise are the usual routes to such agreements, not coercion—which help explain why this is called "modern," "neo," or "societal" corporatism as contrasted with the authoritarian corporatism of the past. Such pacts are mutually beneficial: labor gets more money and benefits, business gets stability and continuous productivity, and the government "buys" social peace.

Neo-corporatism is also present in welfare programs when workers, the unemployed, mothers, older persons, and other groups are brought into a formal consultative role in the administration of social welfare. This entails not just an occasional expressing of views, as in American interest-group pluralism, but a system in which the groups affected become themselves a part of the state agencies responsible for carrying out their programs. Neo-corporatism may also be present when central planning or negotiations over industrial policy is at issue and the state needs to have all the formal interests "on board" for its programs. Or, when wage restraints are necessary and the state wants to assure that both employers and organized labor will accept the new conditions. Neo-corporatism may thus be present in the modern era over a variety of issues—and also in a variety of forms: strong corporatism, as we see in more detail later on, in Austria, Sweden, and Switzerland; weaker corporatism in France, Germany, and Great Britain. But all of them have this in common (which distinguishes corporatism from liberal-pluralism): the formal incorporation of interest groups *into* the actual decision-making apparatus of the modern state, rather than their remaining freewheeling, independent interest groups, as under liberal-pluralism.

5. Corporatism as Social Science Model

Corporatist institutions and practices, we have seen, have now become pervasive in a variety of regimes: developing and developed nations, and authoritarian systems as well as democratic ones. Corporatism and the corporatist approach have become so pervasive, in fact, that they have recently emerged as a distinct model or paradigm in the social sciences. Note that we are here shifting directions in our description and definitions of corporatism. In this fifth and final meaning of the term we are no longer describing a specific regime in a specific region or time frame. Instead, in this last definition we are talking about an approach, an intellectual framework, a way of examining and analyzing corporatist political phenomena across countries and time periods. We are not here trying to present an exact mirror of any single country's corporatist ideology or movement; rather our goal is to provide a general picture, a model, that tells us what to look for if we are interested in studying corporatism.

The attempt here is not to present a formal or mathematical model of corporatism, as is often done in the natural sciences, but to offer a social science model that is necessarily less precise, more informal. Ours is what is called a *verstahen* approach, a way of looking at things, a set of suggestions as to what to look for, an *approach* and a *framework* rather than a quantifiable formula. We seek not some final or absolute model but instead a set of informal guidelines to help direct our thinking, studying, and analysis.

Corporatism is both a description of an existing regime *and* a model, in the same way that both liberal-pluralism and Marxism are, at the same time, both descriptions of existing regimes and models of more general phenomena. When we call a regime liberal-pluralist, it conjures up in our minds such things as elections, checks and balances, competitive interest groups, democracy, and civil liberties. These ingredients are part of the liberal-pluralism *model.* Similarly, when we speak of Marxism or Marxism/Leninism, some of the elements in that model include the labor theory of value, class struggle, the dialectical theory of history, and dictatorship of the proletariat. In like manner we need to ask with regard to the corporatist model, what are the main ingredients in the model and how does that help us better understand distinct political systems?

One of the main ingredients in corporatism is a strong, directing state—either in actual fact or, most often in the developing nations, in aspiration. Along with the strong state, we find a variety of corporate interests: in emerging nations these would include the military, religious bodies, elite groups, and traditional units like the family, clan, or tribe; in developed nations, organized labor, big business, professional associations, modern interest associations, and the like would be included. Under corporatism, the state tries to structure, license, control, and even monopolize this group structure to prevent the competition among the groups from getting out of hand, to better integrate and organize state policy. At the same time, the corporate groups try to maintain some level of autonomy from the state and to bargain with, infiltrate, and/or capture it to promote the best interests of their members. This dynamic between state and society, this tension and struggle, lies at the heart of the theory of corporatism, just as individual freedom lies at the heart of liberalism and class struggle lies at the heart of Marxism.

If the state–society arena is the dominant arena in the theory of corporatism, then how does the corporatist framework help us understand comparative politics and public policy? At this point we are getting close to the usefulness and practicality of corporatism as a theory. Keeping in mind this state–society arena, I have found that using the corporatist framework is especially helpful in thinking and analyzing such public policy issues as social security, labor relations, industrial policy, and wage policy. The corporatist framework in its neo-corporatist form is also useful in examining health care, education policy, housing programs, and a host of other public policy issues.

But more than these public policy issues, I find the corporatist framework assists in examining comparatively the balance of power in society, the relations between labor and management, the increase (or decline) in the power of the state, the interrelations of interest groups and their tie-ins with bureaucratic agencies, which interests groups are rising and falling in influence and power, and how change and development (social, economic, political) occur in society and how these are related to the dynamics of modernization, industrialization, and societal evolution. In short, most of the big issues in comparative politics, in both developed and developing nations, can be usefully studied by using the corporatist framework.[2]

In later chapters we will return to this issue of fashioning a dynamic and rigorous model of corporatism, to the relations between the distinct types of corporatism outlined previously and the processes of economic and sociopolitical change, and to the utility of the corporatist framework in helping us to understand political power relations and public policy.

Issues for Consideration

The above discussion has identified four types of corporatism: (1) natural or historical corporatism; (2) ideological corporatism; (3) manifest corporatism; and (4) neo-corporatism. In addition, we have set forth some preliminary ideas about corporatism as a model or framework for analysis. It is important to keep these four types, the comparative framework suggested, and the definitions and discussions of each clearly in mind as we proceed with the discussion. Building on the discussion of these four types and the framework, we now proceed to ask a series of questions and raise key issues that weave like threads, appearing and reappearing, throughout the book.

1. Where does corporatism come from? Does it emerge out of the history and culture of the society, out of political or institutional needs, from economic requirements, from crises, or from some combination of these and other factors?
2. What are the precise relations of corporatism to state–society relations and to such specific groups as organized labor, business, the armed forces, and so on? What are the implications of a corporatist system of state–society relations versus a liberal-pluralist one?
3. What are the dynamics of change within corporatism? This question implies two additional questions:
   a. How do societies move from one form of corporatism to another (from historical or precorporatism, to ideological corporatism, to manifest corporatism, to neo-corporatism)? Is there a progression and evolution involved, and what are the dynamic factors that account for the change? In other words, we are suggesting not only that the four types listed above are a classificatory outline but that there is often a progressive evolution in society from one type of corporatism to the next.
   b. What are the dynamics of change within corporatism? For while some corporatist regimes prove to be static, others are able to respond to change just as effectively (in some cases more so) as liberal-pluralist regimes.
4. What are the specific implications of corporatism for labor relations, economic planning, social welfare, wage policy, and other

social policies? And how does this differ from a liberal-pluralist or a socialist system?

5. Recently we have begun to see patterns of corporatist representation emerging at the international (for example, in the structure of interest-group representation of the European Economic Community [EEC]) as well as at national levels. Is this a new stage of transnational corporatism, and what does it mean?

6. How widespread is corporatism? Corporatism is present, in different forms, in many European countries, throughout Asia and Latin America, and in many developing nations; the United States seems also to be practicing a form of "creeping corporatism." If corporatism is becoming ubiquitous, present in so many regimes and cultures, of what use is it as an explanatory device? Alternatively, can we distinguish more sharply among distinct types and forms of corporatism?

7. Finally, we wrestle with the big philosophical questions: what are the implications of all this corporatism in terms of bigness and bureaucracy, interest-group competition, individualism versus collectivism, and even democracy itself?

Notes

1. Mihail Manoilesco, *Le Siècle du Corporatisme* (Paris: Felix Alcan, 1934).

2. The revival of interest in corporatism in the 1970s paralleled the revival of interest among comparativists in what was called the "relative autonomy of the state." Under liberal-pluralism the state was often seen as a mere reflection of the interest-group competition; in Marxism the state was supposed to "wither away." But clearly during the 1970s the central state and its bureaucracies were becoming more powerful, not less; hence the interest both in corporatism, which posited a strong, directing state, and in the state's position as an autonomous, authoritative if not authoritarian actor independent from interest groups and the class system.

2

The Corporatist Idea
Throughout History

The idea of a corporate, organic, integralist, and functionally organized society has been around for a very long time. In the Western tradition it goes back to ancient Greece, Rome, and the Bible—in short, to the very founding and main pillars of Western civilization. Corporatism was also present in the structure of the medieval estates and society (clerics, nobility, military orders, guilds, commons) and in the struggle between these groups seeking to maintain their independence and the emerging, centralizing, royal absolutism of the late-medieval period. However it was only in the late nineteenth and early twentieth centuries that a full-fledged corporatist ideology emerged, and only in the period between World Wars I and II that manifest corporatist regimes first came to power. Modern neo-corporatism is a product of the post–World War II period and of the emergence of the welfare state and of central economic planning. That is the history traced in this chapter.

It should be emphasized that in tracing this history, it is the Western conception of corporatism that we are analyzing. We do that because (1) it is the tradition most of us are familiar with and know best; and (2) it is out of the Western tradition that a complete corporatist ideology, manifest corporatist regimes, and modern neo-corporatism first emerged. But we should also be aware that in the African tradition of clan, ethnic group, and local community; in the Confucian/East Asian tradition of societal unity, community, and organic solidarity; in the Indian and broader South Asian conception of integral pluralism; and in the Islamic and Middle Eastern focus on tribe, clan group, and consultation between government and governed, there are parallel corporatist conceptions. In fact, it would make a wonderful scholarly term paper or thesis exercise to trace these non-Western corporatist concep-

tions and compare them with the Western ones. Indeed we return to the
theme of non-Western conceptions of corporatism in chapter 4, where
we talk about the many varieties of corporatism. For now, however, we
look at the Western tradition of corporatism, keeping in mind that this
is just one corporatist conception among several.

Origins

The origins of corporatist theory and sociopolitical organization in the
Western tradition may be found in the very origins of Western civilization itself and in the very first expressions of political philosophy: the
Bible, Greek philosophy, and Ancient Rome.[1] These influences helped
give rise to what we have called natural, traditional, or historical corporatism. Recall, however, that other, traditional, non-Western forms
of natural corporatism were also found in Confucianism, Buddhism,
and Islam.

The biblical conception of corporatism comes mainly from Saint Paul
in his letter to the Christians at Corinth (I Corinthians 12:12–31). In this
epistle Saint Paul suggests an organic conception of society and politics,
with all its functional units integrated, harmonized, and performing their
proper function—just as in the human body all the parts are interrelated.
This image of an integrated, organic, functionally organized body,
whether in human form or in terms of the body politic, would prove to be
one of the enduring metaphors throughout the history of Western civilization. Thus, just as in the human body the arms, legs, heart, and mind must
all be interrelated and function like a well-oiled machine, so in society and
politics all the actors must be similarly integrated: religion and governance, economics and politics, lords and peasants, capital and labor. If this
conception of a unified, integrated, functionally harmonious political system is taken seriously—as it was for centuries and still is in many quarters—one could see that it would not always be conducive to U.S.-style
conceptions of the separation of church and state, division of powers,
unfettered individualism, checks and balances, or the clash of interest
groups. And that is just our point: that many societies organized on a
natural-corporatist basis are likely to have very different institutional features and behavior patterns than those considered to provide the best form
of government in the United States.

The second, early, and profound contribution to corporatist thought
comes from Ancient Greece, with the principal influence from Aris-

totle in his book *The Politics*. First, Aristotle believed that society and politics were natural, beneficial, existing through time, not evil or artificial. But if the practice of politics and governance is natural and good, then there is no reason to introduce limited government and checks and balances as in the U.S. Constitution; instead the state can be integral, unified, and even monolithic. Note how closely this Greek conception dovetails with Saint Paul's admonition and the biblical message of an integrated and organic society. Second, Aristotle advanced the notion that society should be organized along "natural" class and functional lines: warriors, the priesthood, slaves, and rulers. Today we no longer accept Aristotle's notion of a "natural" slave or ruling class; nevertheless, his notions that society should be organized along functional or occupational lines, on an ordered and bureaucratic basis, that each unit of society should perform its proper functions, and that all the parts need to be harmonized into an organic whole would prove very attractive to future corporatist writers as well as political leaders.

The third influence on corporatist theory stemming from ancient times comes from Rome. Roman political theorists built on the Greek conceptions (the organic theory of state and society, the functional organization of society, "natural" inequalities among people), but they also added new concepts of their own. First, while the Greeks preserved the concept of direct citizen participation in their small city-states, the far larger Roman empire had a system of indirect representation; significantly, however, representation was to be in part by functions in keeping with the corporatist conception: so many seats for the military authorities, so many for religious representatives, and so on. It was not a U.S.-style, individualistic conception of one person, one vote; rather, it was mainly groups or societal sectors who were represented. Second, Rome had a much more elaborate and organized system of corporate and societal associations, with a variety of military, professional, and religious institutions (often called *colegios*), each with its own charter; these groups were usually monopolistic in character, but the state exercised control over and governed the relations between them. Third, the Romans also introduced the system of republicanism, under which a strong state vied for power with its component corporate or group units; of course, there were also some periods during which they made famous the structure and method of authoritarianism ("Caesarism"). For a long time the conception of

competition and a just balance between the central state and its functionally organized bodies (religious orders, the military, towns and municipal-
ities) would constitute the corporatist conception of "constitutionalism" or
"democracy." Note again that it is democracy based on group rights and
representation, not on individual rights and representation.

In the biblical, Greek, and Roman conceptions, therefore, we can
already find most of the ingredients of twentieth-century corporatism.
These include the organic or unified view of society, the organization
of that society into well-ordered and integrated functional or corporative units, the "licensing" and regulation of these units by the state for
the common good, and an almost constant and dynamic tension between the top-down, authoritarian, and statist form of corporatism and
a more democratic, pluralistic, representative, and societal form.

The Middle Ages

Following the disintegration of the Roman Empire in the fifth century
A.D. and its conquest by what were called "barbarians," the great tradition of Greek and Roman political theory that had been built up over
the preceding centuries was all but lost and forgotten in the West for
many centuries. The sophisticated social and political institutions,
many of them corporatist, that had developed in the Greco-Roman
tradition disappeared or were reduced to small-scale, less elaborate
forms. Social and economic organization reverted to more primitive
forms. Central political authority unraveled, giving rise to more localized units; the quite sophisticated political infrastructure of Greece and
Rome gave way before the "barbarian" takeover. This was the period
of the Dark Ages.

Historians often divide the Middle Ages into two subcategories: the
"low" or "dark" Middle Ages, from the fall of Rome through the tenth
century; and the "high" Middle Ages, from the eleventh century
through the fifteenth. It is the high Middle Ages that we are primarily
concerned with here, leading as they do into the modern era. Nevertheless, even during the earlier period we can see some ingredients that
would go into the later corporatist philosophy: the idea that property
has a social function and was to be used for the good of all; the nascent
theory of a just price and a fair wage, which would be largely set by
the state; the principle (again) of an uneven hierarchy of laws and
persons; and once more the notion of society organized according to its

natural, corporate bodies. In Western Europe this corporatist conception now gained a Christian form from the dominant religious beliefs at the time; hence, for example, the relations of seller and buyer, employer and employee, were supposed to be governed not by conflict and the impersonal market but by Christian notions of brotherhood and "just price."[2] As we shall see, in the twentieth century these two dominant traditions of corporatism were often present—the ancient Roman statist form and the Christian idea of brotherly love, often complementing each other but sometimes competing for power.

During the high Middle Ages, larger-scale social and political organizations began to reappear. These included the mushrooming religious organizations associated with the Roman Catholic Church, especially the religious orders, monasteries, and brotherhoods; a variety of military orders, which had received a stimulus to growth from the Crusades; the towns and cities that began to grow as trade and populations also grew and that were largely self-governing; the universities (among the earliest, Bologna in Italy, the Sorbonne in Paris, London, Salamanca in Spain, Coimbra in Portugal) that similarly emerged as autonomous organizations; and above all the artisan and craft guilds with their hierarchical systems of apprentices, journeymen, and master craftsmen. The guilds licensed and policed their own members, helped regulate trade and prices, and were essentially self-governing professional associations that helped provide both for progress and social peace. It is to the guild system that later corporatist writers often looked for a model of efficient economic management and class collaboration.

Indeed, a traveler in Europe today can still see many of the remnants of this guild and medieval corporatist system (in Brussels, London, Paris, Madrid, Lisbon, Rome, and other cities) in the location of all the silver craftsmen, goldsmiths, and other occupational or functional groups on a single street; each group with its own flag and uniforms, each licensing its own members, each with its own place in the social hierarchy. The entire system of corporative bodies formed during the late Middle Ages—religious and military orders, self-governing towns, autonomous universities, guilds, and so on, with most of these represented in a parliament, council of state, or *cortes*—provided an attractive model (often idealized and romanticized as more peaceful and harmonious than it really was) for those in later and more conflictual times to look back to for inspiration.

This corporate group system ran parallel to, overlapped with, and often encompassed the system of medieval estates with which we are more familiar. The estate system consisted of the primary estate (nobles), the second estate (clergy), and the third estate (common people). This, too, was a system based on hierarchy, rank, and special privileges. But in many countries the structure of society was more complicated: it had the three estates, organized in terms of hierarchical class layers, plus such corporate groups (organized along vertical lines) as the military orders, towns, and so on. The clergy were both an estate and a functional organization. Medieval society was thus often crosscut by both class (horizontal) and functional or corporatist (vertical) divisions, as can be seen in Figure 2.1. But it was not just these corporative groups that were growing during the late Middle Ages; centralized monarchies in France, England, Spain, and Portugal were emerging as well and increasing their powers. For a considerable period these two developments, the growth of both corporate society and the central state, went hand-in-hand and in parallel fashion.

But eventually these two would conflict, since the autonomy and more localized self-government that the corporate entities sought to preserve clashed with the absolutism and centralizing tendencies of the several emerging monarchies. A great deal of political theory at the time analyzed these complementary yet ultimately conflicting trends in late medieval society. Where an equilibrium could be found between the autonomy of the several corporate groups and the power of the central state, society was said to be in "just balance," even "democratic." Indeed, in Europe the earliest notions of limited government and checks and balances revolved around these notions of corporate group rights serving as a countervailing power to limit royal absolutism. Note that in Europe, even in early modern times, democracy, representative government, and checks and balances mainly involved group rights set against the power of the central state, not so much individual rights as enshrined by the United States in its Declaration of Independence and Constitution.

But eventually, in sixteenth-, seventeenth-, and continuing through most of eighteenth-century Europe, absolute monarchy won out. During this period, in France, Spain, Portugal, and even England (where the parliamentary tradition was stronger), the prevailing monarchies succeeded in centralizing power and developing systems of strong authoritarian rule. In the process, the concept of corporate group rights

Figure 2.1 **The Class and Corporate Organization of Medieval Society**

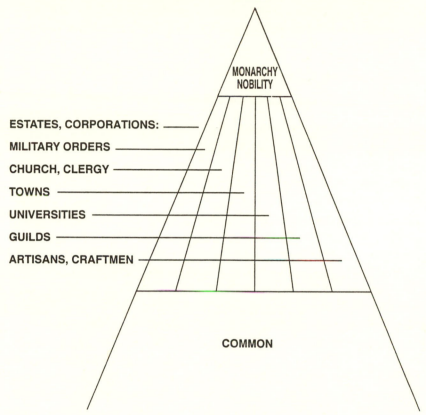

was gradually subordinated to the principles of absolute government. In all the major countries the main corporate groups—military orders, guilds, religious brotherhoods, autonomous towns, independent universities, separate regional authorities, elite families, and the nobility—gradually gave way to the power of the centralizing monarchies. The representative parliaments (*cortes* in Spain), where these groups had often served as a check on encroaching royal absolutism, were all but completely wiped out. The medieval/corporate ideal of representative government and the public good as represented by a corporately organized parliament and well-established group rights serving as a check on royal arbitrariness and tyranny was another victim of the dominant centralizing and absolutist tendencies. The Renaissance, the Enlightenment, the English Revolutions of 1640 and 1688, the rising focus on the individual as opposed to the group in the eighteenth century—were all important influences in the making of the modern age, but for a long time none of them were able to halt this long-range trend, particularly on the continent of Europe, toward absolutism.

The Three Great "Isms":
Liberalism, Socialism, and Corporatism

The French Revolution of 1789 was one of the great turning points in history. Not only did it overthrow the French monarchy and instill the values of liberty, equality, and fraternity (brotherhood) but also, by decree of March 2, 1791, it swept away the guilds and corporate privilege (the special position of the Church and other corporate bodies). The entire structure of a closed, hierarchical, top-down society came tumbling down. Moreover, the abolition of corporate privilege and position in France was followed in subsequent years by their similar abolition in Belgium, Germany, the Netherlands, Portugal, Spain, and other countries. Henceforth it would be individual rights that would receive priority, not so much the corporate or group rights of the past.

By this point we need to start distinguishing between countries, in order to be able to begin to do genuinely comparative analysis. For example, in Great Britain the influence of the older kind of natural or historical corporatism had less of an impact than it did in many of the continental countries. Perhaps that had to do with the more limited impact of the Roman Empire on Great Britain, perhaps with the Magna Carta and the early rise in England of an independent parliament, perhaps with the early democraticizing and liberalizing revolutions of 1640 and 1688. Whatever the reasons, the fact is that corporatism and corporate privilege in England were never as strong historically as they were on the Continent.

Much the same applies to the United States. Because of the absence of a medieval and feudal past, in contrast to the European countries, which experienced feudalism, the estate system, and a tradition of corporate privilege for nearly a thousand years, the United States never had a strong, historical, corporate tradition. Founded in the seventeenth and eighteenth centuries, the United States was "born free," on an individualistic basis, without the legacy of medieval feudalism and corporatism that continental Europe had. We have more to say on more recent, growing corporatism in the United States in chapter 6; here we only need to emphasize that the

United States never had the deeply ingrained natural or historical corporatism that many European countries had.

After France and many other European countries abolished the guilds and corporate privilege in the late eighteenth and early nineteenth centuries, many lamented their passing. The English and French revolutions, and parallel liberalizing developments in other countries, were not necessarily greeted with universal acclamation as ushering in a new era of freedom and democracy. Critics saw society falling apart as a result of this new individualism and its attendant liberties. Some of these critics were political reactionaries who wanted to go back to the stability, discipline, order, and authoritarianism of the ancient (pre-1789) regime. These ranks included many clerics, the nobility, members of the recently deposed royal families, and some military officers. Thus was born in the early nineteenth century the tradition of European conservatism and reaction that persists to this day.

But not all those who lamented the passing of the guilds and corporate society were dyed-in-the-wool reactionaries. Many moderates and thoughtful scholars of society, such as the great French political scientist Alexis de Tocqueville and German legal and sociological scholars Friedrich Hegel, Otto von Gierke, and Max Weber, worried that casting off corporatist organization and the bands that tie society together would result in national disintegration. They feared that, without the social organization of the old regime, and before any new institutions had been created to replace it, society and politics could disintegrate into chaos, upheaval, and civil war. In fact that is what happened in many European countries from the time of the French Revolution of 1789 until society and politics began to settle down and stabilize again around the 1850s.

Until the mid-nineteenth century, the defenders of corporatism were largely in the reactionary camp, but beginning in the 1850s a more realistic and even progressive form and ideology of corporatism began to come to the fore. The major figures in this school included Bishop Wilhelm Ketteler in Germany, Albert DeMun and La Tour du Pin in France, Cardinal Henry Manning in Britain, Karl von Vogelsang in Austria, Giuseppe Bosca in Italy, Kaspar Decurtins in Switzerland, and Monsignor Antoine Pottier in Belgium. Although less well known, this current of corporatist thought began to serve as a popular alternative to the other great currents of contemporary political thought then emerging: liberalism on the one hand and Marxism on the other.[3]

The corporatist writers drew upon some familiar ideas: the utopian communalism of the early nineteenth century, the order-and-national-progress ideas of French philosopher Auguste Comte, the analyses of corporatist social and occupational groups of Hegel and French sociologist Emile Durkheim. They also borrowed from the reformist ideas of French philosophers C.H. Saint-Simon and François LaFarrell, who elaborated guild schemes adapted to the modern age and not just as a throwback to medievalism. Rather than make a sharp break with the past as in the French Revolution, the corporatist writers emphasized a gradual adaption to change, one that blended the benefits of the traditional order with the newer requirements of modernization. New corporative agencies would thus be created for the new middle and working classes as well as for the more traditional groups. In this way corporatism could be flexible, accommodative, and progressive instead of reactionary. Groups rights would continue to be emphasized over individual rights as under liberalism; at the same time, under corporatism class harmony would prevail, as opposed to the class conflict of Marxism.

By the 1870s and 1880s corporatism was emerging as a full-fledged political program and ideology.[4] Although almost entirely unknown in the United States, in Europe the adherents of corporatism were growing in numbers. During the 1870s and 1880s not only was the philosophy of corporatism finding more admirers, but also in France, Germany, and other countries, what were called "Working Men's Circles," which incorporated the corporatist principles of class harmony and employer–employee solidarity, were rapidly being organized as well. Unlike unions, the circles' members included both workers and owners; their goal was to contribute to the good of society as a whole and not just one segment of it.

During this same period, the corporatist ideology, which had largely started in Central and Southern Europe and among Catholic political leaders, developed a Protestant version and adherents and thus spread to the north of Europe as well. Both Catholic and Protestant groups wanted to find a formula that gave social and economic justice to the rising working class (which was rapidly growing in all countries under the impact of industrialization), but without class conflict, revolution, or societal breakdown. Corporatism provided a formula for doing that. Hence, in the last third of the nineteenth century, corporatism steadily gained in popularity and took its place alongside liberalism and Marxism as one of three major ideologies of the nineteenth century (hence the subtitle of this book, *The Other Great "Ism"*).

Corporatism, like liberalism and Marxism, was both a manifest political ideology and a political movement—no longer a system of purely historical interest. In 1881 Pope Leo XIII charged a commission of theologians and social thinkers to study this new ideology and movement in relation to Catholic teachings. They met at the German university city of Freiburg in 1884, and gave corporatism its first official definition as a "system of social organization that has at its base the grouping of men according to the community of their natural interests and social functions, and as true and proper organs of the state they direct and coordinate labor and capital in matters of common interest." Note in this definition that corporatism is now a "system of social organization," that it emphasizes community and groups people according to their "natural interests and social functions," that the corporate bodies that oversee these processes are agencies of the state, and that their role is to "coordinate labor and capital in the common interest."

The Freiburg meeting brought together for the first time corporatist thinkers from different nations, gave their movement international legitimacy and coherence (parallel to and at the same time as the development of the socialist *internationale*), and stimulated the growth of new activities. Another international gathering of what was now called the "corporatist internationale" was held in Berlin in 1890, which gave added impetus to the movement. Then, in 1891, Pope Leo XIII, using these corporatism writings and building on them, issued his famous encyclical (which means it is the official, immutable word of the Roman Catholic Church) called *Rerum Novarum,* otherwise known as the "working man's encyclical." *Rerum Novarum* afforded dignity to labor, gave the blessing of the church for the first time to the organization of trade unions, and indicated that organized labor now had to be recognized as a legitimate social movement and incorporated into the political process. But corporatism, not liberalism or socialism, was the preferred papal means for achieving those goals.

By today's standards, corporatism was not a very radical movement and was often viewed as a conservative alternative to Marxism; but in the context of the nineteenth century and the regimes in power at the time (Bismarck's Germany, Victorian England, Spain under a restored monarchy), it signaled some new departures. Positive conceptions of trade unions and the working class had replaced the earlier negative ones. Workers were now to be incorporated in the political process rather than suppressed, as had often occurred in the past. New concepts of social justice through corporatism came to the fore. Furthermore, the older paternalistic attitudes toward workers and unions—that it was okay to have them but that they should be guided and run by the "better people"—gave way to one in which workers organized their own unions, independent of owners and management, and had the right to employ collective action, including the right to strike. The ideology of corporatism had clearly came a long way from the reactionary years of the early nineteenth century.

All these changes were within prescribed limits, however. Many of the new corporatist groups and unions remained under the guidance of the Catholic Church and were often led by clerics and/or ministers. The activities of these groups were often social and educational rather than militantly trade unionist. And although corporatism had a strong social justice component, it was also seen by its members and clerical backers as providing a counter to the rising Marxist, anarchist, and radical unions. In Europe, corporatism was viewed as opening the door to trade unionism but, as compared to its competitors for the workers' loyalties, it constituted the most conservative of the emerging labor groups.

An added impetus to the rise of corporatism in the decades immediately preceding World War I came from the widespread disillusionment with ineffective parliamentary regimes. In France, Portugal, and even England, parliamentary governments seemed unable to cope with rising social pressures; with the international arms race and competition for colonies that helped lead to World War I; and with political tendencies that pointed toward fragmentation and chaos. This was the period of what historian Barbara Tuchman called the "proud tower" of pre–World War I civilization—the last, dying gasps of an older and more traditional hierarchical order, about to be swept aside by the war and the threat of Bolshevik revolution.[5] This order proved incapable of responding adequately to the rising social demands, including those of organized labor, for which corporatism attempted to provide an answer. Then too, corporatism's rise was aided by the writings of a whole school of antiliberal, antidemocratic, antiparliament writers— Ludwig Gumplowicz, Gaetano Mosca, Vilfredo Pareto, Roberto Michels, Georges Sorel, and others—who offered pointed barbs at the idea that government, as under democracy, should be based on the lowest common denominator of one man, one vote. These and other arguments bolstered the corporatist idea that a strong, well-led state—not the uneducated common man—should be at the forefront of engineering change.

By the turn of the century a great variety of (mainly) Catholic corporatist workers' and social movements had sprung up. In 1895 the first national Catholic trade union movement had been organized in Germany to compete with the socialist unions, and in the first decade of the twentieth century similar corporatist federations were established in a number of other European countries. In addition to Catholic unions, there were now Catholic youth groups, Catholic business associations, Catholic women's organizations, as well as Christian-Democratic (Catholic) political parties beginning to compete for members and power throughout Europe. All this was part of the Catholic revival of the early twentieth century, a movement that gave additional support to corporatist ideas and organizations. And, of course, if the Catholics were reviving and renewing themselves, Protestant denominations had to do the same, which helps explain the parallel rise during this period of Protestant unionism and corporatism in the Netherlands, Germany, and Scandinavia.

Corporatism in Power

The twenty-year period between World Wars I and II was the high point of corporatism in Europe. The flowering of corporatism during this period was due to at least four factors. First, World War I itself had revealed the fragility of parliamentary institutions and parliamentary regimes and thus strengthened the appeal of corporatism in countries where parliaments had been ineffective or threatened. Second, the 1917 Bolshevik revolution in Russia, particularly with its anticapitalist and antireligious ideology and action, severely frightened people throughout Europe and made corporatism look like a viable alternative. Third, the world market crash of 1929–30 and the global depression that persisted throughout the 1930s made it appear that liberalism and capitalism were on their last legs as well and might collapse at any time. The failures of liberalism and capitalism and the unacceptability of socialism and Bolshevism made it seem in the 1930s that corporatism was the only viable option.

A fourth factor stimulating corporatism during the 1930s was the rise of central state planning, increased government regulation of the economy, and new programs such as Social Security. These developments toward greater statism in the economy, stimulated by the fears growing out of the depression, required a further rationalization of society, a stable and disciplined work force weaned away from strikes, and stable employer–employee relations. That was precisely what corporatism seemed able to offer, with its emphasis on close cooperation between capital and labor and with the state managing and directing both the economy and social relations in the common interest. Hence our earlier dictum: whenever there is heavy statism in the economy, corporatism in the social and political spheres is very likely to be there too.

Early, brief, and partial experiments with corporatism were carried out in Portugal in 1917, in Greece from 1917 to 1920, and in Spain in the early 1920s. But the first full-fledged, long-term corporatist regime to come to power in Europe was that of Benito Mussolini in Italy. Mussolini used corporatism as a way to centralize his authority and achieve greater discipline and control over the economy. His famous *Carta del Lavoro,* or labor statute, was used to keep the Italian labor movement under state control and to prevent labor strikes; meanwhile the vigorous (and often radical) independent labor activity of the past was wiped out. Mussolini created a corporative structure to manage the economy, but this turned out to be largely a showpiece meant for people to admire. The real power was in the hands of Mussolini and his totalitarian state, not in the corporatist organization. Hence in the first country where corporatism was implemented seriously, it served as a smokescreen for state power and as a way that a fascist and totalitarian government gained control over all areas of national life. Some started calling Italian corporatism a "fake," a "confidence trick." The Italian corporatist experiment from 1922 to 1939 was a form of state (really dictatorial) corporatism, only vaguely resembling the participatory, societal, and pluralist form that many earlier corporatist philosophers had written about.

Many of the other corporatist regimes in Europe that came to power in the 1920s and 1930s copied features from the Italian "model." In Portugal, under Antonio Salazar and then Marcello Caetano (1928–74), and in Spain under Francisco Franco (1939–75), the labor statutes promulgated bore a striking resemblance (almost a word-for-word translation) of the Italian labor code. Both these regimes in the Iberian Peninsula created corporations, supposedly the capstone of any corporative system, to help manage labor relations and all sectors of the national economy; but these turned out to be agencies without much purpose, since it was the central state that largely directed the economy, not the corporations.[6]

In both regimes the corporative system was used to suppress worker rights and as an instrument of top-down, dictatorial control. Portugal was perhaps the most elaborately corporatist regime in Europe, with a functionally organized Chamber of Corporations alongside the parliamentary Chamber of Deputies; a similarly functionally representative (with military, church, government, and economic elite representatives) and high-level advisory body called the Council of State; and a Corporative Council to oversee the entire process of restructuring society along corporative lines. But none of these agencies, in either Portugal or Spain, ever functioned as the original corporative theory and laws said; they too, as in Italy, served mainly as agencies of centralization and dictatorial state power; and eventually they were largely shunted aside by the regimes in power and ignored.

Similar corporatist regimes came to power in Bulgaria and Lithuania (1926–29); Poland under Jozef K. Pilsudski (1926–35); Albania (1928–39); Yugoslavia (1929); Turkey, Estonia, and Latvia (1934); Austria (1934–38); Greece under Joannes Metaxas (1936–41); Romania; and Ireland (1937). In addition, Vichy France during the years of World War II was organized in part on corporatist principles. And Nazi Germany under Hitler from 1933 to 1945 also instituted corporatism in the running of the economy; but in the German case, even more so than in the Italian, corporatism was completely subordinated to the requirements of Hitler's personal dictatorship and the regime's totalitarianism.

It is striking that during the interwar period, corporatist regimes were concentrated in Southern, Central, and Eastern Europe, and preponderantly in the Catholic countries, but not so much in the Protestant and Northern countries. In fact, during this period the Netherlands, the Scandinavian countries, and Great Britain all had corporatist movements of various sorts and sizes; but none of them came to power or had an opportunity to implement very many corporatist institutional changes (with the possible exception of wartime economic planning, which required greater centralization, greater coordination of social and political forces, and stronger government control). The conclusion is that although corporatism was not exclusive to the Southern European and Eastern European Catholic and more peripheral countries, it was concentrated there. And while this earlier form of statist and authoritarian corporatism had its advocates in the Northern and Protestant countries (and Switzerland), it never came to power in these. The patterns are striking.

Outside of Europe, primarily in Latin America—because of the Spanish and Portuguese examples and again, the Catholic tradition— corporatism also flourished. The regimes of Getulio Vargas in Brazil, Juan Perón in Argentina, Rafael Trujillo in the Dominican Republic, Jorge Ubico in Guatemala, Velasco Ibarra in Ecuador, Arnulfo Arias in Panama, Oscar Benavides in Peru, Carlos Ibañez in Chile, Alfredo Stroessner in Paraguay, Maximiliano Hernández in El Salvador, the Mexican Party of Revolutionary Institutions (PRI), the Bolivian National Revolutionary Movement (MNR), and Peru's American Popular Revolutionary Alliance (APRA) all had corporatist features and influences, although in varied forms. Interesting for comparative purposes is the fact that while most of these were right-wing and conservative movements or regimes, others (APRA, the MNR, the PRI under Lázaro Cárdenas) were more left-wing and progressive. That is, they incorporated labor, peasant and progressive sectors alongside the traditional corporate wielders of power (army, Church, oligarchy) or discarded these latter groups altogether. Another interesting feature of Latin American corporatism, which reflects the area's lower level of economic and institutional development as compared to Europe, is the fact that it combined, or tried to combine, the older quasi-medieval corporatism that still existed in Latin America with the newer social justice orientation of *Rerum Novarum* and *Quadregessimo Anno*. We have more to say about these regional differences in chapter 4.

Post–World War II Corporatism

Rather than the open, democratic, participatory, pluralist, and society-based corporatism of many corporatist theorists, corporatism as it was actually practiced in the 1920s and 1930s was usually authoritarian, often repressive, and statist if not dictatorial. As such, and given corporatism's presence in the regimes of Mussolini and Hitler, corporatism came to be identified in the popular mind with authoritarianism and fascism. In some quarters it is still so identified. And since fascism was both discredited and defeated in World War II, corporatism was discredited along with it. Following the war, most of the corporatist regimes left over from the 1930s, led by Italy and Germany, were removed or replaced, either by their own citizens or by the wartime occupation armies. For a time corporatism as an ideology and popular movement with considerable mass appeal all but disappeared.

Corporatism, albeit in greatly changed forms, managed to hang on in Spain and Portugal (the regimes of Salazar and Franco) for thirty years after World War II. And in Latin America, which for a long time remained isolated from and peripheral to the mainstreams of Western political change, corporatism persisted in a variety of forms—although the term "corporatism" now was seldom used and almost never in a positive way. The Perón, Vargas, Trujillo, and other Latin American regimes mentioned earlier continued many of the practices if not the ideology of corporatism, despite its being discredited. But these were thought of as backward-looking regimes, retrogressive, certain soon to disappear or be overthrown. Hence in the later 1940s and through the 1950s, corporatism seemed to be in permanent if not yet quite total eclipse.

But then three things happened to bring back corporatism and corporatist modes of interpretation. The first of these was the rediscovery of corporatism in Western Europe. Although Europe had formally repudiated corporatism in World War II and thereafter, by the 1960s much of Western Europe had come to practice a disguised form of corporatism—but without calling it that. In a variety of public policy areas such as social welfare, incomes policy, economic planning, and industrial policy, a tripartite group of actors—usually organized labor, management, and the state—often got together to negotiate the shape and direction of the policy. Sometimes this took the form of U.S.-style interest-group politics; but often it went beyond that to include the state organizing, licensing, and policing the interest groups involved, or incorporating the interest groups directly into the regulatory, consultative, administrative, and implementation agencies of the state. These institutional arrangements and functions, we have seen, are at the heart of corporatism theory and practice. It may not have been called that, but corporatism is in fact what it was. It is like that old saying about ducks: if it looks, acts, and quacks like a duck, it probably is a duck. So with corporatism. Eventually a handful of scholars in the 1960s began to call these European practices what they were: corporatism. Actually the term that came to be widely used was neo-corporatism, or new corporatism.[7]

The second development was the resurgence of corporatism in Latin America.[8] Recall that we said earlier that in Latin America several corporatist regimes had been left over from the pre– and World War II period and that they were expected to expire. While many corporatist regimes did leave the scene in the late 1950s and early 1960s, and for a time Latin America enjoyed a brief democratic interlude, by the mid-to-late-1960s a whole wave of military authoritarian-corporatist regimes had come back into power, sweeping away the earlier trends toward democracy and pluralism. In such important countries as Argentina, Brazil, Chile, Uruguay, and others, corporatism and authoritarianism came back with a vengeance, not only eliminating democratic and liberal regimes but also often ruling repressively and with widespread violations of human rights. Note that this is quite different from the post–World War II, social-democratic, neo-corporatism of Western Europe; it was closer to the pre–World War II authoritarian and statist corporatism of Mussolini, Franco, and Salazar.

These differences between the neo-corporatism of Western Europe and the authoritarian corporatism of Latin America help explain why it is so hard to arrive at a clear definition of corporatism and why the literature on corporatism goes in so many different directions: because there are two quite different forms and historical stages of corporatism that we are talking about. The one (neo-corporatism) is, for the most part, democratic, pluralistic, societal, oriented toward social welfare, and a product of the modern planned economy and the welfare state; while the other is authoritarian, monolithic, statist, oriented toward social control, and often a product of underdevelopment and weak institutions. However, both have in common the functional organization of society, the licensing of interest groups, and their incorporation into the machinery of the state.

The third development was the widespread discovery of distinct forms of corporatism in many non-Western and Third World countries. Recall that corporatism, as its history has been traced in this chapter, has largely been a Western phenomenon found mainly in Europe and (since these countries were colonies of Spain and Portugal) Latin America. But now, scholars began finding elements of corporatism in the tribal or ethnic societies of Africa; in the strong connection between business and the state in Japan; in the organic, communalist, and Confucian-based societies of East and Southeast Asia; in the interconnections between the caste associations, political parties, and the bureaucracy in South Asia; and in the often paternalistic relations of leaders and their peoples in Islamic society. This development made corporatism a global phenomenon rather than one limited to just one or two areas. It significantly expanded, as we see in chapter 4, the number, types, and varieties of corporatism—no longer just Western but non-Western as well, in developed countries and in a great variety of developing ones. Corporatism became ubiquitous, seemingly present in a plurality of forms in quite distinct cultural and social settings. But with corporatism so omnipresent, it also proved harder to get a clear handle on it, to define it precisely, and to distinguish it from other types of political regimes.

The discovery and rediscovery (in Europe) of corporatism in so many variations gave rise to a virtual cottage industry of corporatism studies. In the later 1970s and throughout much of the 1980s, it seemed like everyone in the comparative politics field was studying corporatism. And that gave rise, as we earlier saw, to the fifth and final definition of corporatism. Corporatism was no longer just a set of institutional arrangements and practices in certain countries; it had become a paradigm, a social science approach, a whole way of thinking about and studying distinct political systems, that was different from either the liberal-democratic or the Marxian approaches. Few scholars of corporatism went so far as to claim that their approach had replaced the pluralist or the Marxist approaches, or that it provided a complete model of society and politics to the exclusion of other approaches. Rather, most scholars saw the corporatist approach as complementing the other main approaches in the field and found it particularly useful in studying labor and industrial relations, social welfare programs, wage policy, industrial policy, and other public policy programs. For it is precisely in these areas that labor, management, and the state tend to be brought together in a collaborative relationship for integral national development—which is close to our definition of corporatism.

Since this earlier fascination with corporatism, many countries in the Third World have moved away from authoritarianism toward democracy; the interests of many comparative politics scholars have also shifted to studying these transitions to democracy. But even with this shift the study of corporatism remains fascinating, and not just for historical reasons. First, many countries are still practicing one or another form of corporatism. Second, corporatism is growing in many countries, including the United States, that seldom or only weakly practiced corporatism before. And third, even with this movement from authoritarianism to democracy, that does not necessarily mean the abandonment of corporatism. In fact—and it is a fascinating new topic for study—as the transition to democracy occurs, many countries are simply moving from an older-fashioned, historical, medieval, or statist form of corporatism to a newer form of social or neo-corporatism. So even in the transition to democracy, corporatism remains present—in newer forms, perhaps, but still present.

Hence not only is corporatism still with us and probably growing ("creeping corporatism," it is often called) but in many countries it is also evolving, developing, transitioning, changing its spots. Corporatism therefore will likely be with us for a long time to come, and its newer as well as older permutations continue to provide a great variety of fascinating subject matter for students of comparative politics.

Notes

1. The early history may be traced in Carl Landauer, *Corporate State Ideologies: Historical Roots and Philosophical Origins* (Berkeley: University of California, Institute of International Studies, 1983).

2. Corporatism in the Middle Ages is analyzed in Angus McKay, *Spain in the Middle Ages: From Frontier to Empire, 1000–1500* (London: Macmillan, 1977); Archibald R. Lewis, *The Development of Southern French and Catalan Society, 718–1050* (Austin: University of Texas Press, 1965); and Antony Black, *Guilds and Civil Society in European Political Thought from the Twelfth Century to the Present* (Ithaca, NY: Cornell University Press, 1984).

3. More recent, national histories of corporatism may be traced in Ralph H. Bowen, *German Theories of the Corporate State* (New York: McGraw-Hill, 1947); and Matthew H. Elbow, *French Corporative Theory, 1789–1948* (New York: Columbia University Press, 1953).

4. The intellectual and social history is traced and analyzed in Howard J. Wiarda, *Corporatism and National Development in Latin America* (Boulder, CO: Westview Press, 1981).

5. Barbara Tuchman, *The Proud Tower* (New York: Macmillan, 1962).

6. For a detailed case study as well as the broader context, see Howard J. Wiarda, *Corporatism and Development: The Portuguese Experience* (Amherst: University of Massachusetts Press, 1977).

7. A useful survey is in Philippe C. Schmitter and Gerhard Lehmbruch (eds.), *Trends Toward Corporatist Intermediation* (Beverly Hills: Sage, 1979).

8. James Malloy (ed.), *Authoritarianism and Corporatism in Latin American* (Pittsburgh: University of Pittsburgh Press, 1977).

3

Toward a Corporatist Model

In chapter 2, we traced the history of corporatist theory and ideology from ancient times to the present. It is clear from that history that over the centuries corporatism has appeared in several different forms and time frames—ancient, medieval, and modern—with distinct sociological bases and in a variety of political forms. In recognizing these historical differences, we also sought to keep in mind the common features and continuities—such as a strong state role and the group, functional, sectoral organization of politics structured through and often by the state.

In this chapter we shift directions somewhat, looking no longer at history but at the emergence in the 1960s and the blossoming thereafter of an explicit theory and model of corporatism. For during this period, as we have seen already in introductory form, corporatism was employed not just as a descriptive term to portray certain economic and political institutions at various points in history, but also as an analytical framework comparable to liberal-pluralism and Marxism that was capable of explaining new forms of sociopolitical organization and public policymaking that these other major models failed adequately to explain. The first paragraph in the Preface talks about how the study of corporatism introduced a paradigm shift in the social sciences. In this chapter we examine the nature and components of that shift and why it was and is so important.

This is an interesting and colorful story, not just because the ideas and concepts are large and important but also because the personalities and academic conflicts involved in this paradigm shift were sometimes also large. Starting perhaps with James Watkins's portrait of the discovery of the structure of DNA (*The Double Helix*),[1] we now recognize more than before that major intellectual breakthroughs, in both the natural and social sciences, are the products not just of dull, dry, plodding research but also of personalities, academic rivalries, and scholarly conflicts. Hence, there has recently been a trend in scholarship not just to trace the intellectual origins of new approaches and breakthroughs but also to look at the individuals, factions and competing perspectives, their values, their biases, and their rivalries as well. These factors were certainly present in the rise of the corporatism model, a factor that not only makes this a colorful story but also makes it complicated to render accurately because it is, at least in part, autobiographical. The author is not just a chronicler of these disputes but was himself a participant in them.

European Precursors

Recall that in the 1920s and 1930s corporatism had come to power in many of the European countries; it was subsequently discredited mainly because of the fascist and Nazi connections and experiences and the defeat of fascism in World War II. With the demise of these regimes, the entire body of corporatist literature and ideology developed over the previous centuries went into oblivion as well.

Hence, the early writing on corporatism in the postwar period, during the 1950s and 1960s, largely focused on the leftovers of corporatism from that earlier period, on the disguised or renamed forms of corporatism that many European countries were still practicing. But hidden or briefly mentioned in this early literature were also some tantalizing tidbits and analyses that would later form into a full-fledged *theory* of corporatism.

Samuel Beer

Samuel Beer is an American political scientist, a professor at Harvard, and a specialist in British politics. Beer was one of the first scholars to recognize that, even though corporatism had been discredited and abandoned in World War II, it continued to linger in semihidden form in a number of European countries. Rather than interest-group pluralism, which was the publicly stated system of politics, many European countries continued to employ corporatist practices.

Specifically with regard to interest groups in Great Britain, Beer observed that during the period of wartime controls, a number of trade associations had become closely linked to the state, "embedded in the administration," as he put it. He noted more generally that interest groups in Britain were far more closely integrated into the state than they were in the United States. These are precisely among the hallmarks of corporatism identified earlier. Beer went on to say: "In spite of the relaxation of control since the war, there remains a system of 'quasi corporatism' which leaves no important interest group without a channel of influence and a real share in the making of decisions. The main substance of the system is continual, day-to-day contacts between public bureaucrats in the government departments and private bureaucrats in the offices of the great pressure groups."[2]

In subsequent books, significantly entitled *British Politics in the Collectivist Age* and *Modern British Politics*,[3] Beer went beyond his initial analysis. Rather than just being a leftover from the war years, corporatism in Britain was now seen as stemming from modern centralized government, modern economic planning, and from modern social welfare programs. Both central planning and welfare required for their effective implementation that the groups whose members would be most strongly affected by government policies—employers, trade unions, consumers— also be involved in both the formulation and the implementation of these programs. That is the essence of modern corporatism.

Joseph La Palombara

Joseph La Palombara is a professor of political science at Yale, one of the early leaders of the Social Science Research Council's Committee on Comparative Politics (SSRC/CCP)—an influential group in the field that focused on the politics of developing nations—and a specialist in Italian politics. Among the SSRC/CCP group, La Palombara was especially notable because he did not accept the ethnocentric (U.S.-centered) perspectives of several other members of the committee, preferring to study other countries in their own context and within their own conceptual frameworks—which included corporatism.

In focusing on Italy, La Palombara found that although Mussolini's fascist/corporatist regime was overthrown and defeated in 1945 and the institutions of corporatism formally abolished, the practices of patrimonialism and corporatism often continued.[4] Both organized labor and big business were integrated into the state and dependent on it for jobs, wage increases, favors, and contracts. The two main political parties also incorporated various functional sectors of society (unions, farmers, professionals, students, women) into their party structures. At the cabinet/ministry level, the corporate interests had often captured and literally hived off whole sectors of the public bureaucracy for themselves, channeling jobs, favors, and patronage in their own directions. This was corporatism run amuck.

While La Palombara was perceptive in pointing out the persistence of corporatist features even though corporatism itself was supposed to have been ended after the war, he limited his comments to the Italian case. Like Samuel Beer on Britain, La Palombara's analysis of corporatism in Italy was pioneering, but it did not go beyond a single case study to try to suggest a general theory of corporatism.

Stein Rokkan

Stein Rokkan is a Norwegian political scientist and student of comparative politics. Writing in the mid-1960s at about the same time as La Palombara, Rokkan published an oft-cited article entitled "Norway: Numerical Democracy and Corporate Pluralism."[5]

Rokkan's analysis of Norway focused mainly on political parties, elections, and parliament. But he also identified a kind of hidden corporatism among interest groups and their relations to the government that existed alongside the electoral/political party system. Rokkan's analysis, in fact, identified a dual system of political representation, one having to do with democracy, elections, parties, and parliamentary rule; and the other, parallel to it, that focused on interest-group representation and the implementation of public policy, and that was essentially corporatist. However, Rokkan doubted that this "latent corporatism" would become formalized in law and constitution.

Once again, then, in Rokkan's work we have a fascinating insight into the persistence of corporatism even though it had supposedly been discredited in World War II. Moreover, we now have at least three cases of functioning, although partial, corporatism: Great Britain, Italy, and Norway. Soon there would be other discoveries of corporatism in other nations. But no one had as yet put these individual cases together into a general analysis of corporatism.

Andrew Shonfield

A major step was taken toward a general theory of corporatism in Andrew Shonfield's *Modern Capitalism,* also published in the mid-

1960s.[6] Shonfield is a British economist, really a student of political economy. His research focused not so much on interest groups and political parties, as did that of our previous authors, but on the growing role of the state in managing the economies of the modern, mixed (private and public ownership), social-welfare state. The state in modern times has been called upon to stimulate economic growth, assist new industries, control inflation, provide for full employment, regulate economic life, work out partnerships with business, set wages, negotiate labor conflicts, and implement a plethora of social-welfare measures. The modern state by the 1950s and 1960s, in Europe as well as the United States, had become "Keynesian" (after John Maynard Keynes, the British economist and statesman who had urged a strong government role in managing the economy).

But Shonfield recognized sooner than most that a strong and growing state role in the economic sphere would also imply state oversight and/or coordination of interest group activity. The opposite set of characteristics, we need to be reminded from chapter 1, would serve to describe liberal-pluralism: a weak or limited state coupled with strong and independent interest groups. Shonfield, however, wrote that "the major interest groups are brought together and encouraged to conclude a series of bargains about their future behavior, which will have the effect of moving economic events along the desired path." He went on to say that this strategy would indicate the general direction in which the interest groups, *as well as the state,* have agreed that they want to go. This is, in essence, the formula for modern neo-corporatism.

Shonfield, moreover, was under no illusion that it was anything other than corporatism that he was describing. He wrote, "It is curious how close this kind of thinking was to the corporatist theories of the earlier writers of Italian Fascism [as outlined in chapter 2], who flourished in the 1920s." He continued, "Corporatism got its bad name, which has stuck to it, essentially because of its association with the one-party state."[7]

Well there we have it: a recognition that corporatism, instead of disappearing, had continued in postwar Europe; a recognition of corporatism's main characteristics (interest groups coordinated or led by a strong, directing state); and—heretofore lacking in other corporatism writers—an indication of the dynamic factors involved in stimulating corporatism's growth: the economic planning and directing functions, as well as social-welfare programs, of the modern state. To this last set of factors as causative agents, Shonfield added modern, technocratic planning; the growth of large state bureaucracies (that interact in new ways with the interest groups they were designed to regulate); and outright state ownership or joint partnerships (with the private sector) of larger shares of the economy.

But even Shonfield, with all his insights, did not go on to develop a full-fledged theory of corporatism. Moreover, as an economist, he felt less comfortable dealing with the sociopolitical aspects of corporatism—our main concern in this book—than its economic agenda.

Latin American Scholars

As noted, the other area of the globe where corporatism has long been prominent is Latin America. In Latin America, however, the form of corporatism—until recently, when more modern types of neo-corporatism began to emerge—has been mainly medieval corporatism, often up-dated in the 1930s and later to manifest authoritarian corporatism, similar to that of Franco's Spain or Salazar's Portugal. Hence, it is no accident that scholars like Beer and Shonfield, writing about modern, contemporary Europe, stressed the economic and social policy origins of corporatism; while those writing about Latin America, where corporatism reached deep into the feudal past, gave attention to its historical and cultural roots. The differences between these two schools of thought, who have long talked past each other, may be best explained by the different geographic regions, the different time periods, and, hence, the *two different types of corporatism* about which they were writing.

John Leddy Phelan

John Leddy Phelan was a professor of Latin American history at the University of Wisconsin and Duke University. His specialization was colonial Latin America from approximately 1500 to 1800. But Phelan, like many historians of Latin America, was interested not just in that area but in its colonial roots in the mother countries of Spain and Portugal.

At the time of the conquest of the Americas beginning in 1492, Spain and Portugal were both organized on a medieval corporative basis. The principal corporations were the military orders, the Roman

Catholic Church and the various religious orders, the nobility or economic elites, the medieval towns and various regional governments,
the university, and the powerful sheep-herders' guild called the *mesta*.
These corporate units existed in a situation of a centuries-long conflict
over their autonomy and self-government with the centralizing monarchies of both countries.

Not only did Phelan trace these developments in Spain and Portugal
but he also showed how the corporative principles and institutions
were carried over by the colonial powers to their systems of imperial
rule in the Americas.[8] Society in Latin America was similarly organized on a functional or corporate basis (military, religion, education,
administration or bureaucracy, towns, even indigenous Indian groups),
under the hegemonic control of the Crown. In Phelan's analysis, this
corporative system locked in place for over three hundred years of
colonialism was in power for so long and was so strongly entrenched
that it became part of Latin American society and culture. Hence, when
Latin America achieved independence in the early nineteenth century,
while the outward forms (laws and constitutions) became republican
and ostensibly democratic, many practices and institutions remained
true to the earlier and stronger corporatist tradition—for example the
power of the Church, the army, and oligarchy.

Richard M. Morse

Richard M. Morse is another historian of Latin America and a long-
time professor at Yale. In his various writings Morse has recognized
the corporative basis of Latin American society and politics during
both the colonial and the independence periods, while also putting
Latin American corporatism in larger terms.[9]

Morse's research broadly explores the historical, religious, legalistic, cultural, and sociopolitical basis of Latin America. Much of that
tradition is organic, hierarchical, authoritarian, corporatist, and top-
down. Morse traces that tradition (as we did in chapter 2) to its origins
in Aristotle and imperial Rome; to the medieval Catholic philosophers
St. Augustine and St. Thomas; to medieval Spain and Portugal; to the
sixteenth-century Spanish Jesuit Suárez, who joined traditional Catholic corporatism to modern, state-building royal authority; to the political philosophers Machiavelli and Rousseau; and on into the modern
papal encyclicals *Rerum Novarum* and *Quadregessimo Anno*. All this

organic-corporatist tradition stood in marked contrast to the North American tradition of limited government, individualism, and checks and balances as found in John Locke, James Madison, and U.S. liberalism and pluralism. Moreover, Morse demonstrated the seamless web, with adjustments, of this tradition throughout Latin America's colonial history, after independence, and on into modern times.

Lyle N. McAlister

Lyle McAlister is yet another historian of Latin America, at the University of Florida. McAlister has made two major contributions to our understanding of Latin American corporatism.

First, he is very much in the traditions of Phelan and Morse in tracing the origins of Latin American corporatism to the medieval mother countries of Spain and Portugal, showing how the institutions of Hispanic centralism and corporatism were carried over to Latin America and their persistence into the modern era.[10] But McAlister also provides some new dimensions: he shows that Latin America was based on corporatism on the one hand but that it was also based on a system of class relations that had caste (Indian, African, European, and the various mixes of these) implications. In other words, Latin America was only partially corporatist and could only partially be understood by using the corporatist framework; other models would have to be used to understand these other aspects of Latin America.

McAlister's other major contribution was to analyze in detail one of Latin America's most important and influential corporate bodies, the military.[11] In examining the *"Fuero Militar"* (the corporate legal status and rights of the armed forces), McAlister showed the origins in medieval Spain of the concept of a separate military largely independent of civilian authority, exercising self-government over its own internal affairs, coexisting with but not necessarily subordinate to civilian authority, with special rights and responsibilities of its own, and operating (in American terms) like a separate, fourth branch of government. McAlister demonstrated clearly the corporate nature of the Latin American militaries and that, within this corporatist context, they operate autonomously and not in accordance with U.S. notions of the military being under civilian control. His contribution is one that all students of corporatism and the Latin American military should read.

Howard J. Wiarda

The present author, who was a student of both Morse and McAlister and was trained in the classic historical literature of medieval Spain and Portugal and colonial Latin America, also wrote some early studies of Latin American corporatism but without—at least initially—elevating these into a more general theory. Like the early studies of European corporatism, the early studies of Latin American corporatism—now being written by political scientists as well as historians—were case studies of single countries rather than of corporatism as a broader model.

The author's earliest writing dealing with corporatism was a 1962, unpublished, graduate student seminar paper dealing with the authoritarian regime of Alfredo Stroessner in Paraguay and focusing particularly on the high-level, corporately organized (with representatives from the Catholic Church, military, university, agriculture, business, industry, and government) Council of State. That same year, in writing my master's thesis on the similarly authoritarian regime of Rafael Trujillo in the Dominican Republic, I collected data on Trujillo's corporatist ideology and the corporatist underpinnings of his regime, but did not use these materials until the thesis was published in book form in 1968 and a chapter was included on corporatism.[12] Meanwhile, in 1963, I did research on Mexican corporatism, then went back to the Dominican Republic in 1964–65 to write a doctoral dissertation that included materials on corporatism,[13] and then in 1966 examined other forms of corporatism in Argentina, Brazil, and Peru.

In 1968 we were again in Brazil doing research on the semicorporatist regime of Getulio Vargas, the corporately organized Brazilian Catholic labor movement, and the entire system of Brazilian industrial and labor relations that retained its corporatist features long after Vargas had left power.[14] By this time I had seen so much corporatism in Latin America in so many different kinds of regimes (military, civilian; left, right; multiparty, single party) that I was convinced a general theory of Latin American corporatism should be fashioned. The first papers dealing with what I called "the corporatist framework" were written in 1969–70; the arguments of these papers are summarized later in this chapter.

Philippe C. Schmitter

Another Latin America case study that would potentially have larger implications was Philippe Schmitter's doctoral dissertation on Brazil, written at the University of California, Berkeley, and published in book form in 1971,[15] the same year that the present author's "Corporatist Framework" paper was delivered at the American Political Science Association. Brazil had had virtually every form of corporatism: natural or historic corporatism going back to Portugal and the colonial period; a flurry of Catholic-corporatist ideological writings going back to the early twentieth century; manifest corporatism during the regime of Getulio Vargas, 1930–45, who patterned his regime on Salazar's Portugal; and even the beginnings of modern neo-corporatism. Along with Argentina and Mexico, Brazil was one of the centers of Latin American corporatism.

Schmitter managed to capture much of this corporatist and interest-group activity in his dissertation/book, which represented a real *tour de force*. Written with verve and enthusiasm and originally numbering 900 pages, the dissertation dealt broadly with the subject of interest-group conflict and political change in Brazil. Schmitter interviewed 149 persons representing 108 different associations: labor, business, professional, student, bureaucratic; with many groups that he could not interview, he administered a questionnaire. The result was a major and innovative study of Brazilian interest groups—major because of the wealth of data generated and innovative because of its use of corporatism concepts as well as the more familiar liberal-pluralist ones. Schmitter's book was, to that point, the most thorough and innovative study of corporatism in a single political system.

Despite this pathbreaking work, a number of issues and problems arose in the Schmitter book. First, the term corporatism was never clearly defined, nor were its distinct meanings in different historical time periods spelled out. Second, Schmitter was unclear about the causes of corporatism, talking about natural and historical as well as contemporary corporatism and, surprisingly, given his later criticisms of others who wrote along the same lines, seeming to locate corporatism within the long patrimonialist tradition of Brazil, which was embedded in the political culture. Third, in this book Schmitter captured the messiness of corporatism to which European scholar Martin Heisler (see below) also referred, its incompleteness in actual practice and lack of institutionalization, its hybrid nature, its frequent overlap with liberal-pluralism, the distinction between neat corporatist schemes fashioned by intellectuals and the governments they serve *and* the frequent uneven implementation at grassroots levels. Many scholars, however, found this nuanced picture of a messy, disorganized, incomplete corporatism far more realistic than the neat (perhaps too neat), logical (too logical), ideal-type model of corporatism present in Schmitter's later writings.

Toward a General Theory of Corporatism

To summarize, during the 1960s (even earlier in Samuel Beer's case), a number of scholars in both Western Europe and Latin America had thus begun to rediscover corporatism. Largely discredited because of the fascist and Nazi experiences and because of the Axis's defeat in World War II, corporatism was widely thought to have disappeared. But in Europe, we have seen, a growing number of case studies were beginning to reveal that several countries had continued to practice a disguised form of corporatism that was hidden behind liberal-pluralist institutions and values; or else, under the pressures of centralized economic planning and advanced social-welfare programs, were practicing a revived form of corporatism but not calling it that. In Latin America during this same period various corporatist features and institutions were also rediscovered: some countries continued to follow a quasi-medieval form of corporatism, while others practiced an updated, 1930s-style manifest corporatism—or, most often, some combination of the two.

The next task, following on the heels of these case studies of corporatist practices in diverse countries, was to fashion a model of analysis that (1) provided a more general framework for examining and understanding corporatism comparatively across political systems; and (2) provided a dynamic model that linked Latin American, European, and presumably other forms of corporatism and explained why these distinct types emerged when and where they did. The first issue is taken up here; the second is explored in chapter 5.

Howard J. Wiarda

During the 1960s the author spent a great deal of research time in diverse countries of Latin America, and in the early 1970s in the mother countries of Spain and Portugal as well. Wherever he went in the Iberian (Spain and Portugal) and Latin America world, in right- and left-wing regimes, in military-dominated or civilian governments, he found many of the same persistent and characteristic features, namely organic, integralist, top-down, statist, and corporatist institutions and practices that stood at considerable odds with the generally prevailing orthodoxy that proclaimed liberalism and pluralism as *the* model of developmentalism. After finding corporatism, organic-statism, authoritarianism, patrimonialism, and these other features so omnipresent in so many regimes, the author determined that there was a distinct model of corporatist or organic-statist (the terms were often used interchangeably) development "out there" that was particularly characteristic of Iberia and Latin America. Moreover, this model stood in marked contrast to the liberal-pluralist and Marxist models, both of which had proved inadequate for a full understanding of Latin America.

My "corporatist framework" model was thus aimed at going beyond the earlier case studies to encompass the broader culture-area of Iberia and Latin America.[16] The Iberian countries of Spain and Portugal as well as Latin America shared so many features—language, law, religion, culture, history, colonialism, economy, society, class system, and politics—that it seemed useful to consider them as part of a common corporatist model. This was, hence, to be theory building at the intermediate, culture-area, or middle-range level: more ambitious than a single country study but less pretentious than a model that presumed to offer universal categories. Hence, when I referred to Latin America and Iberia as sharing a "unique tradition," I did not mean that other areas might not have corporatist institutions but only that Latin America was very different from North America and from the liberal-pluralist model that we in American social science usually use to interpret ourselves and the rest of the world. By "unique" I also meant the particular Catholic, Thomistic, Hispanic, neo-scholastic *weltanschauunglich* (historical or political-cultural and institutional) form of corporatism that had long been dominant in Latin America, without implying there were not other forms. And even when I used the term "corporatism," I had in mind not a formal model or definition (assuming that everyone knew that corporatism meant the functional, rather than individual, organization of society) but a more generic and shorthand term that encompassed a number of closely related traits.

Wherever I had gone in the Iberic-Latin world, I had been struck by the functional, sectoral, or *corporatist* organization of political society. The main "corporations" in modern Spain, Portugal, and Latin America included the armed forces, the Roman Catholic Church, business and elite groups, the bureaucracy, the university, trade unions, and eventually peasants, women, and indigenous elements—the latter now organized similarly in a corporatist manner. Each of these groups, in order to function legitimately and to bargain politically in the system, had to have its "juridical personality" or right to existence recognized by the state; each existed in a contractually defined relationship to the state (usually in Latin America called an *organic law,* which occupies a place in the hierarchy of laws just below the constitution) that defines the rights and responsibilities of both the corporate group and the central government. This is what is involved in traditional Latin American corporatism.

In addition to these manifest features of corporatism, there were other, related features of Iberic-Latin political society that seemed to be closely associated with it. These included a top-down and authoritarian structure and system of political relations; a rigid and unyielding class structure; a system of mercantilism or *dirigisme* in the economic sphere; a set of social relations dominated by patrimonialism and patron-client relations; a bureaucratic system by which interest groups, rather than dealing with each other directly, were all integrated into the state; and a political culture, strongly Catholic in almost a medieval and still quasi-Thomistic sense, that emphasized discipline, order, hierarchy, rank, and each individual or group accepting its place within the system. To me, then, in this initial formulation, corporatism was not just a specific institutional arrangement of state–society relations; it was that, but it also came embedded in an entire set of socioeconomic and political-cultural practices and institutions that served to reinforce and perpetuate the institutional corporatist features. For just as in liberal-pluralism both the political and the economic systems need to have a high degree of freedom, individualism, and laissez faire, it is also true that under corporatism, in parallel fashion, it appeared that statism was dominant in both the economic and political spheres, with the two mutually reinforcing each other. In Iberia and Latin America, let us be clear, this was *state corporatism* that I was studying; in the 1960s and early 1970s modern societal or neo-corporatism had not yet made its appearance in Spain, Portugal, and Latin America as it had (as we see below) in Western Europe.

In thinking back about this formulation and the debate that swirled (and continues to swirl) around my general but still area-specific formulation of the corporatism concept, plainly I could and should have provided a clearer definition of the term. I should also have made it clear that I was writing about a particularly Thomistic-Catholic, Iberic-Latin American, and state-centric form of corporatism, and tried to distinguish this form more sharply from other forms. Finally, I should have followed up this initial formulation immediately with a more detailed exposition exploring the dynamics, varieties, and nuanced forms of corporatism. But by then I was already involved in other research projects, did not at that time want to take time out to elaborate on the corporatism theme, and, mistakenly as it turned out, decided to leave it to others to flesh out the bare-bones skeleton that my early corporatism papers had provided.

Martin O. Heisler

Many of the scholars working on corporatism in the late 1960s and early 1970s arrived at their initial formulations quite independently. Several scholars from Beer onward had noticed the emerging and spreading corporatism phenomenon in individual countries; by the early 1970s published versions of more general and theoretical models of corporatism had begun to appear. But these were still the individual efforts of scholars working independently who were unaware of each other's work. Only in later years would there begin to be cross-fertilization between the major scholars working in the field.*

One such writer working entirely independently on corporatism themes was political scientist Martin O. Heisler of the University of Maryland. Heisler was a Europe scholar; his conclusions and my own derived mainly to that point from Latin America were arrived at completely independently, even though they complemented each other nicely in most respects. But that is frequently how scholarly advances move forward in the natural as well as social sciences: individual scholars working independently who discover or are struck by the same phenomena or patterns of phenomena. Only after these initial

---

*My own paper on the "Corporatist Framework" of Iberian-Latin American politics, for example, had been written initially in 1969–70 at the Mershon Center at Ohio State University, presented there to a faculty seminar, and presented in revised form at the American Political Science Association (APSA) Annual Meeting in 1971, before being published in *World Politics* in January 1973. As late as 1971, Schmitter, I, and others beginning to work on developing a model of corporatism were not aware of each other's work on the subject.

discoveries does the work of mutual enrichment by various scholars working on the same issue from different points of view begin to take place.

In the European context, Heisler was impressed by how widespread the phenomenon of sectoral or corporate representation had become. He was also impressed by how far this pattern of corporate representation diverged from the more familiar liberal-pluralist model. He went beyond the earlier discoveries by Beer, La Palombara, and Rokkan of the presence of corporatism in individual countries. Instead, Heisler saw corporatism as a general, European-wide phenomenon. He noted the growing presence of representatives from organized labor, business, and other interests in public policy decision making and as members of the vast web of regulatory agencies that are part of the modern industrialized state.

Like Shonfeld, Heisler recognized the general causes that contributed to this trend, although he emphasized both the economic trends toward a modern, planned economy *and* such political trends as the growing bureaucratization of the modern state and the increased numbers and complexity of modern, interest-group pluralism. Rather as I had done for Iberia and Latin America, Heisler developed an area studies approach and called his formulation the "European Polity Model."[17] In other words, corporatism had now taken its place alongside parliamentarism, political parties, and interest-group pluralism as one of the fundamental and essential features of European politics. Moreover, Heisler even used the term "neo-corporatism" to describe this phenomenon. And, again like me, assuming that everyone was familiar enough with the term to know that it meant the sectoral or functional organization of society, Heisler neglected to provide a clear definition of what he meant by corporatism and neo-corporatism.

But Heisler's intent was clear. He had set out to present a model of the modern European political system. One essential ingredient of that model was a system of sectoral representation, which he called both neo-corporatism and corporate pluralism. The increased importance of corporatist politics, he argued, was related to the decline in importance of more traditional channels of political activity (political parties and parliament) and the rise of such institutions as the large state, bureaucracy, administration, welfarism, and central planning. He pointed correctly to these vertical, structured, pillared corporate sectors as playing key roles in the new-style administrative or bureaucratic state, and showed how they had been integrated into the decision-making apparatus of the modern state. But Heisler was careful also not to claim too much for his formulation: he called it a "pre-theory" rather than a full-blown model, he limited it to the European area, and he did not try to argue exaggeratedly that his was a complete and all-inclusive explanation to the exclusion of all others.

Heisler's pioneering work, however, was largely and inexplicably ignored by other, later theorists of corporatism. In part this was due to the absence of a clear definition of such terms as corporatism and neo-corporatism; in part it was due to the fact that Heisler emphasized broad cultural, social, and political causes of corporatism's rise and not just its economic causes. In part also, it may have been due to Heisler "getting there" first, a fact that caused some jealousy on the part of other scholars working on European corporatism. Then too, while Heisler wrote about corporatism, he was not himself a true believer in corporatism, choosing instead to emphasize his preferred liberal-pluralist orientation.

Years later, Heisler wrote a strong critique of corporatist theory as it had developed in subsequent writers. He argued from a pluralist perspective against the emerging political theory of corporatism. He suggested that the way in which corporatist scholars who came after him (Schmitter and a number of European writers) had constructed their premises made them self-fulfilling. Instead of offering ideas to be genuinely tested empirically, these theorists mainly offered propositions that would be demonstrated on the basis of their own built-in assumptions. In general, Heisler's own research found much more "messiness" (complexity and disorder) in European policymaking than did the too-neat formulations of corporatist theorists. As a result of both his ideas about corporatism and his later criticism of the dominant "school" of corporatist theory, Heisler found himself on the outs with other corporatism writers.

Philippe C. Schmitter

The most influential early essay written about corporatism was undoubtedly Philippe C. Schmitter's "Still the Century of Corporatism?" published in 1974, the same year as Heisler's book.[18] Written in a provocative, challenging, and pizzazzy style, this ambitious article was another *tour de force*. It set forth no less than a global or universal theory of corporatism. Not only did it elevate corporatism into a general, all-encompassing model of the modern polity but it also pointedly rejected other interpretations besides the author's own. Undoubtedly the style used, as well as the substance, contributed to the essay's attractiveness—and the controversy it inspired—among scholars.

Schmitter began by straw manning and then rejecting—a good debater's strategy—other formulations of corporatism besides his own. Rather than locating corporatism in the sociocultural tradition, as I had done in part, or in the policymaking realm à la Heisler, or in political institutions and processes as both Heisler and I had done, Schmitter found the causes of corporatism in its economic determinants. These included, à la Shonfield, the need of the modern state to ensure labor peace; the growth of central planning; the requirement that all modern economies ensure political stability and rationalized decision making; the desirability of bringing both labor and capital into the decision-making process and of integrating them into the state; the usefulness to the state of having labor and capital regulate, license, and police their own members; and the advantages of using these corporate groups to help implement government social and economic programs.

These causal factors in the growth of corporatism and the functions that corporatist institutions performed have an authoritarian, statist, and top-down ring to them that undoubtedly derived from Schmitter's main research experiences to that point: Brazil under military dictatorship and Salazar's authoritarian *Estado Novo* in Portugal. These same authoritarian, top-down features are present in the celebrated definition of corporatism that Schmitter offered, which is worth quoting in its entirety because it is frequently cited:

> Corporatism can be defined as a system of interest representation in which the constituent units are organized into a limited number of singular, compulsory, noncompetitive, hierarchically ordered and functionally differentiated categories, recognized or licensed (if not created) by the state and granted a deliberate representational monopoly within their respective categories in exchange for observing certain controls on their selection of leaders and articulation of demands and supports. (p. 93)

Note especially in this definition the terms that seem to point toward the association of corporatism with dictatorship of the sort that Schmitter had previously studied: limited number, singular, compulsory, noncompetitive, hierarchically ordered, recognized or licensed by the state, representational monopoly, controls. All of these terms suggest coercion, not democratic participation. To complete his taxonomy of types of regimes, Schmitter went on to contrast corporatism with pluralism:

> Pluralism can be defined as a system of interest representation in which the constituent units are organized into an unspecified number of multiple, voluntary, competitive, nonhierarchically ordered and self-determined (as to type or scope of interest) categories which are not specially licensed, recognized, subsidized, created or otherwise controlled in leadership selection or interest articulation by the state and which do not exercise a monopoly or representational activity within their respective categories. (p. 96)

With Soviet-style monism:

> A system of interest representation in which the constituent units are organized into a fixed number of singular, ideologically selective, noncompetitive, functionally differentiated and hierarchically ordered categories, created, subsidized and licensed by a single party and granted a representational role within that party and vis-à-vis the state in exchange for observing certain controls on their selection of leaders, articulation of demands and mobilization of support. (p. 97)

And with syndicalism (which seemed to be Schmitter's preference):

> Syndicalism could be defined as a system of interest aggregation (more than representation) in which the constituent units are an unlimited number of singular, voluntary, noncompetitive (or better hived-off) categories, not hierarchically ordered or functionally specialized, neither recognized, created nor licensed by state or party, nor controlled in their leadership selection or interest articulation by state or party, not exercising a representational monopoly but resolving their conflicts and "authoritatively allocating their values" autonomously without the interference of the state. (p. 98)

Schmitter's purpose was to create a generic model of corporatism, one that applied to all corporatist regimes, as well as to neatly contrast corporatism with other types of systems. But given the experience of fascist corporatism in the Europe of the 1930s, as well as the persistence and even resurgence of often dictatorial forms of corporatism in Latin America in the 1960s and 1970s, Schmitter needed to differentiate this form from the more modern, social-welfare-oriented, democratic neo-corporatism of contemporary Europe. The result was a useful distinction between *state corporatism* (authoritarian, top-down, dictatorial) and *societal (neo-)corporatism* (participatory, pluralistic, democratic). The trouble was, as several specialists in modern European politics pointed out, the supposedly generic definition—derived from Schmitter's heretofore research experiences—was far closer to the coercive, statist-authoritarian form than it was to the societal type. This caused numerous problems in applying the model in such democratic countries as Switzerland, Austria, the Netherlands, Sweden, and Norway. This bias continues to plague the corporatism concept and its presumed universality even today.

There were other problems with the Schmitter formulation. Some critics suggested the economic-determinist perspective was too simple, giving insufficient attention to sociocultural and political-institutional factors. Other critics thought the distinction between corporatism and pluralism was too sharply drawn, suggesting that corporatism was perhaps an extension of interest-group pluralism or that the term corporate-pluralism was useful, that corporatism and pluralism could be complementary rather than antithetic. Many saw in Schmitter's formulation a political agenda, not only in his apparent personal favoritism toward syndicalism but also a social-democratic preference that seemed to rescue trade union movements from the realities of decline that they were already experiencing, and to restore them under corporatism to a position of full and coequal power. Still other critics said the theory claimed too much, both in its pretensions to universality and in its claim to represent an entirely new and exclusive approach in the field. These critics suggested the insights of the corporatist approach were useful in enlightening *some* areas of decision making and policy implementation (labor and industrial relations, social-welfare policy), but that corporatism should not be elevated into a single and all-inclusive explanation. They argued that corporatism offered a valuable contribution in explaining *some* aspects of modern politics, but that other approaches (for example, interest-group pluralism, class conflict, bureaucratic behavior, others) should be used *in conjunction with* the corporatist one to provide more complex, *multicausal* explanations.

Nevertheless, even with Schmitter's exaggerated claims for his model and the criticisms leveled against it, there can be no doubt of the importance and impact of his explanation. Schmitter's essay, along with the writings of the other scholars previously mentioned, set off a veritable explosion of new research and writing on corporatism. For a time, in fact, the corporatist approach became the most exciting and innovative one in the comparative politics field, and perhaps the dominant one. Part of its attraction was its newness and freshness, and part of it was Schmitter's ebullient writing style, but undoubtedly the major cause for the new receptiveness of corporatism as a scholarly framework was the serious one that it fitted the new facts of modern society and politics better than other explanations and offered a handle for understanding these new phenomena that these others failed to provide. On this basis, the corporatist model, and particularly Schmitter's formulation of it, spread like lightning throughout the world, inspiring a host of studies of corporatism—some in areas that had never thought of corporatism before (chapter 4).

The European School

Schmitter's presentation of the corporatist model found a particularly strong reception among European comparativists. The reception was especially warm in Great Britain, where an entire school of corporatism studies sprang up, but the reception on the Continent was almost as strong. The reasons for the receptivity were, once again, Schmitter's challenging style, the fact that the model neatly put into perspective some new facts that were readily observable—most importantly the gradual replacement of interest-group pluralism and political parties by corporatist decision making—and the social-democratic perspective that made the model attractive particularly to European academics.

In general, European academic political discourse has tended to be farther to the left than is American political science. This fact has been reflected in the debate over corporatism. For example, in Great Britain Leo Panitch and Bob Jessop presented Marxist versions of corporatism. As scholars they recognized corporatism's growing influence, but from a Marxist perspective they argued that under capitalism the state would never be a neutral referee between labor and capital; instead it would consistently side with capital to the disadvantage of workers.

Quite a number of other British writers on corporatism were close to the country's Labor Party. They often wrote on corporatism from a left or social-democratic perspective; they saw the coequal treatment of labor and capital that corporatism advocated as a way of getting greater bargaining power for labor, higher wages, and expanded social welfare. Some of these benefits began to be seen as budget entitlements: permanent benefits for the lower classes that politicians should not tamper with. But this politicization of the discussion of the corporatism issue carried dangers as well since, when conservative Margaret Thatcher became prime minister of Great Britain, she not only reduced the entitlements to various interest groups but also, as part of her advocacy of free markets, attacked corporatism in general and corporatist institutions as well.[19] Because the political and economic stakes were so high, involving not just theoretical discussion among academics but real public policy issues with major national impacts on millions of people, the debate over corporatism was often hot and heavy, carried out in the popular press as well as in scholarly journals.

On the continent the debate was only slightly less intense. The key countries and areas where the debate over corporatism was most vigorous were Austria, Belgium, Germany, Holland, and Scandinavia. There was less discussion of corporatism in France and Italy—in France's case because the country was less corporatist than some of these others, in Italy because the country had long practiced a disguised form of corporatism and did not think it was a big deal. Spain and Portugal were, at that time (mid-1970s), beginning to break out of their old-fashioned, Franco- and Salazar-style authoritarian state corporatism; and, as democracy flowered in these two countries, they saw corporatism not as a new phenomenon to be analyzed or celebrated but as a very old and by-then despised philosophy, associated with the old regime, to be rejected and discarded. Only later, and with great difficulty because of this political baggage, would these two countries begin to come to grips with modern neo-corporatism.

As in Great Britain (and unlike in the United States), the debate over corporatism on the continent involved not just academics discussing alternative theoretical models but real-life social, economic, and political issues. These included the place of organized labor in the political system, wage policy, welfare policy, entitlements, central planning vs. privatization, social security, and austerity and layoffs. These were big issues, with major socioeconomic and political implications. The political stakes in these debates were high since they involved fundamental questions of the future organization and direction of the country. In these discussions corporatism and its various forms were hot, charged, political issues.

Among the continental European writers on corporatism, two in particular stand out: Gerhard Lehmbruck and Claus Offe. Lehmbruck was a frequent collaborator with Schmitter in some useful edited volumes that offered distinct interpretations of corporatism.[20] He was particularly interested in incomes policy and how the state regulates the material conflict (wages, benefits) between business and labor. Offe's contribution, which went back to some earlier literature, was that there are *degrees* of corporatism that emerged from a complex political process.[21] That is, the state may delegate certain responsibilities—for example, in implementing policy—to various corporate groups which thus gives them greater independence from the state. Offe seemed to be moving away from the rigid definition of corporatism ("singular," "compulsory," "monopolistic," etc.) offered by Schmitter.

In fact, within the European school of corporatism, there was a dawning realization during the 1980s that the Schmitter definition, based heavily on his research experiences in authoritarian Brazil and Portugal, was not very useful in their countries. Schmitter's formulation had spirit, but in its emphasis on top-down corporatism it may not have been entirely accurate in describing the democratic, pluralistic, inclusionary, socially just, and less rigidly structured countries of North and Central Europe. Hence, a newer school of European writers began to talk about voluntary corporatism, democratic corporatism, and corporate pluralism, thus undermining the perhaps too-sharp distinction Schmitter had drawn between corporatism and pluralism. In these writers' views, the emphasis on neo-corporatism as a new phenomenon in the modern state was valid, but not Schmitter's confining definition or its key terms, which made corporatism sound too heavy-handed and top-heavy to fit their socially just and democratic societies.

Up to this point almost all the studies of corporatism had focused on the national or macro level: grand theory, the state, the peak associations of labor and capital. But increasingly during the 1980s, scholars began to use the theory of corporatism to look at the micro level: decisions on the individual factory floor, specific wage or welfare policies, policies in specific sectors of the economy (automobiles, steel, etc.) and studies of individual social policy arenas (education, health care, social security) to see how the makeup of the various corporate groups consulted changed from issue to issue. For example, the groups involved in education reform might be quite different from those involved in welfare policy; those corporate interests consulted on industrial policy would be different from those consulted on health care reform. Some scholars began referring to this as "floating corporatism," because the lineup of interests involved and consulted—no longer just labor and capital—would vary from issue to issue. This shift toward studies of microcorporatism represented a triumph of the overall corporatist approach, however, not a repudiation of it. It signaled an acceptance and further refinement of corporatism studies, but it was one that was still within the corporatist approach.

The Explosion of Corporatism Studies

By the late 1980s, an explosion of corporatism studies had occurred. More and more scholars and students were using the corporatist approach in their writings. At least four elements were involved in this. First, the corporatist framework was being used in studying more and more countries; by the late 1980s there were numerous studies of Austria, Belgium, Canada, Denmark, France, Germany, Great Britain, Italy, Japan, the Netherlands, Norway, Portugal, Spain, Sweden, and Switzerland—all using the corporatist framework. Second, the corporatist approach was being increasingly used to study the specific structuring and strategies of individual interest groups or to examine specific policy issues (education, health, social welfare, wage policy, welfare, industrial policy, etc.)—the micro approach.

Third, the corporatist approach had achieved a degree of acceptability that had not been present before. The early works on corporatism written in the 1970s had been pioneering; now corporatism had been integrated into the field and was used regularly, routinely, and without great controversy or long accompanying explanations. And fourth, the corporatism concept had now spread beyond its original geographic confines (Latin America on the one hand, Western Europe on the other, some attention to Japan) to encompass research and writing on Africa, other Asian countries, some Middle Eastern countries (primarily Egypt), and even the (formerly) Marxist-Leninist countries of the Soviet Union and Eastern Europe. It is to this last topic, the spread of the corporatism approach to new, heretofore unexplored areas—and the great variety of corporatist forms and practices analyzed—that we turn in chapter 4.

Notes

1. James Watkins, *The Double Helix: A Personal Account of the Discovery of the Structure of DNA* (New York: New American Library, 1968).
2. Samuel Beer, "Pressure Groups and Parties in Britain," *American Political Science Review* 50 (1956): 1–23.

3. Samuel Beer, *British Politics in the Collectivist Age* (New York: Knopf, 1965), and *Modern British Politics* (London: Faber, 1969).

4. Joseph La Palombara, *Interest Groups in Italian Politics* (Princeton, NJ: Princeton University Press, 1964).

5. Stein Rokkan, "Norway: Numerical Democracy and Corporate Pluralism," in Robert Dahl (ed.), *Political Oppositions in Western Democracies* (New Haven: Yale University Press, 1965).

6. Andrew Shonfield, *Modern Capitalism* (London: Oxford University Press, 1965).

7. Ibid., p. 233.

8. John Leddy Phelan, *The Kingdom of Quito in the Seventeenth Century: Bureaucratic Politics in the Spanish Empire* (Madison: University of Wisconsin Press, 1967).

9. Richard M. Morse, "The Heritage of Latin America," in Louis Hartz (ed.), *The Founding of New Societies* (New York: Harcourt Brace and World, 1964).

10. Lyle N. McAlister, "Social Structure and Social Change in New Spain," *Hispanic American Historical Review* 33 (February 1963): 349–70.

11. Lyle N. McAlister, *The "Fuero Militar" in New Spain, 1748–1800* (Gainesville: University of Florida Press, 1957).

12. Howard J. Wiarda, *Dictatorship and Development: The Methods of Control in Trujillo's Dominican Republic* (Gainesville: University of Florida Press, 1968).

13. The dissertation was finished in 1965; the three-volume book appeared ten years later: Howard J. Wiarda, *Dictatorship, Development, and Disintegration: Politics and Social Change in the Dominican Republic* (Ann Arbor: Monograph Series of Xerox University Microfilms, 1975).

14. Howard J. Wiarda, *The Brazilian Catholic Labor Movement: The Dilemmas of National Development* (Amherst: University of Massachusetts, Labor Relations and Research Center, 1969).

15. Philippe C. Schmitter, *Interest Conflict and Political Change in Brazil* (Stanford, CA: Stanford University Press, 1971).

16. Howard J. Wiarda, "Toward a Framework for the Study of Sociopolitical Change in the Iberic-Latin Framework: The Corporatist Model," *World Politics* 25 (January 1973): 206–35, and *Corporatism and National Development in Latin America* (Boulder, CO: Westview Press, 1981).

17. Martin O. Heisler (ed.), *Politics in Europe: Structures and Processes in Some Postindustrial Democracies* (New York: McKay, 1974), especially part 1.

18. Philippe C. Schmitter, "Still the Century of Corporatism?" *The Review of Politics* 36 (January 1974): 85–131.

19. In Thatcher's memoirs, she repeatedly attacks corporate elements, by which she meant parasitic interest groups that reap money and benefits from their close association with the state; see her *The Path to Power* (London: HarperCollins, 1995) and *The Downing Street Years* (London: HarperCollins, 1993).

20. Gerhard Lehmbruck and Philippe C. Schmitter (eds.), *Trends Toward Corporatist Intermediation* (Beverly Hills: Sage, 1979) and *Patterns of Corporatist Policy-Making* (London: Sage, 1982).

21. Claus Offe, "The Attribution of Public Status to Interest Groups: Some Observations on the West German Case," in Suzanne Berger (ed.), *Organizing Interests in Western Europe* (Cambridge: Cambridge University Press, 1981).

4

The Varieties of Corporatism

Corporatism, we have seen, may be present in a variety of forms in a great variety of countries and culture areas—areas with different religions, different histories, and quite different social, economic, and political forms. In chapter 2, we traced the evolution of corporatist political theory, but recall we only focused on the Western tradition of corporatism; clearly that focus needs to be corrected. Then in chapter 3 we analyzed the emergence of a social science model and theory of corporatism as it emerged mainly in Western Europe and Latin America, but note also how the early work on corporatism in these two areas stimulated a flood of letters and eventually papers and books suggesting the corporatist model also had relevance for East Asia, South Asia, the Middle East, and sub-Saharan Africa. To understand corporatism in *all* its manifest variations, therefore, we need now to go beyond the Western world and examine corporatism in its non-Western versions as well.

As we examine these several varieties of corporatism, we also need to keep in mind that there is often a progression from one type to the next. That is, the type of corporatism that a country or region has is related to the level of development of that country or region. There are both less-developed and more-developed versions of corporatism, just as there are both less-developed and more-developed institutions and economies. In chapter 5 we will be discussing the dynamics of how a country moves from a less- to a more-developed form, including to a more modern and developed form of corporatism. In this chapter, then, we will be looking comparatively at the different forms of corporatism in distinct areas; in the following chapter we will be examining the change process by which a country moves from one form of corporatism to the next.

Western Europe

Western Europe has gone through, at different stages in its history, all the forms of corporatism discussed in chapter 2. But these forms have varied from country to country and from region to region. Moreover, there are patterns in the kinds of corporatism that have appeared and in the countries where corporatism, in its various manifestations, has been present.

The first stage was historic or natural corporatism. By this we mean the corporations such as military orders, religious organizations, guilds, estates, parishes, independent towns, universities, and so forth, associated with feudal and medieval Europe. Probably all the European countries had such medieval corporations in one form or another. But in some countries they were stronger and better organized than others. Italy, Spain, France, Austria, and Germany (most of these were part of the Roman Empire at one time and had its corporatist influences) had among the most developed corporative institutions in medieval times, while northern Europe and Scandinavia (not part of the Roman Empire and its earlier corporative system of *colegios*) had fewer, less well organized corporative institutions.

Following the French Revolution of 1789 and the destruction or outlawing of many of Europe's historic corporative institutions, Europe next experienced in the nineteenth century the growth of a manifest corporatist ideology to rival liberalism and Marxism. Recall that initially the corporatist ideology was reactionary and heavily influenced by Roman Catholic social and political doctrine; later on it became more forward looking, secular and pluralistic.

The third stage in Europe's experience with corporatism, manifest or state corporatism, came in the interwar period of the 1920s and 1930s. In this period many regimes came to power based in whole or in part on corporatist organizational principles: Mussolini's Italy, Franco's Spain, Hitler's Germany, Salazar's Portugal, Dolfuss's Austria, Metaxas's Greece, Pilsudski's Poland, Vichy France, and others. These corporative systems were eventually and generally discredited, both by their defeat in World War II and by the dismal performance and character (authoritarian or even totalitarian) of most such corporative regimes.

Following World War II, most of the interwar corporatist regimes (Spain and Portugal excepted) repudiated corporatism even while continuing to practice some aspects of it in new form. The new, updated, modernized form came to be called neo-corporatism. It mainly involved the *incorporation* of such groups as business, labor, and agriculture into the decision-making and policy implementation structures of the modern state. The growth of central economic planning and expanded social-welfare programs were the main causes of this new form of societal corporatism. Governments did more than consult with these interest groups (which would be called interest-group pluralism); it actually brought them into the decision-making and implementation process and often gave them formal representation in the state's various policy and regulatory agencies.

While all of Western Europe practices neo-corporatism to some extent, some countries have stronger forms of corporatism than others.[1] It is useful for comparative purposes to distinguish between them and to try to understand why some are more corporatist than others. The criteria used to distinguish these types and levels of corporatism are:

1. historical experience with corporatism
2. organization of corporatist institutions
3. degree of centralization and concertation
4. corporatist politics and policies

Strong Corporatism

Austria is usually thought of as having the strongest corporatist institutions in Europe. Austria has a long history and tradition of corporatism; the corporatist ideology was strong in the nineteenth and early twentieth centuries; and Austria's experience with corporatism has not been an entirely unhappy one. Organizationally, Austria's interest associations are compulsory, monopolistic, and self-governing; they and their functions are established in public law, and the associations enjoy the right to give their opinion on all bills and to participate on quasi-official advisory boards. Both business and labor are centralized and well organized. The central clearing agency for corporative activities is the Joint Commission on Wages and Prices, which operates at the highest level, under the presidency. Agreements are often worked out on an informal but still corporative basis between the representatives of business, labor, agriculture, and the state. These functional groups also exist in close symbiosis with the political parties; the parties generally have sections for each corporate group, and often the interests groups are represented directly in the Parliament through their influence in the parties. Public policy in such areas as income policy and social welfare is similarly determined through a corporative "social partnership" between these groups and the government; this system has functioned quite smoothly for over forty years. Thus, Austria would seem to be strongly corporative on all four of the criteria listed above.

Other strongly corporatist countries are Sweden and the Netherlands. While neither country has quite the long and deep corporatist tradition of Austria, both do have systems of well-organized interest groups strongly integrated into the state bureaucracy. The Netherlands has a powerful Social-Economic Council, a part of the state, which incorporates these groups and is a key decision-making body. Sweden lacks a similar body but nevertheless has other strong corporatist institutions. In both countries interest associations are closely tied into the political parties and are strongly centralized, though not in so monopolistic a manner as in Austria. Public policy, particularly in the areas of social policy and wages, is similarly hammered out on a corporative basis. Both these countries, therefore, have strong corporatist systems that are not quite as strongly corporatist as Austria's.[2]

Intermediate Countries

West Germany (now united with East Germany) and Denmark are usually thought of as medium or intermediate corporatist countries; Great Britain also possibly fits into this category. Germany has a long history of corporatism going back to the Middle Ages, but it was discredited by the Nazi experience. Germany has both publicly sponsored (corporative) chambers of industry and commerce and free or voluntary associations. The corporative groups are often consulted by government decision makers and are involved in policy but, unlike in Austria, their inclusion is not compulsory. In addition, the ties of the interest organizations to the parties are often uneven. Germany, more than many European countries, has a free-enterprise style economy, so its corporatism also tends to be weaker.

Denmark's interest groups are organized in a way closer to those of Sweden (a fellow Scandinavian country) but do not enjoy the same type of representational monopoly. Moreover, Denmark still has many craft unions that are pluralistic, whereas Sweden's labor system is dominated by more monopolistic industrial unions. Danish public policymaking on social and economic programs, however, does bring all the interest groups together under official auspices to try to forge a common, consensual policy.

In Great Britain there are some corporatist traditions but also a tradition of individualism and of the sovereignty of Parliament, which is organized on liberal and pluralist lines. In contrast, corporatist involvement in decision making has been strong on incomes, social, and industrial policy. Moreover, since the early 1960s a framework for the tripartite (labor, business, the state) organization of decision making has been present, and there are often close ties between interest groups and the parties—especially between the dominant Trade Union Conference and the Labor Party. Nevertheless, corporatism has been a hotly debated political issue in Britain (unlike in most of our other countries, where it is widely accepted) and, as we see in chapter 7, came under strong attack especially from conservatives like Margaret Thatcher.[3]

Weak Corporatism

France is usually considered by comparativists an example of weak corporatism, but I am not so sure. France has a long tradition of natural and historic corporatism; it has a strong statist and mercantilist tradition, a long history of corporatist thought and ideology, and it was in France that the idea of economic concertation (bringing all groups into the effort for integral national development) was invented. France thus possesses the conceptual and institutional framework for corporatism, but its corporative institutions are weak and do not work in the disciplined, centralized, and efficient ways that they do in Austria, Sweden, or the Netherlands. For example, France has a coordinating Economic and Social Council, but it has not had much power or worked effectively for decades. In addition, French trade unions have long been deeply divided ideologically, the business associations are not well organized, and there are few effective mechanisms to bring labor, business, and the government together. The strikes that all but closed France down in late 1995 showed a low level of concertation and demonstrated that the integral system of corporatist, tripartite collaboration was not working.

Italy is another mixed case. As in France, there is a long and strong corporatist tradition and history that would seem to provide a solid base for corporatism. But—as in France—Italy's trade unions are deeply divided and highly ideological, business groups are not well organized, and conflict rather than corporative collaboration has long marked the relations between the two. If anything, Italy may have passed to a new stage, that of syndicalism, in which, in contrast to the integrated and collaborative development of corporatism, the groups are spinning in completely separate orbits—or else some of them have hived off and almost literally "captured" for themselves whole sectors of the public bureaucracy, for example labor groups in the Labor and Social Welfare ministries, which have been turned into large-scale patronage and sinecure agencies.[4]

Spain and Portugal are also examples of weak corporatism but for special reasons. Both countries have long histories and traditions of corporatism, strong corporatist ideological influences, and long-term corporatist regimes that came to power in the 1930s. But because these regimes—of Franco in Spain and Salazar in Portugal—stayed in power too long, were associated with fascism, and were discredited, the corporatist institutions associated with them were also discredited and repudiated. With corporatism in these two countries carrying such negative overtones, in the new era of democracy Spain and Portugal have been slow in developing the newer, updated, *neo*-corporatist institutions comparable to those elsewhere in Europe.

Recent Trends

Three recent trends in European corporatism deserve brief mention. First, there has been (as we see in chapter 7) a strong attack on corporatism by Margaret Thatcher and the neo-liberal economic strategists, who argue for freer economic and political arenas. These attacks and their accompanying policy changes have weakened corporatism in several countries of Europe. Second, with the fall of the Berlin Wall, the end of the Cold War, and the tearing down of the Iron Curtain, the Central and Eastern European countries have become more integrated into the rest of Europe and are just beginning to experiment with and develop new institutions, including corporatist ones. The third trend is the growth of corporatist representation at the international level in such agencies as the European Parliament and the organs of the European Economic Community (EEC), where representation by functions (labor, farmers, business) has been instigated. It almost seems that as corporatism has declined at the national level, it has grown at the level of the larger, international European Community.

Special mention should be made here of Russia and other countries that once formed the Soviet Union. Recent events in Russia, the Commonwealth of Independent States, and some areas of Eastern Europe suggest that attempts to implement a liberal-pluralist and democratic political order and capitalist economic system are precipitating significant social unrest and economic crises in these countries. Corporatism may offer an attractive way to control the unrest, avoid crises, and serve as a middle ground between a nascent but still weak democracy and a reversion to full-scale communism. But the danger in the use of such corporatist control mechanisms, now as in the past, is that it may imply manifest or authoritarian corporatism rather than a participatory and democratic kind. Clearly this is a promising area for further research; we need to keep an eye on Russia and other formerly communist countries to see if corporatism is on the rise there.

Latin America

Latin America has a long history of corporatism, but it is more disorganized and less disciplined than in Europe and has not reached the European level of modern neo-corporatism.[5] Latin American traditional corporatism was mainly imported from Europe during the long (1492–1820s) colonial occupation of the continent by Spain and, in the case of Brazil, Portugal. The main corporative institutions during this period were the Roman Catholic Church, the Spanish or Portuguese colonial armies, the economic elite, the colonial bureaucracy, and the cities and universities. But in addition to the impact of imported corporatism from the Spanish and Portuguese colonial regimes, Latin American corporatism also had a basis in the large indigenous civilizations of the area—Aztec, Maya, Inca—which were similarly organized on a corporative functional or sectoral basis: priests, warriors, laborers. Even today, in the form of the *ejido* or self-governing indigenous community, Latin America continues to exhibit corporatist influences from its indigenous as well as its European past.

But up until recently, Latin America never had anything comparable to the French Revolution, which destroyed the old, medieval basis of society and, with it, the historical basis of corporatism. Instead, when independence came to Latin America in the 1820s, the established, conservative, traditional, semifeudal basis of historic corporatism— Church, army, oligarchy—largely continued. Unlike the United States, where independence from Britain was accompanied by a real liberalizing revolution, the independence movements in Latin America were conservative movements aimed at preserving the institutions of traditional society rather than destroying them. While the power of the Church gradually declined over the course of the nineteenth and twentieth centuries, the other main corporative groups, the army and the oligarchy, only increased in strength. For example, the *fuero militar* (the military "right," a feudal concept) of the army, coupled with the weakness of other civilian institutions, is what helps explain the frequent coups and military dictatorships in Latin America in the nineteenth and twentieth centuries.

Latin America, unlike Europe, did not have a long history of corporatist ideological writings in the nineteenth century, but it did have positivism. With its emphasis on order, progress, top-down, and integral rule, positivism in Latin America was ideologically parallel to corporatism and also helped to perpetuate the power of Latin America's elite groups. Corporatist ideology only came to Latin America in the early decades of the twentieth century, mainly in its Catholic and Southern European forms, when it had a major impact mainly on the structure of labor relations and social welfare programs.[6]

Beginning in the 1930s, corporatism began to exert a major influence on Latin American political institutions. There were new, functionally representative councils of state, corporately organized trade union movements, corporative regulatory agencies, and even some legislative bodies organized (as in Portugal) on a corporative or functional (so many seats for the military, the Church, etc.) basis. The main influence on Latin American corporatism at this time was the Catholic encyclicals (*Rerum Novarum* and *Quadregessimo Anno*) as well as the corporatist regimes of Mussolini, Franco, and Salazar. The most prominent corporatist regimes in Latin America were those of Getulio Vargas in Brazil, Juan Perón in Argentina, and the Mexican Party of Revolutionary Institutions (PRI), which is organized on a tripartite functional basis consisting of worker, peasant, and popular (everyone else) sectors. But virtually every other government in Latin America during the period of the 1930s and 1940s had some corporatist influences (which were often mixed and overlapped with liberal and republican institutions): Bolivia, Chile, Colombia, Costa Rica, Cuba, the Dominican Republic, Ecuador, El Salvador, Guatemala, Honduras, Nicaragua, Panama, Paraguay, Peru, Uruguay, and Venezuela.

Following World War II, when corporatism was either repudiated or practiced in disguised form in Europe, it continued largely intact in many Latin American countries. Because Latin America had not participated in the war on the Axis side (most Latin American countries had allied themselves with the United States), and because Latin America's form of corporatism had not been associated with fascism or Nazism, corporatism in Latin America continued to be practiced— again often mixed with republican and liberal influences. As Latin America became somewhat more democratic in the late 1950s to early 1960s, corporatism declined somewhat in influence but never disappeared. Then, when a wave of military regimes came to power in the 1960s and 1970s based on the familiar principles of discipline, order, authority, and top-down, integral or coordinated development, corporatism came roaring back—often with a vengeance as many of these regimes (for example, that of Augusto Pinochet in Chile) employed authoritarian and human rights–abusing techniques. This was the high-point of Latin American *state corporatism.*[7]

State corporatism in Latin America was a controlling and a co-opting device. As the Latin American countries began industrialization and accelerated modernization from the 1930s on, they often looked for a formula that would enable them to develop economically without the usual concomitants of modernization—powerful trade unions, organized peasants, greater pluralism and democracy, perhaps even social revolution—from growing or getting out of hand. Corporatism provided just that formula. For corporatism stood for integral national development but it also provided, through official, state-run agencies, a means to control the groups and pressures to which development gave rise. Hence, what many Latin American corporative regimes did from the 1930s on was to create official, government-sponsored labor organizations, businessmen's associations, and so on, and channeled certain benefits such as social security, wage increases, and government contracts to them. In this way Latin American economic development could advance, but without the frequently disruptive tendencies of real pluralism. Hence, corporatism often co-opted the new, rising interest groups into the political system, but in so doing it also kept them under control. In this respect, their corporatism was very much like—and was often patterned after—the top-down, authoritarian state corporatism of Spain's Franco and Portugal's Salazar.

Latin American corporatism, while showing these general characteristics, often came in a variety of forms. The regimes of Perón (Argentina) and Vargas (Brazil) were probably closest to the European system of manifest corporatism of the interwar period. There were in Latin America both military authoritarian-corporatist regimes and civilian (generally less authoritarian, more Catholic) corporatist regimes. Some Latin American corporatists were bloody tyrants (Trujillo in the Dominican Republic), others were more benign. Most of these incorporated corporatist institutions in the state machinery, but in some countries such as Venezuela or Peru a type of corporatism or sectoral organization of society (workers, peasants, students, businessmen) was embedded in the main political parties.

A special category of Latin American corporatism might be called *populist corporatism* (which we will revisit in other regional contexts) or even *revolutionary corporatism.* In this category we would put Mexico after its revolution in 1910, Bolivia after its revolution in 1952, Peru under a radical military regime 1968–75, Nicaragua (in part) after its revolution in 1979, and Cuba (in part, we say in part because in these regimes corporatism overlapped with Marxism or Marxism-Leninism) after its 1959 revolution. What these populist or revolutionary corporatist regimes had in common was that they destroyed (in whole or in part) the old and conservative corporatist groups (Church, oligarchy, sometimes the army) while elevating the newer or revolutionary groups in importance (workers, peasants, the popular sector—hence the term "populist"). Mexico's ruling PRI is the most institutionalized of these, with its tripartite organization of peasants, unionists, and other popular sectors. Nicaragua and Cuba both had full-scale socialist revolutions, but it is significant that even after their revolutions the sectoral or functional organization of society (women, peasants, students, workers) was reconstituted in new forms.

The present situation of corporatism in Latin America is one of often conflicting currents. On the one hand, Latin America has become considerably more democratic in the 1980s and 1990s; with that has come a decline in the older corporatist institutions associated with dictatorship and authoritarianism. On the other hand, the underlying political-cultural and historic currents of corporatism (centralism, organicism, statism, integralism, the functional organization of society and politics) continue to be present; and, much like in Europe after World War II, a disguised form of corporatism often continues to be practiced. Then too, continued economic crisis in Latin America in the 1990s has often meant a continued strong state role in the economy and, associated with it, the continued practice of corporatism.

At the same time, the term corporatism in Latin America is now often used disparagingly to refer to groups (military, business, unions, in some countries virtually all groups) who have their "hooks" into the political system and are using their access and privileged positions to milk jobs, patronage, contracts, special favors, second (or third or fourth) government salaries, privileges, sinecures, and outright graft out of it. But while criticizing such activities in public, many Latin Americans continue these practices in private—either because that is the only system they know or because their own, newly created liberal and democratic institutions are still too weak to be relied on entirely.

The result in Latin America is a great deal of confusion and overlap: liberal and republican in some institutions but corporatist in others; repudiating corporatism at some levels but still practicing it at others. At the same time, the type of corporatism that Latin America is arguing about is still, mainly, the statist, bureaucratic, top-down corporatism of the past. Only in a few countries have initial steps been taken toward the development of modern, European-style neo-corporatism—a process made more difficult by both the strong influence of U.S.-style liberal institutions in Latin America and the association now of corporatism with the discredited authoritarianism of the 1970s. The best estimate is that Latin America will continue to develop in this way, with a mix of liberal and corporatist institutions and practices, and will transition gradually from an older, 1930s-style corporatism toward more modern forms of neo-corporatism.

Asia

In chapter 2 we traced the history of corporatist theory and ideology, focusing on the Western tradition because that is the most familiar. But now it is time to go beyond the Western tradition and look at the cultural bases of other kinds of corporatism in non-Western societies. We begin with Asia.

Recall that when discussing the early history of the Western concept of corporatism, we stressed its group or communalist origins: the

Greek system of "natural" inequalities among groups of persons; the Roman *colegios;* and the estates, guilds, and orders of the medieval period. Then in the eighteenth century, with its emphasis on individualism, the group or corporatist organization of society came under strong attack, culminating with the French Revolution and thereafter in other countries, when corporate privilege was largely outlawed. At the time many writers in the West lamented and warned against this attack on traditional group solidarity, arguing that it would fragment and tear apart the bonds of society and produce conflict and disintegration. It was out of this fear of the social and political consequences of excessive individualism and liberalism occasioned by the end of corporate group solidarity that the modern Western theory and ideology of corporatism developed.

Much of Asia is still based on notions of society, community, and group solidarity that have been declining in the West at least since the eighteenth century. In Asia it remains the group and the broader community that are most important, not so much the individual, as in the West. Asia has never, even in modern times, placed such great stress on the autonomous individual as has the West. Although this is now changing toward greater individualism in Asia, the stress is still heavily on communalist values and group cohesion to which individual personalities should be subordinated.* This communalist basis of culture and society provides a strong foundation for corporatism.[8]

The main intellectual/religious/cultural basis to Asian communalism and what we earlier called historical or natural corporatism is Confucianism. Just as we located a part of the cultural/intellectual basis of Western corporatism in Greek and Roman political ideas and in traditional, Southern European Roman Catholicism, so we can locate a part of basis of Asian corporatism in Confucianism. But remember the differences as well: Confucianism is not a single set of religious beliefs

---

*This point was brought home to the author when he was traveling in China and conducting an ongoing seminar of cross-cultural exchange with his guide/translator, who was also a political science graduate student. At one point she told the author that she was "working on developing her individual personality." This comment sounds strange to Western ears, because we take it for granted that we are born with individual personalities, that individual personalities are natural to us, and that we always have our individual personalities. But to the Chinese, with their heavy emphasis on community, such individualism is not "natural"; it has to be "worked on" and "developed."

as is Catholicism, nor is it a formal body of ideological beliefs like Marxism. Instead, Confucianism is a "secular religion" whose perspective and "mood" help define everything from family relations to the structure of industry and the political system.

Confucianism began in mainland China over two thousand years ago; over the centuries it gradually spread to Korea, Japan, Taiwan, and much of Southeast Asia (but not the Philippines or Indonesia). In the last three centuries it has become quite secularized; it is also deeply ingrained in the broader Asian culture. Confucianism is a system of ethics that is important to an understanding of Asian corporatism in two main ways. First, groups are more important than individuals. Confucian thought stresses group loyalty, solidarity, and obedience to communal norms; it stresses the human error of individualism and the many advantages of working with and through the group.

Second, Confucianism stresses that society should be organized hierarchically. Confucianism also spells out the appropriate relations between the various elements and levels in the hierarchy: husbands and wives, parents and children, employer and employee, government and governed. Each person in the society must occupy his or her designated place and behave toward both superiors and inferiors in accord with accepted ways; in this manner social conflict can be avoided. The avoidance of conflict is strongly emphasized, because conflict means the entire hierarchy of society is unraveling, which therefore must be avoided at all costs.

The implications of these value and culture underpinnings for Asian corporatism and politics are many. First, the emphasis on group and communal values means that corporatism—similarly group based—will have a particularly fertile breeding ground in Asia. Second, the emphasis on solidarity and on the avoidance of conflict is also conducive to corporatism. Third, there is great attention to national unity and to avoiding polarization that might tear society apart—such integralism being another important ingredient in corporatism. Fourth, the system of hierarchy, of top-down authority, and of accepting one's position in life will have an effect on the type of corporatism that exists in Asia. It is interesting that all these features—emphasis on communalism, solidarity and unity, and hierarchy—have also been strongly present in Latin America historically, where corporatism has been particularly prevalent.

Corporatism in Asia, like corporatism in Latin America during the period of military rule in the 1970s, has been most closely associated with authoritarian regimes. These may be military-authoritarian regimes or civilian-authoritarian regimes; the predominant form of corporatism in Asia is thus state corporatism. The most prominent examples are South Korea under military rule, Taiwan under the single-party Kuomintang regime, Singapore under authoritarian Prime Minister Lee, and Hong Kong. In all these regimes, as in the Latin American state-corporatist regimes, corporatism involved both integral national development and the effort to harness and control the new social and political forces to which modernization and industrialization give rise: emerging labor organizations, new businessmen, professionals and their associations, university students, and former peasants who have flocked to the cities in search of jobs.

All these groups are considered possibly disruptive and potentially destabilizing. Rather than risk disruption or instability, the regimes in these countries sought instead to control them and their participation in the political process by enveloping them in a network of officially sanctioned, government-run interest associations that were corporative in character and organized and run by the state. At times, coercive measures were used to keep these groups under control. The system was not one of democracy, pluralism, or modern societal or neo-corporatism as in Western Europe; rather it was one of top-down, authoritarian, or state corporatism.[9] Asian corporatism has thus been far closer to the Latin American model than to the Western European one.

But note that these regimes—South Korea, Taiwan, Hong Kong, and Singapore—are also referred to as the "Four Tigers," or NICs (newly industrialized countries): they are among the most successful countries in the world in terms of economic development. Their economic successes, moreover, have often been associated with their authoritarian regimes and with their particular forms of state corporatism. The ability through corporatist institutions to coordinate, harness, and control the social forces that modernization sets loose without producing disruption or instability is often viewed—certainly by many Asians—as among the most important factors in enabling them to achieve their miracle economic growth rates of often 8, 9, or 10 percent per year. Here we have, then, the essence of the Asian model of economic development: not the pluralist, democratic model that the United States prefers but a top-down, integral, sometimes authoritarian, and state-corporatist route to development. We may not appreciate the authoritarian methods sometimes used, but the economic results have certainly been impressive. And it is these undoubted accomplishments that lie behind the recent Asian assertion that they have found a model of development that is uniquely Asian and that demonstrates that their culture and accomplishments are superior to those of the West.

In recent years, however, these Asian regimes have begun to move away from authoritarianism and state corporatism and toward more democratic and pluralist regimes. South Korea is now more democratic than before, Taiwan has allowed more competitive elections, and Hong Kong and Singapore have relaxed their authoritarian controls somewhat. It seems likely—and is already occurring—that as these countries move from authoritarianism to greater democracy, they will also move from a system of strict state corporatism to one of greater societal or neo-corporatism. The fact is that as these countries have achieved successful modernization, the logic of maintaining such strict corporative controls over their group and associational life has weakened. We are likely to see in Asia, therefore, an evolution toward a more European and pluralist form of corporatism. But it is still the case that many Asians take great pride in their earlier developmental experiences—which were definitely not democratic in character—and present the authoritarian-corporatist system as a model for other developing nations to emulate, especially during the early or transitional stages of modernization.

Two other state-corporatist regimes in Asia merit mention here, those of Indonesia and the Philippines. Neither of these are Confucian societies, so they lack some of the cultural bases for natural corporatism that other Asian societies have; nonetheless they created definite corporatist regimes. We refer specifically to Indonesia under Suharto and the Philippines under Ferdinand Marcos. Both of these were long-term authoritarian regimes; both leaders presided over periods of considerable economic development. But development usually gives rise to new social and political forces (businessmen, labor unions, a variety of professionals) who often begin to demand a voice in the political process and who may threaten the use of force if their demands are not met. Rather like the state-corporatist regimes of Latin America, therefore, these regimes used corporatism as a way to control the sociopolitical forces that modernization set loose. Instead of allowing pluralism and democracy to develop, these regimes employed a set of official, state-directed institutions and associations (corporatism) to channel, direct, and oversee the new groups that the modernization process produces. In this way, development could go forward, authoritarianism be preserved, and democracy and pluralism be avoided—at least for a time.

A special case is Japan, which is special in at least three respects. First, Japan is the most successful of all the Asian countries; it is a modern, developed nation, a world economic power, and impressive in other ways as well. Second, Japan, in contrast to the East Asian and Southeast nations already considered, is a democracy, with regular elections, a multiparty system, and well-respected freedoms. Third, while Japan has many of the ingredients of other modern corporatist systems, it remains very different from the Western European systems.

These differences between Asia and Europe can best be understood by looking back at the European experience. The model system of modern corporatism, as presented in this book, developed first in Western Europe. European corporatism emerged out of a particular historical, cultural, and institutional context. That context included the development of mobilized, class-conscious trade union movements, fears of the disruptive effects of class conflict during times of economic development and external challenges (for example, the Cold War), and close links between organized labor and a number of socialist or social-democratic political parties that sought to bring labor and business together into a corporatist arrangement for purposes of smoother, peaceful, public policymaking.[10]

In Japan, as in other Asian societies, the Confucian ethic of harmony and community was present, helping give rise to an Asian form of historical or natural corporatism. But many of the ingredients of the European model pattern of modern neo-corporatism were absent: no Marxian tradition, no history of class conflict in the European sense, no strong revolutionary threat from the working class that needed to be co-opted through corporatist arrangements, no alliance between a strong trade union movement and a strong or governing socialist party. In fact, Japan has weak trade unions and therefore lacks one of the essential ingredients of European-style corporatism. By culture, historical circumstances, and institutional arrangements, therefore, we should expect Japanese corporatism to be quite different from that of European.

The Japanese system of corporatism grows out of both the Confucian tradition of harmony and, in modern times, the close, collaborative, institutional relationship between business and the government. That relationship is a symbiotic one, with both business and the state feeding off each other and so closely intertwined—as in the Ministry of Trade (the famous MITI)—that it is impossible to separate them. This close and essentially corporatist relationship also gives rise, incidentally, to the often-heard charge in the United States that the Japanese state subsidizes and protects its business sector, giving it an unfair advantage in competition with U.S. business. At the same time, since organized labor in Japan is relatively weak, it is not part of the usual tripartite (labor, business, the state) relationship that characterizes modern European corporatism. And, as we know from popular television programs, Japanese labor relations are usually based on agreements reached *within* the firm, on a consensus basis (the Confucian pattern), not on a nationwide or sector-by-sector system of bargaining and co-optation between organized labor and organized business (too conflict oriented for Japanese taste). The result is that Japan has a system of partial or only half-corporatism, with business included but labor dealt with under a more paternalistic system of employment and social guarantees.

India is also a special case. India has a system (actually, several systems) of natural and historical corporatism that grows out of its Buddhist and Hindu traditions. These traditions, and in more recent times Gandhi, emphasize harmony, consensus, and community—in contrast to the pluralistic and/or class conflict models of the West. There are numerous writings in India that suggest neither the capitalist nor the communist models (both Western and European in origin) are suitable, that argue for a system of politics, society, and economy based on Indian traditions.[11] One corporative agency that frequently receives mention in this respect is the caste associations, particularly as these have begun to evolve into modern interest associations.[12] Indian writers, parallel to their East Asian counterparts, often argue for a system of closely interrelated societal units integrated into the state (called "integral pluralism"). The traditional Indian corporative conception often includes regional and ethnic groups, caste groups, and religious groups, as well as the modern institution of labor, employers, and the state. But this often remains vague and is as yet not well institutionalized. As India continues to develop and modernize, it will doubtless develop more of the interest groups and institutions of modern corporatism; but at present it remains a mix of traditional and modernizing influences.

No discussion of Asia would be complete without mentioning China (one-fourth of all mankind!), even though China's corporative arrangements are still at a quite primitive level. First, China is, like the rest of East Asia, a society strongly influenced by the Confucian tradition, so the familiar emphasis on family, community, solidarity, and harmony is present. But second, China remains in many respects a communist country (one of four left, along with North Korea, Vietnam, and Cuba) so it does not permit real, independent interest associations. And third, China remains underdeveloped. As China both develops economically and opens to the outside world, it will doubtless come up with some form of corporatist institutions; but for now it has only the most rudimentary base. Much the same could be said for a number of other countries of Southeast Asia that are just beginning the development process.

Islamic Society

It seems as though all the world's major religions place heavy stress on such concepts as community, society, solidarity, and communalism. The focus on community, as we have seen in the cases so far of Christianity, Confucianism, Buddhism, and Hinduism, helps give rise to the phenomenon of traditional, natural, or historical corporatism. Similarly with Islam: the Koran also contains a strong call to brotherhood, solidarity, and community. Moreover, in the great writings of Islamic sociopolitical thought, heavy emphasis is placed on the just ruler who must consult regularly with the groups that make up his kingdom.[13] Some have seen in these injunctions the roots of both corporatism and a kind of Islamic democracy.

The main natural corporate groups in a traditional kingdom like Saudi Arabia are the desert tribes. Saudi Arabia and the other sheikdoms of the Persian Gulf are not developed enough that they have strong labor unions and the other institutions of modern corporatism. Instead, the kingdom is organized on a tribal basis with the king exercising ultimate authority. The king consults with the tribes that make up his kingdom; indeed, King Fawd of Saudi Arabia, for example, still does so, periodically taking his entourage from the capital, Riyadh, out into the desert to consult with the tribal chiefs. The king will often bring his tent (large and royal) along, set up his court at a desert oasis, and hold discussions with the clan leaders that make up Saudi society. Such consultations between royal authority and tribal organizations have been referred to as a "primitive" (traditional, historical, natural) form of corporatism or, alternatively, as a precursor to democracy.

If we move to a larger, more diverse, more developed Islamic state such as Egypt, a different form of corporatism appears. The foremost student of the subject, Robert Bianchi, calls Egypt a system of "unruly corporatism."[14] As Egypt has modernized and developed economically in recent decades, the web of its associational and corporate group life has also expanded. The main corporative groups in *modern* Egypt (as distinct from *traditional* Saudi Arabia) are the labor unions, businessmen's associations, religious groups, agricultural cooperatives, and professional agencies.

As in many emerging, developing corporative systems, there is in Egypt a long history of tension between these corporative groups, which are seeking to enhance their power and preserve their autonomy, and the Egyptian state, which also seeks to expand its power— often at the expense of these groups and by controlling their organizations (again, state corporatism). Former strongman Gamal Abdel Nasser, who also thought of himself as a revolutionary, sought to give a populist thrust to Egyptian corporatism by showering benefits on the lower class groups; his successors Anwar Sadat and Hosni Mubarak returned to a less populist, more exclusionary style of state or top-down corporatism.

Other Islamic states—Morocco, Tunisia, Libya, Algeria, Syria— have similarly begun to move from a more primitive kind of clan corporatism to a more modern kind. But often the new associational groups are weakly organized and are sometimes attacked and suppressed by the state. Indeed, as in East Asia and Latin America, there is almost always a dynamic and sometimes violent tension in these countries between the strong state reaching for still greater power and the efforts of these groups to maintain some degree of independence. It must also be remembered that the balance among these corporate groups (as well as vis-à-vis the state) varies over time; currently religious groups advocating Islamic fundamentalism appear to be growing in size and power. They may try to seize the reins of state power for themselves and use that power to snuff out other groups and even the principle of pluralism itself; meanwhile, the central government may try to suppress these groups. Corporatism in the Islamic world, therefore, often remains both underdeveloped and threatened.

Africa

In Africa, as in the Middle East, the main focus of corporatism research and political organization has been the tribe, the clan, or the ethnic group. The system of ethnic groups is the African version of natural or traditional corporatism.[15]

Much of Africa south of the Sahara desert is organized on such a clan, tribe, or ethnic group basis. In some of Africa's larger states there may be hundreds of ethnic groups within a single country. At the same time—and this is a key problem for many African states—the national boundaries drawn by the colonial powers do not correspond to ethnic group boundaries. Quite a number of African states have been torn apart by these ethnic conflicts, which at times degenerate into civil war and violence. Kenya, Ethiopia, Zaire, Liberia, Rwanda, Somalia, Uganda, and Burundi are among the countries that have been all but destroyed by cross-ethnic violence.

Africa has had two basic responses to this kind of destructive clan violence. The first response has been to try to snuff it out, either through force or by persuasion. The use of force implies strong state power, a strong army, and often dictatorship. The dictatorships may try to balance out the competing ethnic groups, using either repression or a quasi-corporatist system of having each group represented in the regime. But more democratic and pluralist solutions are also possible.

In Tanzania, for example, which has over 120 ethnic groups (most of them, fortunately, separated by some distance; they are also relatively balanced numerically, so no one group can dominate), clan loyalties have been de-emphasized. People are urged not to ask about each other's tribal affiliations; political candidates are discouraged from appealing to clan loyalties.

Tanzania's relative ethnic harmony is part of the enduring legacy of Julius Nyerere, who established policies aimed at de-emphasizing ethnic differences during his reign of twenty-four years, from independence in 1961 until he stepped down in 1985. Nyerere sought to emphasize national unity over ethnic solidarity. He made Swahili the official language and outlawed the teaching of tribal languages in school. He wrested power away from the clan chiefs and refused to allow civil servants to work in their home areas where they might show special favoritism to members of their own clan. He also made sure cabinet positions and military officerships went to persons from a variety of tribes. In the capital city of Dar es Salaam, interethnic marriages, businesses, and neighbor-hoods are common. A single-party system brought unity to the coun-try—but at the cost of competitive democracy.

More recently the institution of tribe, clan, or ethnic group has been undergoing reevaluation and is viewed not in such negative terms. After all, many African political parties and interest groups have their basis in tribal organization. In addition, justice, social welfare, police protection, health care, education, and other positive public policies are often administered through communal or tribal networks. Hence, many African politicians and intellectuals are now suggesting that instead of wishing the tribal phenomenon away or trying—usually futilely—to snuff it out, let us acknowledge and deal with it realistically. For exam-ple, instead of the unitary, centralized political systems bequeathed by the colonial administration or adopted by African leaders immediately after independence, why not a federal or decentralized system of politi-cal authority? That at least would be a realistic way of dealing with tribalism. Representation in national government institutions would be based on a form of corporatism organized through the diverse clan groups. Such a plan would also enable the African states to develop truly indigenous political systems instead of relying on outside models. Of course, a proper balance would still have to be drawn between the central state and these decentralized units and between the rival clans themselves. But perhaps a form of federal system with representation through a corporatist structure might help save some African nations from the kind of fratricidal violence that has led to national disintegra-tion. One can easily see in these ideas an African form of state–society relations, an African form of corporatism.

But corporatism takes different forms in Africa, as it does in other areas.[16] South Africa has the most developed economy in the region; it also has the most developed system of corporately organized interest associations, now encompassing both white and black members of the society. Angola and Mozambique, both former Portuguese colonies, still show remnants of the kind of Catholic/bureaucratic corporatism that Portugal's dictator Antonio Salazar tried to export to the colonies in earlier decades.* We also find different political and institutional

---

*In 1973 the author was living in Portugal writing a book on Portuguese corporatism. But he became so fascinated with Portugal's colonial situation in Africa that he dreamed up a research project to study the attempt to export

arrangements depending on whether the country was a former Belgian, British, French, or German colony. Nevertheless, African corporatism, reflecting the area's relatively low level of economic and institutional development, is still in its early stage.

From this analysis it is clear that there is a great variety of corporatisms. The differences between them are based on a combination of cultural, historical, and institutional factors. Across regional boundaries, in Europe, Latin America, Asia, Islamic Society, and Africa, corporatism shows both great variation and some interesting common features.

But corporatism also varies according to level of economic and social development. There are parallel patterns in the way corporatism emerges and grows above and beyond cultural factors. It is to these common dynamics in the growth and development of corporatism that we now turn.

Notes

1. The analysis here follows in part that of Gerhard Lehmbruch, "Introduction: Neo-Corporatism in Comparative Perspective," in Gerhard Lehmbruch and Philippe C. Schmitter (eds.), *Patterns of Corporatist Policy-Making* (London: Sage, 1982).

2. Some key studies include Alfred Diamant, *Austrian Catholics and the First Republic* (Princeton, NJ: Princeton University Press, 1960); and Peter J. Katzenstein, *Corporatism and Change: Austria, Switzerland, and the Politics of Industry* (Ithaca, NY: Cornell University Press, 1984).

3. Useful comparative studies include Lehmbruch and Schmitter (eds.), *Patterns of Corporatist Policy-Making;* Ilja Scholten (ed.), *Political Stability and Neo-Corporatism: Corporatist Integration and Societal Cleavages in Western Europe* (Beverly Hills: Sage, 1987); and Andrew Cox and Noel O'Sullivan (eds.), *The Corporate State: Corporatism and the State Tradition in Western Europe* (Cambridge: Cambridge University Press, 1988).

4. See the earlier, conceptual study by the author, *From Corporatism to Neo-Syndicalism: The State, Organized Labor, and the Changing Industrial Relations Systems of Southern Europe* (Cambridge: Harvard University, Center for European Studies, 1981).

5. The major studies are James Malloy (ed.), *Authoritarianism and Corporatism in Latin America* (Pittsburgh: University of Pittsburgh Press, 1977); and

---

Portugal's corporative system to the overseas colonies. The project was approved and funded, but the 1974 revolution in Portugal not only ended the older Salazar system of corporatism but also led to independence for the Portuguese colonies. Hence, the project was never carried out.

Howard J. Wiarda, *Corporatism and National Development in Latin America* (Boulder, CO: Westview Press, 1981).

6. See, by the author, *The Corporative Origins of the Iberian and Latin American Labor Relations Systems* (Amherst: University of Massachusetts, Labor Relations and Research Center, 1976); and David Collier and Ruth Berins Collier, *Shaping the Political Arena: Critical Junctures, the Labor Movement, and Regime Dynamics in Latin America* (Berkeley: University of California Press, 1991).

7. Kenneth P. Erickson, *The Brazilian Corporative State and Working Class Politics* (Berkeley: University of California Press, 1977). The earliest corporatist paradigm for Latin America during this period was set forth in Howard J. Wiarda, "Toward a Framework for the Study of Political Change in the Iberic-Latin Tradition: The Corporative Model," *World Politics* 25 (January 1973): 206–35.

8. See, among many works, Peter R. Moody, Jr., *Tradition and Modernization in China and Japan* (Belmont, CA: Wadsworth, 1995).

9. Harmon Zeigler, *Pluralism, Corporatism, and Confucianism: Political Association and Conflict Regulation in the United States, Europe, and Taiwan* (Philadelphia: Temple University Press, 1988).

10. Lehmbruch, "Introduction," 25.

11. For example, Vrajenda Raj Mehta, *Beyond Marxism: Towards an Alternative Perspective* (New Delhi: Manshar Publications, 1978).

12. Lloyd Rudolph and Suzanne Rudolph, *The Modernity of Tradition* (Chicago: University of Chicago Press, 1967).

13. Anwar Syed, *Pakistan: Islam, Politics, and National Solidarity* (New York: Praeger, 1982). Syed's rich analysis is important beyond the Pakistan case.

14. Robert Bianchi, *Unruly Corporatism: Associational Life in Twentieth-Century Egypt* (New York: Oxford University Press, 1989).

15. Crawford Young, *The Politics of Cultural Pluralism* (Madison: University of Wisconsin Press, 1976).

16. Julius E. Nyang' oro and Timothy M. Shaw (eds.), *Corporatism in Africa: Comparative Analysis and Practice* (Boulder, CO: Westview Press, 1989).

5

The Dynamics of Change in Corporatist Systems

In chapter 4 we focused on corporatism and corporatist systems in different regions of the world. Such a focus is usually referred to in comparative analysis as a cross-cultural or horizontal approach. It is a picture, a snapshot, of a variety of countries in different areas of the globe at a given point in time—in this case, the present. We were concerned in that chapter with the variety and types of corporatism that exist in distinct countries and regions in the contemporary context.

But countries and regions can also be studied comparatively over time, or vertically. That is, we can look back as well as forward and trace the forms of corporatism in a given society as they have evolved from one historical phase to the next. Even more challenging, we can take the form of corporatism that exists in one society at a given stage in history and compare it with another form of corporatism in another society at another stage. In other words, we can also trace comparatively the form of corporatism from one stage to another, relating each form to the country's level of development, industrialization, social differentiation, or overall level of modernization. In this way we can assess corporatism both comparatively *and* over time, in distinct societies *and* distinct historical time periods. We can also predict with some degree of accuracy how, under a given set of similar conditions, one form of corporatism may evolve into another, more advanced form.

The forces driving the transition from one form of corporatism to the next are complex. The main stimulus in such change is often economic development, industrialization, and the overall modernization of society that usually accompanies economic development. These in turn ordinarily give rise to new classes and social groups, such as trade unions, business groups, and professional associations—to greater *dif-*

ferentiation among the social levels and groups in society. It is this greater social differentiation and the rise of new classes and socioeconomic groups that often stimulate more advanced forms of corporatism as a way of incorporating and thus often controlling these new groups' participation in the political process. Political institutions may also be influential in shaping the type of corporatism that emerges.

But as we have already seen in examining corporatism in a variety of culture areas, the precise form that corporatism may take in a given society is shaped by that society's culture and history as well as by economic and institutional factors. For example, we have seen that corporatism in Southern Europe and in Latin America was influenced heavily by Roman Catholicism; in Asia the Confucian ethos helped determine the kind of corporatism that exists. But sometimes the causation is even more complex: economic factors will sometimes shape the political institutions and the cultural patterns; at other times the culture may help influence the political and economic structures; and all of these factors—economic, social, political, and cultural—often interact in complex and ever-shifting ways to determine the practice and form of corporatism. So as we trace the evolution of corporatism through distinct historical stages, we need to be aware of this complex web of causation.

Traditional Corporatism

Traditional, historic, or what we have called natural corporatism may come in a great variety of forms. Traditional corporatism refers to the basic, historic, grassroots organizational units on which early society is structured. Of course, these may take different forms in different culture areas, but the basic units are usually the family; the clan or extended family; and the tribe, parish, caste association, or neighborhood group. Note that these units are usually limited in size and geographic distance; they existed before the onset of modern communications, transportation, and bureaucratic organization enabled larger units to be brought together. Such small-scale, grassroots organizations also lack a principle of representation. Cultural anthropology teaches us that most, if not all, societies had these forms of rudimentary organization, which usually encompassed both geographic and some kind of primitive functional organization. Although the precise form and cultural traditions of these early societies varied significantly, such units as the family, clan, or extended family were well nigh universal. We refer to this first or earliest stage within traditional society as *primitive corporatism*.

But in most such traditional societies, significant processes of change sooner or later begin to occur. For one thing, as these societies grow and develop, they often come to govern a larger geographic territory. For another (and related), they come to govern a larger group of people. Plus, as these societies grow and expand, they also become more complex, requiring greater differentiation of roles, greater specialization of functions, and, hence, a principle of representation. For example, society and its functions may differentiate between a warrior group, a priestly group, artisans, craftspeople, farmers, and so on. As society begins to develop, these different groups begin to emerge, with each group performing specialized functions, and a new and more complex system of group and corporate representation begins to emerge. For that reason, traditional corporatism needs to be thought of as encompassing two stages: early or primitive corporatism, as described above, and a somewhat more developed (medieval or feudal) corporatism, as society begins its early processes of change.

All societies seem to go through these processes; Europe provides us with a readily understandable or paradigm case. Early Europe was organized on the quite primitive family, clan, and tribal basis as outlined earlier; there was little geographic or occupational specialization or representation. With the fall of the Roman Empire, much of early medieval Europe reverted to this primitive form. But in the twelfth and thirteenth centuries. Europe began to experience renewed prosperity after the dismal, centuries-long experience of the Dark Ages, and also the consolidation of larger territorial states.[1] To this point European society had consisted mainly of two classes, lords and peasants, with agriculture being the predominant occupation. The new prosperity of the later Middle Ages, however, led to a considerably greater social differentiation and to new social classes: artisans, craftsmen, and merchants. In addition, and in conjunction with the Crusades, new religious and military orders were created, providing greater social complexity. At the same time, the growing towns and cities as well as regional governments, newly organized universities, and the merchant guilds negotiated for greater independence from encroaching central government authority.

In the language of the time, all these groups—artisans, craftsmen, guilds, religious orders, military orders, towns, cities, universities, regions—were known as "corporations"; hence, the origin of the term "corporatism." That is, these groups were chartered in law like a modern joint-stock corporation; their "juridical personality" was recognized; and, usually in return for loyalty and service to royal authority, they were given jurisdiction to govern their own internal affairs and afforded the right to bargain in the political process—which frequently involved disagreements with the central state over the degree of their own autonomy. It was out of this greater social differentiation and the organization of new groups in society that the system of representation by estates—nobility, clergy, common—developed in the Middle Ages. The estate system provided a modicum of popular participation and of national integration; but since class lines were still rigidly drawn and since no group was willing to accept the decisions of a majority within a single representative body, the estates met and voted separately and then had to negotiate among themselves over issues of common concern.

But several forces were at work undermining the structure of estates and the system of nascent or traditional European corporatism on which it rested. The first factor was the emergence of royal absolutism and strict centralized control that was growing at the same time as the more decentralized corporative structure. Absolute monarchies throughout Europe, after a long struggle, either abolished the estate assemblies altogether—and with them much of the independent corporate group life—or let them function for a time, but stripped of their power. Royal absolutism undermined the foundations of medieval corporatism by destroying allegiance to a particular social or corporate group and substituting for it absolute loyalty to the monarchy.

Then, in the seventeenth and eighteenth centuries, came the growing emphasis on the individual rather than on the group—the second factor in weakening traditional European corporatism. Out of the Renaissance, the Reformation, and the Enlightenment came the notion that it was the individual that was most important, not so much a person's estate, corporate, or community loyalties. This emphasis on the individual reached its most dramatic point in the American (1776) and French (1789) Revolutions, when the idea of democratic, individualistic *citizenship* triumphed over the earlier, feudal, and corporate concept of *subject*. The French Revolution resulted in 1791 in the outlawing of the system of estates and its corporative underpinnings; most of the other European countries shortly thereafter similarly abolished their corporate group rights and representation by estates. In Germany, however, where the American and French notions of persons endowed with individual rights without regard to their membership in a social group was still viewed as strange, the system of representation by estates hung on for a time until, after a new round of European revolutions in 1848, it, too, was abolished in favor of a modern parliament based on geographic representation. So ended, for the most part, traditional, feudal, or medieval European corporatism.[2]

Although the historical record of the evolution of traditional corporatism in non-Western areas is not as complete as it is in the paradigm European context, there are interesting differences from the European case as well as similarities. First, the differences. Ever since the French Revolution and the subsequent destruction of premodern European social structure based on estates and corporative organization, the notion has been widespread in sociology and political science that traditional society is, like that of France in 1789, a hard, inflexible, unbending shell. It must either give way peacefully under the impact of modernization or it will crack and be destroyed by revolution. In both cases, the assumption is that traditional society must disappear.

But in most non-Western societies, which lack both the forces (Renaissance, Reformation, Enlightenment) that led to the triumph of individualism in the West and the destructive impact of the French Revolution, traditional society has not disappeared. Rather than giving way through a quick surrendering of power or, alternatively, succumbing to revolution, traditional society and its corporative bonds have proved remarkably permeable and flexible in much of the Third World, bending to and absorbing change rather than giving way before its supposed onslaught. Whether one is talking of African or Middle Eastern clan groups, Indian caste associations, East Asian Confucianism, or Latin American patrimonialism and clientelism, the pattern has been that these traditional institutions have proven to be amazingly malleable and accommodative, absorbing new social forces, practices, and public policy issues rather than being destroyed by them. In fact, the pattern of persistence of traditional institutions has been so powerful in so many distinct culture areas that one is forced to conclude that *it* is the modal pattern and not so much the supposedly paradigmatic European case. It turns out that Europe is the exception—at least in the short run—and not necessarily as inevitably the model for others to emulate.

This idea of the persistence of traditional institutions and ways of doing things and their continuation in modified form into the era of modernization (as distinct from the European pattern, which implies a sharp break with the past) gives rise to an entirely new sociology and politics of modernization. It forces us to study traditional institutions as long lasting and perhaps semipermanent, as distinct from our usual, Western dismissal of them as doomed to failure and collapse. It forces us to examine their accommodative and adaptive mechanisms rather than simply to assume they will fade away. And it obliges us to consider traditional institutions as agents of change even though that sounds to Western ears like a contradiction of terms.

Indian caste associations, for example, which are usually thought by Americans to be wholly traditional and retrogressive institutions, have, in fact, demonstrated themselves to be partly modernizing institutions, evolving into more modern interest associations and helping India bridge the gap between the past and the future.[3] Similarly in Asia, the traditional Confucian ethos, which was once thought to be inimical to modernization, is now, with its emphasis on discipline, family, education, organization, and hard work, thought to be one of the most important factors in the incredible success stories of the East Asian nations. In Africa the institution of the clan, tribe, or ethnic group, previously viewed by Westerners and many Africans alike as wholly traditional and in need of obliteration, is presently seen more favorably as administering police and judicial functions in many local communities, providing social services in a continent plagued by famine and disease, and perhaps providing the foundation of a new, decentralized political system.

In Latin America many of the same themes apply. Latin America's "traditional" institutions include the extended family as well as vast patronage and clientelistic networks. Often in the past (and still in some quarters today), these institutions were thought of as belonging to history and requiring obliteration if Latin America was to progress. But we are now discovering that extended family networks can serve as the basis for interest groups, political parties, and economic and political viability; that patronage and clientelistic networks can be extended to include trade unions and peasant associations as well as elite groups; that such patronage systems are not necessarily incompatible with democracy; and that entire, functioning, complex political systems (such as those of Mexico or Brazil) can be constructed on a vast patronage basis. Clearly these comments force us not only to rethink our common notions of "traditional" institutions but also the entire issue of how nations modernize and develop. For even traditional systems with their historic corporative features as described here, instead of standing in the way of change, have shown remarkable abilities to bend, accommodate, absorb, and even lead their societies on the route to modernization.[4]

We have been talking so far of the differences between the Western and the non-Western experiences, but we also need to focus on the similarities. For in *all* these societies, what provoked traditional corporatist institutions into their efforts at modernization were the beginnings of economic development, social change and differentiation, and, especially among today's developing nations, the intrusion of outside influences and pressures. Economic development and eventually industrialization tend to set new social forces loose, to make society more complex, and to give rise to new social pressures. Faced with these new pressures, traditional corporatist institutions can either try to resist change and stand in its way, or they can seek to accommodate and thus control it in their own ways. When faced with this choice, most traditional corporative institutions have reacted in similar ways— which leads to the next stage both in our analysis and in terms of corporatist development.

Dealing with the "Social Question"

Recall that in chapter 2 we showed that, after the French Revolution and the formal outlawing of traditional, medieval corporatism, writings on corporatism in the early nineteenth century tended to be very reactionary. The advocates of corporatism harked back to an idealized version of medieval corporatism from before the French Revolution; they sought to turn the clock back, to restore the *status quo ante*. Theirs was a wholly unreconstructed and often romantic vision of the earlier form of corporatism, of a stable, even static society in which everyone knew their place and accepted their station in life. If you were of the nobility, then that was God's will and part of the "natural" order of the universe; if you were a peasant, you were similarly obliged to accept that as your permanent societal position. One's place in the social order was thus determined by birth or status.

But, of course, by the nineteenth century that kind of stable, static social order no longer existed in much of Europe, or it was rapidly giving way to new pressures. This period, after all, of the early nineteenth century was one of vast and profound economic and social change throughout Europe. This was the age of the Industrial Revolution, of technological breakthroughs in manufacturing and other areas, and of accelerated economic growth. It was also an era of political revolution, of stirring ideals stemming from the French and American Revolutions, of vast social change, of the uprooting of traditional, peasant-based communities in rural areas and their migration in massive numbers to the cities and sweat shops where the great new industries and jobs were located. It was one of the most change-oriented periods in all of history, certainly in the history of the Western societies; by the mid-nineteenth century, so much had been transformed that it would be impossible to restore the *status quo ante* as the reactionary corporativists were arguing, to turn the clock back to an earlier, "sleepier" time, to resurrect the Middle Ages. Europe had clearly entered a new, industrialized era. On all these changes one can read any of a number of profound thinkers and authors: Balzac, Durkheim, Max Weber, Charles Dickens, or Marx.

One of the new social groups to which all this urbanization and industrialization gave rise in the nineteenth century was trade unions. Trade unions were a new phenomenon; they did not fit into the medieval conceptions of the proper ordering of society concocted by the reactionary corporatist writers of the time. What to do with them? Where to put them? Where do they fit? This was the "social question" as it began to emerge in Europe from the mid-nineteenth century on. What to do with this new social class that obviously did not fit medieval notions of a well-ordered, stable society—and yet could not be ignored either.

Out of these questions gradually emerged a new, more modern conception of corporatism. Moreover, corporatism was no longer just a theory or an ideology; corporatism was about to become a social movement, a way of handling change, of dealing with this new phenomenon of organized labor. The patterns of this new corporatist development, with local variations, were the same almost everywhere; they therefore deserve detailed consideration. For whether we are talking about European corporatism in the nineteenth century or the corporatism practiced by many developing nations in the 1960s and 1970s, the responses to the "social question" ran remarkably parallel across time periods and culture areas. These responses were also crucial to our understanding of how the modern structure of society and politics in today's world were hammered out.

The first response to the rise of trade unions on the part of many European nations in the nineteenth century and many developing countries in the mid-twentieth century was to try to suppress them. To send the police out to beat them up. Not only did these labor organizations not fit in the still-prevailing conception of society, but they also lacked legitimacy. They had no "juridical personality"; their right to participate in the political process had not (yet) been recognized. The early history of trade unionism, thus—whether we speak of Great Britain, France, Germany, or the United States in the late-nineteenth and early-twentieth centuries; or Asia, Africa, and Latin America in the mid-to-later twentieth—is almost universally one of repression, violence, and efforts to snuff out organized labor movements. As President Washington Luís of Brazil once said in a stark statement of how trade unions were viewed in this earlier stage, "The problem of labor is a problem for the police."

But this solution, though possible (if unconscionable) in the short run while labor unions were small and weak, would not do as a response in the long term. For as industrialization continued, the urban proletariat and their organized labor groups continued to grow and become more powerful. It was one thing to suppress a few hundred "uppity" workers, but it was quite another in terms of the social and political costs involved to suppress thousands or even millions. Not only were the *numbers* of organized workers growing, but in Marxism, anarchism, syndicalism, socialism, and eventually Bolshevism they were finding ideologies that gave them organizing and unifying principles that frightened the traditional power holders to their foundations. Hence, there began to grow in the late nineteenth century, principally on the part of elite groups, a less repressive, more positive view of the social question. Instead of suppressing the ever-growing unions by sending the police or army out to squash them, the new strategy was to bring them into the fold, to incorporate them into the political system but under state control. The strategy would now involve *both* repression (in some circumstances) *and* co-optation, both carrots (inducements) and sticks (restraints). How best to do this? The answer was a new, revived form of corporatism.

The corporatist solution as proposed by a host of writers in the late nineteenth century and by Pope Leo XIII in *Rerum Novarum* in 1891 was to set up a corporatist system of representation including labor, capital, and the state, in which the state, still controlled by the elites, would be the decisive partner. It should be recalled that at this stage, "out-of-control" capitalistic entrepreneurs were seen by the state and by the pope as almost as much of a threat (but not quite!) as were "undisciplined" but now newly organized workers. This concern reflected both political preoccupations about an added or new social group (big business) that was growing increasingly wealthy and powerful, and also traditional Roman Catholic sensibilities going back to the Middle Ages about capitalism as representing illegitimate usury.

Hence, both organized labor and owners and management were to be brought into the political system on a supposedly coequal basis, but under the state's direction and control. Class harmony would be substituted for the looming, Marxist threat of class conflict. A well-ordered society would thus be maintained (evoking the medieval ideal), but new and threatening groups (labor and capital) would be co-opted in. The existing social structure (of Victorian England or Bismarckian Germany) would be maintained, but new corporatist "pillars" would be added on to the system. This "corporatist solution" to the social question, in addition, soon spread beyond the mainly Catholic officials and intellectuals who had been instrumental in promulgating it in its early years to include many Protestant writers and officials as well as nonreligious or secular officials. To all these groups, this updated version of corporatism was tremendously attractive because it both preserved traditional power hierarchies while also adjusting to change. It provided a means to absorb new and rising groups into the political system but without this producing fragmentation or breakdown. It is small wonder, therefore, that corporatism would be so attractive.

An important sociological change now occurred in corporatism that is crucial in our understanding of this and later developments. Recall that traditional corporatism was based mainly on status. That is, in the Middle Ages, one was born and lived all one's life in a certain status (lord or peasant), one was obliged to accept this station in life as according to God's will for the universe, and the medieval corporatism system of estates (nobility, clerical, commons) was similarly based on a rather rigid hierarchy of statuses. But the new corporatism was to be based on function or occupation, not status. For example, labor, capital, and eventually corporatively organized religious, military, bureaucratic, and other groups were represented in political decision making not on the basis of birth (status) but on the basis of what they did. This shift from status to functionally based corporatism would be an important indicator in all societies of the transition from traditional to more modern forms of corporatism.

The process by which new corporatist groups were brought into the political system occurred, approximately, as follows (note that we are here, as in other contexts, using a somewhat simplified "ideal type" or "model"; we cannot possibly provide all the complexities and all the variations of all the world's political systems). The process involved both co-optation (rewards) and coercion (punishment). In the early stages of union organization, when the labor groups were small, weak, and poorly organized, coercion was a common tool, as when governments or employers used police, military, or private security agencies to break up the unions. But as the labor organizations grew larger and better organized, it proved unproductive to use force to try to suppress the unions. New political strategies were called for.

Here is where the corporative, co-optive mechanisms come in. Government representatives would meet with the labor organizers; a deal would be offered. The precise ingredients would, of course, vary from country to country, depending on such circumstances as the strength of the unions or the strength of the government; but the essential elements of the deal would include the following. First, the government would recognize the "juridical personality" of the unions. That phrase continues to sound strange to American readers, but remember the countries involved are usually those with long histories of natural or historical corporatism; they are accustomed to dealing with societies on a group rather than an individualistic basis. Granting juridical personality to a group gives it legality, legitimacy, and the right to participate openly in the political process. Without that grant of juridical personality, the group has no legal rights and can still be suppressed—the "stick," or coercive, side of this political deal, which is still held in reserve and can be used if the group proves disruptive or fails to go along.

A second and major concession on the government's side was to include members of the union in the new social security and welfare programs then being enacted for the first time (such as health care, housing provisions, unemployment compensation, etc.). In a corporative system, only those organized into duly recognized groups (those with juridical personality) would be eligible for such programs. Mere individuals or members of nonrecognized groups were not eligible for these benefits. The promise of such benefits was, therefore, a powerful incentive for a group to enter into such a corporative arrangement with the state.

A third government concession in these fledgling corporative systems was that the state would use its influence (and the convenient fact that employer groups were being brought into the corporative system under state guidance at the same time) to persuade management and owners to grant wage increases to workers in return for a pledge that they would not strike. Under corporatism, both strikes and lockouts of employees by employers were often deemed illegal. Furthermore, under corporatism, rather than labor unions and employer groups bargaining directly with each other, these negotiations were to be handled indirectly through the state, usually through the ministry of labor. The state became the third and often the most powerful party in labor disputes. If it wished, the state could pressure employers to grant bigger wage increases than would be likely if these were only two-party (employers and workers) negotiations. This could be a tremendous benefit to the workers. But, in fact, such agreements were often implemented irregularly; experience in later decades showed that corporative systems usually put more pressure on labor unions to grant concessions than they did on employers, mainly because business groups were often able to persuade state officials that their unrestricted economic activities were necessary for the health of the entire national economy.

Entering into a corporative arrangement with the state and employers thus had the *potential* to be significantly beneficial to organized labor, but labor also had to make concessions. First, it surrendered its autonomy. For under corporatism the unions came under the control of the state or were reorganized as official state-run unions; they generally lost part or all of their independence. Second, they had to give up what may be their primary bargaining instrument: the right to strike. Third, the unions had to agree to abide by what we will call the "rules of the existing political game"—i.e., to relinquish their often revolutionary ideologies, to abandon their goals of a total transformation of society, to moderate their own demands, and to accept the existing (sometimes democratic, sometimes authoritarian, sometimes mixed) system of society and politics.

These were difficult concessions, but note that the benefits for labor of entering into a corporatist arrangement were also significant: increased wages, participation in social security, health care, a seat at the political table. In addition, for those labor groups that refused to accept the corporative "contract," the state still held "in reserve" its full coercive apparatus that it could either threaten to use or actually use against unions that refused to go along. Countries where the labor groups refused to accept the corporative compromise often broke down into confusion or became full-fledged dictatorships in the 1920s and 1930s, when unions were *forced* to accept these *or worse* provisions.

This early phase of corporatism had one further effect on labor: it split the labor movement. To this point most of the trade union movements in Europe, although still by and large weak, had been quite radical and even revolutionary: Marxist, anarchist, communist, and anarcho-syndicalist. But beginning in the 1870s a number of what were called Working Men's Circles were also organized, beginning in France and then spreading to Belgium, Austria, Germany, Italy, and most of the rest of Europe. The circles were closely linked to the Catholic Church and were often founded and led by priests; they served as the prototype for the corporatist labor organizations legitimated by Leo XIII in *Rerum Novarum.* Though not necessarily reactionary, the Workers' Circles were more conservative than the other existing labor groups. For example, they often organized dances and social activities as a way of alleviating what Marx had called the "alienation" of the working class under capitalism. The Workers' Circles, as well as other Catholic groups, later came together to form the Christian-Democratic parties of such countries as Austria, Germany, and Italy.[5] Moreover, it was these Workers' Circles (initially largely organized by Catholic workers; later there would be Protestant and nonreligious comparable movements) that were most likely to accept the corporatist contract and thus enter into corporative agreements with employers and the state. Whereas many other labor groups were seeking confrontations with employers and/or the state, the Workers' Circles, believing in class collaboration rather than class conflict, sought to work out mutually beneficial arrangements (corporatism) with both management/owners and government officials.

These differences in approach and ideology split the labor movement into more conservative and radical factions, one willing to work with employers and the state, and the other often seeking to overthrow them. Moreover, by giving wage increases and benefits to the more cooperative corporative labor groups, factory owners and government officials learned they could attract more workers to the conservative groups and thus weaken radical labor elements. The corporative contract thus involved not just a tripartite cooperative arrangement among labor, employers, and the state, but it was also consciously used as a political instrument to weaken the radical unionists, who then often felt the state's coercive wrath for being "uncooperative," while strengthening those labor groups that proved amenable to state/employer initiatives.

These are the general outlines of the corporatist solution to the "social question" existing pre–World War I, but in point of fact a great variety of regimes and solutions could exist under this umbrella. In Bismarckian and Wilhelmian Germany, the political system remained authoritarian but paternalistic, keeping strict controls over all political groups but often granting wage increases and social benefits to its workers. In Victorian England some corporative compromises were made, but these coexisted alongside a more liberal, party-based, and increasingly democratic political system. In France the unions were more radical and Marxist and refused to give up either their autonomy or their revolutionary ideologies. But in Spain, where industrialization was less advanced and the unions weaker, the government still used the police and army to quell worker agitation.

On a broader societal and political level, the corporatist solutions of the pre–World War I period also had major implications. In most of the advanced, industrial, or industrializing societies of Western Europe or the United States, organized labor had by now—more or less, often partially, sometimes reluctantly—been brought into the political process. Labor was no longer an "outlaw," a "problem for the police." Instead, labor had been incorporated, often co-opted. Labor had become a part of an emerging, more participatory, more pluralist, and thus more democratic political system. Though only partial at first, this process of incorporation was largely completed during the next two decades, the interwar period, of manifest corporatism. The gains for labor were many, but the costs of this "corporatist bargain" were significant as well.

For look what happened to labor. First, by accepting the benefits of the corporatist contract, labor gave up its revolutionary aspirations. Second, labor lost both its autonomy and the strike weapon, as the state became the dominant force in labor bargaining. Third, labor *de facto* accepted the existing, bourgeois social order and its lower-class place in that order. And fourth, along with that, labor accepted the existing power structure. That implied a top-down system of power in which already established elites, the powerful middle class, the wielders of industrial and economic power, and the state that was largely controlled by these groups would be dominant. And as we see in the next section, under manifest corporatism that power structure would often cost labor dearly.

Manifest Corporatism

Europe

World War I was a major turning point in European history—and not just in a military sense. The collapse of the Austro-Hungarian empire and of Wilhelmian Germany at the end of the war led to the destruction of what historian Barbara Tuchman called the "proud tower" of traditional, conservative, "Victorian," elitist society.[6] The long dominant hierarchical and aristocratic social structures in Europe under which the first corporatist labor and social experiments had been carved out were now either undermined (in such countries as Spain and Portugal) or collapsed completely (as in Russia).

After World War I, the new middle class, or bourgeoisie, would emerge as the dominant class. But in the meantime, and in fact stimulated by wartime production, the working class and its labor organizations also continued to grow. Rather like the elites in previous decades, the newly dominant middle class now faced the question of what to do with, how to handle, this new and sometimes threatening working class—except now the trade unions were far larger and better organized than previously. The answer was a new stage or phase in corporatism: full-scale or manifest corporatism.

Up to World War I, as we have seen, a number of countries had experimented with corporatism and the corporative contract, but this was usually limited to a handful of industries and select labor and employer groups. During the war itself, the needs of wartime production as well as the government's need to closely regulate wages, prices, and production stimulated some further steps toward corporatism in most of the major countries. These steps were viewed as temporary and short term, however, scheduled to end as soon as the war itself ended. It was generally thought that most countries would go back to the basically laissez faire, open-market economies that had prevailed before the war.

But with the war over, the crisis atmosphere that had prevailed during the war often continued. First, in 1917, came the communist revolution in Russia. Then in 1918–19 there were unsuccessful revolutionary upheavals and movements in Germany, France, and Italy that, despite failing, severely frightened established elites and the middle class, which was now emerging as dominant. Next came the wild spending, the inflation, and the boom-and-bust economies of the 1920s. Economic uncertainties, fears, and failures culminated in the world market crash of 1929 and the depression of the 1930s, which seemed to augur the failure of liberalism and capitalism and to revive fears of worldwide (at least in the industrialized countries) Bolshevik upheaval. Meanwhile, the looming clouds of World War II were gathering overhead, plain for all to see. Political upheaval threatened to accompany the economic tempests. Even in the historically stable and nonrevolutionary United States, President Franklin D. Roosevelt—like many other national leaders in Europe—felt compelled to issue a reassuring statement (which actually was meant to counter fears of upheaval in America) that "the only thing we have to fear is fear itself."

In the 1920s and 1930s, therefore, a large number of countries determined to adopt corporatist policies or a full-scale corporatist restructuring. They were prompted to do so both by the now even more pressing issue of what to do about organized (and often revolutionary) labor as well as by fears of general societal, economic, and political breakdowns. In Italy, France, Germany, Great Britain, Belgium, Austria, Holland, Scandinavia, Switzerland, Spain, Greece, Portugal, Poland, Hungary, Romania, Latvia, Estonia, Lithuania—virtually everywhere (including the United States, as we shall see in chapter 6)—either corporatist regimes came to power or else the governments adopted one or another of the corporatists' recommendations. This new, full-scale, or manifest corporatism went considerably beyond the limited corporatist experiments of earlier decades, beyond the earlier corporatist contracts. It often encompassed a complete and total reconstruction of the social, economic, and political system.

Many of these corporatist movements and efforts sprang from considerable idealism. After all, many of them grew out of the Catholic ideologies and well-meaning religious movements, both Catholic and Protestant, of the nineteenth century. But right from the beginning there were several and mixed motives involved, not all of them idealistic and aimed at solving the plight of the working class. Even the early Catholic leaders who advocated corporatism, for example, while clearly concerned to solve "the social question," wanted to do so paternalistically under state and elite auspices (doing good *for* the poor, but not of and by them), which all but guaranteed that labor would be a less-than-equal partner in the corporative contract. Similarly, the emerging middle class, while often in favor of giving certain benefits to the poor, wanted to do so in ways that would guarantee and enhance their own power while simultaneously keeping the labor movement in check. This was part of what historian Charles Maier, in writing about this period, called "the recasting of bourgeois Europe": corporatism provided one of the instruments by which the European middle class sought to restructure social relations so as to protect its own newly achieved dominance while putting organized labor in a subservient position.[7]

Sometimes in conjunction with these middle-class aspirations and sometimes separate from them, other European leaders used corporatism to help construct a full-scale authoritarian or even totalitarian state. In Italy, Mussolini in the early 1920s put in place most of the institutional features of a corporative state, including provision for the coequal representation of labor and business interests. But corporatism in Italy seldom functioned as the laws stated, and instead it became a smokescreen for Mussolini's totalitarianism. Rather than serving as a way to bring labor into the political coalition, Italy's corporative system came to function only as one of several means by which Italian fascism maintained *total* (hence, the term totalitarianism) control over all groups, including both business and labor. Similarly, in Nazi Germany, where Hitler began his regime by putting in place a set of corporative institutions designed to regulate economic life and sociopolitical relations. But Hitler was ideologically less committed to corporatism even than Mussolini had been: either the corporative institutions failed to function or else they served as a further instrument of control for Nazi totalitarianism.

Elsewhere in Europe—Spain, Portugal, Greece—the experience with corporatism in the 1920s and 1930s was not much different; nor was it happier. Almost everywhere, corporatism was used as an instrument to control the working class as well as other groups, not to bring labor into a more democratic and pluralist social and political order. In many countries corporatist institutions were used as a means to control both organized labor and big business, as well as all other groups. Interestingly, in Spain and Portugal, the regimes of Franco and Salazar, respectively, used corporatism to control both left-wing labor groups and the right-wing fascist groups that were jockeying for power. In all these regimes corporatism came to be identified with state power and dictatorship; it was a system of top-down, authoritarian, *state corporatism* rather than the more pluralistic and democratic *societal corporatism* advocated by earlier writers on corporatism.

Other countries adopted limited corporatist-inspired legislation but never put in place a full-fledged corporatist system. Nor did they all employ authoritarian or totalitarian methods. In Great Britain, Holland, and Scandinavia, for example, there were admirers of the Mussolini and German systems, but these were not the dominant political views. Instead, corporatism in these countries was generally limited to labor-management coordinating councils, functionally representative regulatory agencies, wage-price boards, the incorporation of functional groups as sectors within the political parties, or joint (government, labor, employers) agencies to generate employment or to stimulate industrialization. Hence, there were many *degrees* of corporatism in the Europe of this time. The discussion also serves to illustrate how widespread corporatism was, and not just in the fascist countries; corporatism *did* come to be associated, however, with the fascism phenomenon.

Corporatism in this milieu was seen as a system of strict state controls, a means of regulating not only wages, prices, and production but also the nation's socioeconomic interest-group life as well. And despite the use by some governments of the corporative institutions to control right-wing fascist elements as well as left-wing challenges, everywhere (because of the Mussolini and Nazi experiences) corporatism came to be identified with fascism. Now, we have already seen that corporatism can come in a variety of forms—liberal, pluralist, conservative, Christian-Democratic, socialist, and social-democratic—but because of the experiences of the 1920s and 1930s, corporatism was usually linked with fascism in the popular mind. As such, it was thoroughly discredited; it would not be able to survive beyond the end of World War II and the defeat of the fascist countries. Except that, it *did* survive, but only in disguised form and by not using the word "corporatism." This postwar form of European neo-corporatism is a thread that we will pick up in the next section, but first we need to analyze the emergence of manifest corporatism in Latin America.

Latin America

Corporatism arrived later in Latin America than it had in Europe, reflecting the lower level and delayed timing of economic development and industrialization in Latin America as compared with Europe. Nor did Latin America use the term *corporatism* very often; it preferred such terms as *justicialism* (Argentina) or *guided democracy* (various countries). Corporatism in Latin America was never as totalitarian as it was in Europe, nor was it as closely identified with fascism. One additional difference is that Latin American corporatism was never as rigidly and tightly organized as it was in Europe; instead, corporatism in Latin America usually came mixed with liberal and republican forms. It also served somewhat different purposes from what it had in Europe.

Corporatism as an ideology appeared in Latin America in the first decades of the twentieth century, several decades after its initial appearance in Europe. At this time (let us say the period leading up to World War I) Latin American industrialization was still in its very beginning stages. Because of this, trade unions were also only beginning to form and then only in a few countries; hence, there was at this time little perceived threat to the elites and middle class from the labor groups and little need to begin harnessing them. One can detect in some of the earliest labor and social welfare legislation in Latin America traces of corporatism's influence.[8] But through the end of World War I there was little industrialization, only fledgling labor organizations, and hence no need for corporatism.

There was more Latin American interest in corporatism in the 1920s, reflecting its rise in Europe, but still few corporatist political movements or institutional changes. A major transformation occurred in the 1930s, however, which, not coincidentally, was also the period of Latin America's first large-scale industrialization. Industrialization, of course, gave rise to significant labor movements and, as in Europe again several decades earlier, raised the "social question" for the first time and the familiar issue of what to do with labor, how to handle this new social force. As organized labor in Latin America began to grow in size and strength and could no longer be viewed realistically as in the past as simply a "problem for the police," Latin America began to search for a formula to deal with the emerging trade unions. As it had in Europe earlier, corporatism emerged as the answer.

The Latin American version of corporatism was never fully totalitarian or fascistic, however. Rather it was generally closer to the milder, Catholic, authoritarian corporatism of Franco and Salazar than to the fascist regimes of Mussolini and Hitler. For example, Getulio

Vargas in Brazil, 1930–45, enacted a corporatist system of labor relations and even promulgated a corporatist-style constitution in 1937 (which, however, was never fully implemented). Nevertheless, from that moment on Brazil's industrial relations system was dominated by corporatist rules and institutions. In Mexico, the populist government of Lázaro Cárdenas, 1934–40, adopted a left-wing system of corporatism favoring and giving special access to labor, peasant, and popular groups while excluding more traditional (religious and oligarchic) elements. The more common experience in Latin America in the 1930s, however, was the association of corporatism with right-wing and authoritarian regimes that came to power during the crisis of the depression. In fact, as in Europe, virtually every regime in Latin America in the 1930s adopted some form of corporatism (a labor statute, a new constitution with corporatist features, corporatism-inspired social welfare legislation, a functionally representative council of state, or a partially functionally organized legislative body). But because of Latin America's republican tradition, and perhaps because of U.S. influence, fully realized corporatism like Italy's or Portugal's failed to materialize; instead Latin America adopted partial corporatism, combining it with liberal and pluralist forms.

Unlike in Europe, these manifest (though partial) experiments with corporatism continued after World War II. Because Latin American corporatism was more a pragmatic adjustment to new circumstances (industrialization and the rise of organized labor) than a reflection of a deep ideological commitment, and because Latin America had sided (although not always enthusiastically) with the Allies in World War II, corporatism there was never as closely identified with discredited fascism as it had been in Europe. In fact, corporatism in Latin America continued to expand in most countries through the late 1940s and 1950s.

The prototype was the regime of Juan Perón in Argentina (1946–55). Perón was a military officer and a nationalist and populist whose base of support was the heretofore neglected Argentine labor movement. As a young officer, Perón had spent time in Italy, and his model for corporatism was a populist, pro-labor version of Mussolini's fascism. But because fascism and corporatism were, after World War II, out of fashion, Perón invented his own ideology, which he called "justicialism" or "justice-ism." Justicialism was a mishmash of corporatism and authoritarianism; along with his wife Evita, Perón benefited labor with new social programs. But in the process he ruined the economy of the most prosperous nation in Latin America, ruled in an authoritarian and imperious manner that resulted in increased opposition, and was eventually overthrown by the armed forces in 1955.

Perón's was the most complete case of corporatism in Latin America, but many other authoritarians in power in the 1940s and 1950s—and some democrats as well—borrowed their philosophy and institutions from the corporatism closet. For example, almost all the labor codes and social security programs enacted during this period show the emphasis of the corporatist ideas of harmony (often dictatorially enforced) between labor and capital, of the requirement of state recognition of labor unions before they could function legitimately, and of group rights taking precedence over individual rights. Social security, for instance, was often extended to categories of workers (not individuals) as a way of tying them to the regime that gave them these benefits and as a way of co-opting the labor movement. Many countries, in addition, maintained corporative or functionally representative councils of state (in Paraguay, a typical case, the council of state consisted of the heads of the three armed services; the Catholic archbishop; the rector of the national university; the heads of the farmers', industrialists', and businessmen's associations; the president of the country; and three cabinet members with economic responsibilities), economic regulatory agencies, or other institutions that showed the still-strong influence of manifest corporatism. But in Latin America these corporatist practices and institutions were usually combined with the institutions of a liberal and republican polity: political parties, more or less regular elections, a congress based on geographic representation, and private, laissez faire business associations that were *not* forced into a corporative contract.

Corporatism in Latin America went into eclipse in the 1960s during the U.S.-inspired Alliance for Progress with its emphasis on liberal, democratic political development. Many Latin American leaders, while seldom repudiating corporatism, thought it best not to emphasize their corporatist practices and thus antagonize their large benefactor, the United States. However, in Brazil, Argentina, Mexico, and other important as well as smaller countries, labor relations, social welfare, and other programs continued to be heavily impacted by corporatist institutions and practices.[9] The facade was often liberal and democratic in accord with U.S. and European wishes, but the underlying practice was often corporatist. Or else, in most countries, it showed a mixture of corporatism and liberalism.

In the later 1960s and 1970s, accompanying a new wave of authoritarianism in Latin America, corporatism returned—often with a vengeance. The Chilean regime of Augusto Pinochet was perhaps the most prominent example of a government using corporatism as a way of suppressing the trade union movement, eliminating political parties and interest groups as expressions of hated liberalism, and restructuring the political system. In less extreme ways, the military governments in Argentina, Bolivia, Brazil, Ecuador, Uruguay, and Central America followed much the same path. But in Peru from 1968 to 1975, a military regime followed a left-wing and nationalist path, using corporatism as Cárdenas in Mexico had done in the 1930s: not to suppress labor but to incorporate peasants and workers into the regime.

Beginning in the late 1970s and continuing to the present, many of these military regimes in Latin America were replaced by civilian, elected, democratic governments. These governments legalized political parties once again, moved to liberalize the system of labor relations, and removed many of the restrictions on free interest-group activity. In the transition toward liberalism, however, it is striking how many corporatist influences and institutions still remain in place: the concept of a top-down and organic state, the emphasis on "social pacts" to tie both labor and employers into state-directed development efforts, continuing restrictions on labor union activities and on interest groups in general ("limited pluralism"), the valuation of group benefits over individual human rights, the requirements of the state recognizing a group's "juridical personality" before it could legitimately function in the political process, and so on. It is clear that even in this new era of transitions to democracy in Latin America, corporatism is by no means dead.

By now, corporatism in its various forms and halfway houses has been around in Latin America for so long—since the 1930s—that its original purposes have been considerably extended and, at the same time, perverted. Remember that corporatism first arose in its modern form as a way of responding to "the social question," of dealing with the rise of organized labor. That issue was largely dealt with in Latin America in the period from the 1930s through the 1960s, during which cooperative labor movements were co-opted in corporatist fashion into the state apparatus, while noncooperative unions were excluded and repressed. But since then, other social groups—peasants, women, indigenous movements, domestics—have also risen to the fore, putting pressure on the political system for recognition and benefits. It is striking—and a measure of corporatism's pervasive influence in Latin America—that all these groups have been dealt with in much the same corporative way that labor unions were: first, with some repression, then with co-optation—but only of cooperative groups, who were granted recognition and eligibility for social benefits; meanwhile, noncooperative groups were excluded.

The methods used to deal with these newer corporative groups, in other words, followed almost exactly the same coercion/co-optation techniques used earlier by Latin America in dealing with organized labor and by Europe in the pre–World War I and interwar periods in handling its social question. Moreover, the political bargain struck, or "corporative contract," was also the same with these newer groups: recognition of their juridical personality and making them eligible for social benefits from the state in return for the group agreeing to moderate its political demands and to abide by the existing, nonrevolutionary rules of society and of the political game.

At some levels, the Latin American countries are liberal, pluralist, democratic, free, republican, and laissez faire; I and other authors have written about their transitions to democracy at length.[10] But our main concern here is with their continuing corporatist features. So alongside the democratic systems with which we are familiar, we need also to envision Latin America as consisting of a second, parallel, sometimes overlapping system of power and authority that is essentially corporatist. That system should be envisioned, as in Figure 5.1, as hierarchical and pyramidal. The original, quasi-medieval "corporations" in Latin America consisted of the oligarchy, the Church, and the military. Then, early in the twentieth century, the rising business/commercial groups were, quietly and peacefully, incorporated into the political system. Next, in the 1920s and 1930s, came the middle class and its professional associations—such as lawyers, doctors, engineers—who were similarly incorporated. From the 1930s on it became the term of organized labor—a bigger group and one made more complicated by its radical ideology. More recently it has become the turn of the newer, more recently mobilized groups: peasants beginning in the 1960s, women and domestics in the 1970s and 1980s, indigenous elements today. Each new social group has been progressively added on to the political system in pillared, functional, corporative fashion.

Figure 5.1 **Corporative Organization of Latin America**

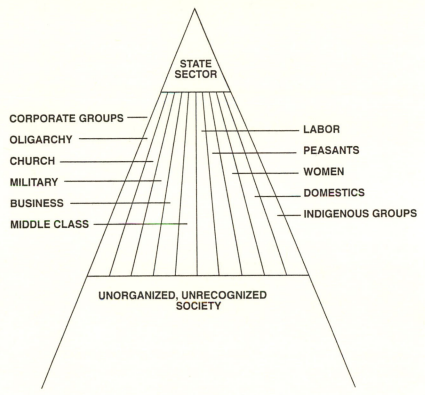

While this implies considerable change in the Latin American systems as new groups are appended to the system, note also what remains the same. Society is still often organized on an elitist, top-down,
and hierarchical fashion. There is greater pluralism, but it is still limited, still largely organized and controlled by the state. The elitist and
bourgeois social order remains in place. Progressive and/or revolutionary groups are either co-opted (if they have accepted the corporatist
contract) or repressed (if they have not). The result is that Latin America continues to have two power structures: one democratic and the
other corporatist. And while our analysis shows that it is possible to
have considerable change within such a corporatist system as the new
groups are continuously added on, there are also severe limits and
costs involved. But that is what the corporative contract is all about: to
get certain benefits, a group also has to give up certain things. Differ-

ent leaders have and will come to different conclusions as to their willingness to accept the costs *and* benefits of these arrangements.

This lengthy analysis of manifest European and Latin American corporatism is important both as a means to understand the processes and dynamics involved and because, as perceptive readers will have already seen, there are clear patterns of development involved. Societies tend to move from traditional, natural, or historical corporatism; to manifest corporatism; to, as we see below, modern neo-corporatism. Moreover, and this is critical, many societies appear to go through the same or roughly similar stages at different points in time. Europe broke with traditional, status-based corporatism in 1789 and thereafter; then it slowly developed manifest corporatism; now it is in the stage of neo-corporatism. Latin America, less developed than Europe, broke with traditional, status-based corporatism only in the 1930s, then developed manifest corporatism (mixed, however, with both liberalism and some continuing traditional-corporatist features), and is only now making the beginning steps into neo-corporatism.

Neo-Corporatism

Corporatism can take many different forms. In thinking about and summarizing the previous discussion of manifest corporatism, we can say that corporatism can be *exclusionary* (often excluding certain groups from the political process), as it was under European fascism in the 1920s and 1930s or Latin American bureaucratic-authoritarianism of the 1960s and 1970s; or it can be *inclusionary*—designed to bring new groups into the political process. Corporatism can take the form of *state corporatism* (dictatorial, top-down, heavy-handedly controlled and regulated by the state) or *societal corporatism* (based on a pluralism of free and independent interest associations). Corporatism can take a traditional, *unmobilized,* or demobilized form, in which few interests are involved and the rest are discouraged from organizing, or it can take a mobilized and more *participatory* form. We can also have *authoritarian* corporatism, again as in Europe in the 1930s and Latin America in the 1960s and 1970s, or we can have *democratic* corporatism.

It will be apparent that each of the first set of traits in the four dichotomies analyzed above—exclusionary, statist, unmobilized, authoritarian—points toward a corporatism that is not very attractive: dictatorial if not totalitarian, top-down, bureaucratic, statist, nonparticipatory, nondemocratic. Fortunately, that kind of corporatism largely met its demise in Europe with the close of World War II and the end of the Salazar, Franco, and Greek colonels' regimes in the mid-1970s. And it began to fade in Latin America with the fall of military bureaucratic-authoritarianism in the late 1970s and early 1980s and the restoration of democracy. These events paved the way for a new kind of corporatism that was reflective of the second set of traits in the four dichotomies offered above: one that was inclusionary, societal, participatory, and democratic. These adjectives are precisely the words one would use to describe modern neo-corporatism.

After World War II, even though corporatism had been discredited and repudiated for its association in the popular mind with fascism, many European countries continued to practice a disguised form of corporatism. They didn't talk about it much for obvious political reasons (no leader wanted to be associated with an unpopular ideology), but many corporatist practices and institutions left over from the earlier era persisted. Just as in the aftermath of World War I, many of these corporatist mechanisms, even in the democratic countries, were carryovers from wartime controls and regulations or from wartime mobilization that required all groups to subordinate their private interests to the larger national war effort. Some of them also grew out of Marshall Plan and Point Four economic assistance of the late 1940s and 1950s, which often required a strong state role in the economy. Or they emerged from economic development requirements of the 1950s, when Europe was still recovering from the wartime destruction and struggling to get back on its feet. Some corporatist controls also grew out of Cold War considerations and the need to control left-wing labor organization. By the late 1950s and 1960s, as we saw in chapter 3, some analysts were already writing about these continued or revived corporatist practices.

Modern neo-corporatism is both an extension of the earlier practices and a new and altered form of corporatism. Neo-corporatism grew out of the new prosperity of Western Europe in the 1960s and 1970s, not out of poverty, deprivation, and limited resources as the earlier, 1930s-style corporatism had. Neo-corporatism tends to come in modern, developed, industrial nations, not in traditional or transitional ones. Whereas the earlier forms of manifest corporatism were products of industrialization and the new social groups it spawned, neo-corporatism is the product of what some call postindustrialism or the modern welfare state. Neo-corporatism is also democratic, participatory, and social-justice oriented; it seeks to bring in and involve in democratic, participatory decision making the very groups that the earlier corporatism sought to regulate and control. Modern neo-corporatism, in short, was a product of the prosperous, more affluent 1960s and of modern, postindustrial social welfarism.

Manifest or statist corporatism had in considerable measure grown out of the *fear* that rapid social change might get out of hand, out of the perceived *threat* that radical trade union movements seemed to pose, and out of the *crisis* atmosphere of the 1930s when war, depression, and economic and political breakdown and catastrophe loomed. This form of corporatism sought either to exclude organized labor (and other groups) from the political process or to bring it in under co-optive mechanisms and with severe restraints on its activities. But by the 1960s Europe was back on its feet and prosperous. The fear of social upheaval or Bolshevik revolution had largely passed, there was no longer a crisis atmosphere, and organized labor was no longer viewed as a threat. In fact, a variety of European socialist and social-democratic parties, now either in power or about to come to power, welcomed labor in, saw it as an ally, and began the process of developing a modern welfare state. It was in this changed atmosphere that modern neo-corporatism emerged.

Modern neo-corporatism involved four major policy areas—and the list kept expanding. One was economic policy, which also came to include industrial policy. On such issues as wages, working conditions, hours, pensions, vacations, and the targeting of industrial priorities, organized labor was not only consulted on the major questions but was also *brought into* the processes of economic planning and even implementation. Similarly on social security and welfare policy: not only were labor and the other beneficiaries of these programs consulted but they were also brought into the decision-making process and often given formal representation on the regulatory boards and government agencies that decided such policies. Much the same occurred with health care, education, and other public policies. The groups affected were not only consulted but literally got a seat at the table and were incorporated into both decision making and the actual implementation of the policy. This is clearly a more inclusionary, more participatory form of corporatism. In fact, the changes were so significant that they represented a new type of corporatism.[11]

Under neo-corporatism, corporate groups perform at least four major functions. First, they *represent* the interests of the group and serve as intermediaries between the group and government agencies. Second, since they sit in on and often have seats assigned to them in these government agencies, they perform *deliberative* functions, helping to hammer out government policy on specific issues. Third, these groups have *regulative* functions, especially the regulation, policing, and setting of professional standards for their own members. And fourth, these groups perform *implementation* functions, helping to carry out the very programs that they have helped design. In other words, under neo-corporatism the corporate groups are involved in all facets of the policymaking process as it affects their particular policy areas: from initial identification of problem areas, to consultation and drafting bills to lobbying and exerting political pressure, to implementation.

Under neo-corporatism, therefore, business and labor are no longer just private interest associations, as they are under interest-group pluralism. Rather, they cross the line to become quasi-public or even fully public agencies. They regularly receive subsidies from the state for their activities, their leaders and staffs are often paid by the state, and they frequently lobby the state—now from their inside-the-bureaucracy positions—for greater funds and resources. While this kind of constant, neo-corporative interaction between the state and corporative groups can be and often is efficient and beneficial, one can see all kinds of potential conflicts of interest arising from these arrangement. For these are now public or quasi-public agencies, but to whom are they responsible? To whom are they accountable? Not to the electorate, which has no say in determining the policies or leaders of these groups, and maybe not even to their own members, from whom the leaders are often insulated. And what of the conflict involved in these groups using public funding to lobby from inside the government for even greater funding for their own activities, again with no or limited public knowledge of these activities or accountability? In becoming fully or quasi-public agencies, these neo-corporatist arrangements have probably improved public policymaking but at the cost of less public scrutiny and oversight. In a democracy this is a dangerous development.

In fact, what grows up under neo-corporatism is a dual power structure. On one side is the democratic structure—and, recall, these are democratic countries—of political parties, regular elections, parliament, and prime minister. But on the other side is the structure of neo-corporatism: corporative groups, regulatory agencies, government offices, cabinet ministries, and the bureaucracy. These two power structures exist side-by-side as two parallel pyramids. They rarely touch, interrelate, or have much to do with each other—except perhaps when corporative groups also present their case to the parliament. But that does not solve the conflict-of-interest problem, since often these groups have blocs of votes in the parliament that protect their interests and shield them from public scrutiny. For example, in the British Labor Party, fully 40 percent of its representatives in Parliament come directly out of the Trade Union Congress (Britain's major labor group), which is more than enough to protect organized labor's interests. Moreover, the fear is growing that under this dual power structure and in this current age of large-scale lobbying and large-scale bureaucracy, the corporative-bureaucratic side of this power structure is inevitably growing, while the democratic-accountability side is shrinking.

Another problem with these new (since the 1960s) neo-corporative arrangements is the political bias that may be involved. For just as in the 1930s when in Europe the manifest corporative arrangements that were meant initially to solve the "social question" were manipulated by dictators and authoritarians to keep labor down and enhance their own power, so in more recent times has modern neo-corporatism had its own—but quite different—biases. Most of the neo-corporative plans of the last three decades were initiated by labor, socialist, and social-democratic parties and their supporters. Instead of viewing labor as "the enemy," as earlier corporatists had often done, these parties saw labor unions as their friends and political allies. Naturally, then, they tried to do favors for those they viewed as electoral supporters by bringing them into the government and its various jobs, welfare, and social programs. These parties lavishly handed out neo-corporative arrangements and entitlements (guaranteed jobs, lavish welfare programs, free health and education, elaborate pension and retirement programs) as a way of cementing labor and popular support for the parties.

But what would happen when these "insider" neo-corporative arrangements were discovered and denounced by conservative parties, or when the conservative parties as under Margaret Thatcher in Great Britain or Helmut Kohl in Germany came back into power and moved through their own neo-liberal ideologies to dismantle corporatism and corporative arrangements? It is an issue to which we return in chapter

7; here let us only say that it was very risky and perhaps downright dangerous for one particular form of neo-corporatism to be identified so closely with one side of the political spectrum. For, in fact, a non-partisan neo-corporatism is a product of modernity, of advanced industrialization or postindustrialism, and of the modern bureaucratic, planned welfare state, and not necessarily of any one particular party or group of parties. It will therefore be around for a long time, even after the party-of-the-moment has been defeated at the polls.

An even graver threat is that under neo-corporatism the political system becomes so overloaded, so saturated with corporative interest groups now located inside rather than outside the bureaucracy and the structure of decision making, that the entire system goes into gridlock, becomes paralyzed with competing interests, and breaks down into chaos and ungovernability.[12] As we will see in chapter 6, that may now be becoming the situation in such countries as Argentina, Great Britain, Italy, or the United States where, instead of improving public policymaking, neo-corporatism has led instead to such an embedded system of entitlements and special privileges for the groups involved that it is producing political sclerosis and breakdown. Powerful, entrenched, but competing interests that are located *inside the political system* (the essence of neo-corporatism)—that are so evenly balanced that each has veto power over the others, thus producing paralysis, and at a time of declining public revenues and disillusionment with often wasteful and inefficient government programs—especially those in which a quasi-private, quasi-public neo-corporative group proves greedy, enjoys lavish entitlements, or squanders public resources; these are the elements that are fueling our own public malaise and the profound dissatisfaction of voters with government, especially big government. But these are precisely the features that characterize neo-corporatism. Our present political crisis is, therefore, in essence, a crisis of neo-corporatism.

Corporatism: The Next Phase?

Neo-corporatism is a product of modern societies; it arose in the 1960s, and already it seems to be in deep political trouble. We need to ask, therefore, what the next stage of corporatism is likely to be. I see three main possibilities.

The first is that corporatism moves to a new stage of neo-syndicalism.

Syndicalism was a political philosophy often related to anarchism that was popular in the early twentieth century under which the corporate groups or "syndicates" (labor, peasants, other groups) would rule directly, through a coordinating council but without the need for a large government or bureaucracy. Italy, Argentina (the legacy of Perón), and some other countries in limited ways moved in this direction; that is, certain groups, primarily labor, became so entrenched and so dominant in such key ministries as Labor and Social Welfare that they virtually "captured," hived off, and monopolized these agencies for themselves. However, it was not just labor or business groups that sank their talons into the system, but *all* groups: journalists, teachers, artists, military officers, religious officials, almost everyone—all living off the entitlements and special privileges that recognition by the state had given them.[13]

Not only do many of these corporatized groups control all the jobs and patronage within these agencies, but also the public policies these agencies administer are aimed almost exclusively at benefiting the selfsame corporative groups that have taken them over. One wonders if the dominance in the United States of the Department of Commerce by business groups, the Department of Agriculture by farm groups, or the Department of Labor by trade union organizations might not also be a sign of this advanced stage of corporatism or neo-syndicalism in this country. Such entrenched corporatism, with so many groups carving out whole areas of public policy for themselves, often leads to corruption, an emphasis on satisfying private interests over serving the public interest, and a further blurring of the lines between private and public pursuits. With so many groups involved, it can also lead to saturation, paralysis, gridlock, and ungovernability. We shall have more to say on these themes in chapter 6.

A second possibility for the next stage of corporatism is at the international level. Here we refer to the agencies of the European Economic Community (EEC) in Brussels and Strasbourg or to the multilateral agencies established under the North American Free Trade Agreement (NAFTA), which includes Canada, Mexico, and the United States. In the EEC, for example, representation on its many regulatory boards and agencies is often on a corporative or functional basis: wheat growers, bankers, wine producers, hoteliers, industrialists, fishermen, and so on. In NAFTA, representatives not just from the government but now also from semiprivate corporative groups (the AFL-CIO labor organization, the Chamber of Commerce business group) are appointed to oversight boards that regulate in such areas as pollution and environmental controls, enforcement of labor laws, and business practices. In many such cases, a corporative structure at the international level has been purposely structured so as to reflect the internal corporative organization of the nations that are part of the international organization involved. But is also seems that, since international organizations change more slowly than their member states, at a time when corporatism is under attack at various national levels, it is still thriving at the international level. (We will also have more to say on this theme in chapter 7.)

The third possibility for corporatism in the future is its dismantling. In a number of countries, particularly (but not only) those where corporatism has reached syndicalist and saturation levels, efforts are under way to reverse the trends toward corporatism. The repudiation of entrenched corporatism in Argentina, levels of party and interest group corruption in Italy that are beyond the pale, and pressures for privatization and a reduced government in Great Britain, France, Germany, the United States, and elsewhere, are all signs of reaction against entrenched corporatism and of an effort to reverse the course of growing corporatism. The neo-liberal attack on entrenched corporatism has by now become a global phenomenon. But it seems that even in the countries that are most strongly corporatist, reductions of corporatism in one public policy arena are usually accompanied by increases in corporatism in other arenas—or that the agencies designed to dismantle corporatism (such as Vice President Gore's Restructuring Government campaign) are often themselves corporately organized. Meanwhile, the march toward greater corporatism still goes on in scores of countries around the globe, at the same time that the trends toward privatization, state-downsizing, and greater participatory democracy would seem to be pointing in the opposite direction.

Summing Up

While corporatism can appear in different forms in different countries in different stages of history, there are definite patterns in the types that appear and their evolution. Traditional corporatism can exist in many different forms: families, tribes, clans, caste associations, feudal groups, patronage groups, and so on. Modernization, economic development, and industrialization—along with their accompanying cultural and social changes—are usually the motor forces driving new kinds of corporatism. They produce labor and other social groups that societies must deal with and that need—somehow—to be accommodated to the political system.

Manifest corporatism often provides the mechanism for doing so. At first, these new groups are frequently suppressed; as they grow they are usually brought into the system through corporative agencies that provide both benefits and some costs to the new groups. In Europe, because of the French Revolution and its impact, there was a sharp break between traditional, semifeudal corporatism and the newer kinds of manifest corporatism; but in most non-Western societies, being less individualistic and lacking a revolutionary tradition, traditional and more modern forms of corporatism have often been fused during these transitional phases. In many cases, however, the newer versions of manifest corporatism produced not a happy, pluralistic, democratic corporatism but an unhappy, statist, authoritarian kind.

Once organized labor and other groups had been accepted into the political system, as in Europe following World War II, neo-corporatism appeared. Neo-corporatism was a product of affluence, prosperity, postindustrialism, and the welfare state. It was democratic, pluralist, and socially just. But neo-corporatism was often also tied to the political agenda of the socialist and social-democratic parties, and it often produced corruption, clientelism, and government paralysis. It was strongly attacked by neo-conservative political movements that sought to dismantle the corporative state. And yet, at both the national and international levels, corporatism is not only still present but still growing. Corporatism remains attractive because it provides a means to absorb new groups into the society, to provide thus for change while also maintaining stability.

To this point we have had little to say about corporatism in the United States. The reason is that, historically, the United States is one of the few countries in the world without either a corporatist tradition or a corporatist movement or ideology. But as the hints in this chapter make clear, in recent decades corporatism has also been growing in the United States: what we call here "creeping corporatism." Hence, we now turn to the subject of the distinctive and now quite advanced system and practice of U.S.-style corporatism.

Notes

1. Norman F. Cantor, *The Civilization of the Middle Ages* (New York: HarperCollins, 1993).

2. Carl Landauer, *Corporate State Ideologies: Historical Roots and Philosophical Origins* (Berkeley: University of California, Institute of International Studies, 1983).

3. Lloyd Rudolph and Susan H. Rudolph, *The Modernity of Tradition* (Chicago: University of Chicago Press, 1967).

4. A.J. Somjee, *Parallels and Actuals of Political Development* (London: Macmillan, 1986); and Howard J. Wiarda, *Ethnocentrism in Foreign Policy: Can We Understand the Third World?* (Washington, DC: American Enterprise Institute for Public Policy Research, 1985).

5. Ralph H. Bowen, *German Theories of the Corporative State* (New York: McGraw-Hill, 1947); Matthew Elbow, *French Corporative Theory, 1789–1948* (New York: Columbia University Press, 1953).

6. Barbara Tuchman, *The Proud Tower: A Portrait of the World before the War, 1890–1914* (New York: Macmillan, 1966).

7. Charles Maier, *Recasting Bourgeois Europe: Stabilization in France, Germany and Italy in the Decade after World War I* (Princeton, NJ: Princeton University Press, 1988).

8. Howard J. Wiarda, *The Corporative Origins of the Iberian and Latin American Labor Relations Systems* (Amherst: University of Massachusetts, Labor Relations and Research Center, 1976).

9. Kenneth P. Erickson, *The Brazilian Corporative State and Working Class Politics* (Berkeley: University of California Press, 1977).

10. See Howard J. Wiarda, *The Democratic Revolution in Latin America: History, Politics, and U.S. Policy* (New York: The Twentieth Century Fund, Holmes and Meier Publishers, 1992); as well as the bibliography in this book.

11. Gerhard Lehmbruch and Philippe C. Schmitter (eds.), *Patterns of Corporatist Policy-Making* (London: Sage, 1982).

12. This is the argument of Mancur Olson, *The Logic of Collective Action: Public Goods and the Theory of Groups* (New York: Schocken Books, 1976); Olson, *The Rise and Decline of Nations: Economic Growth, Stagflation, and Social Rigidities* (New Haven: Yale University Press, 1982).

13. Jorge Bustamante, *La República Corporativa* (Buenos Aires: EMECE Editores, 1989).

6

Creeping Corporatism in the United States

Of all the advanced-industrial or, as we called them in the last chapter, postindustrial nations, the United States is usually cited as the least corporatist. In all the anthologies and writings on corporatism in recent years, the United States is seldom mentioned; or, if it is mentioned, it is in the context of the United States being an exception to the corporatist trends evident in other countries. In addition, most of the research and writing on corporatism in recent decades has come from scholars of Europe, Latin America, and increasingly other areas; seldom has corporatism or the corporatist model been used to analyze the United States.[1]

In fact, we do not like to talk about corporatism very much in the United States. It is not mentioned in polite company, in part because of its association with fascism. But more than that, corporatism does not fit our ethos, our historic and familiar image of ourselves. We like to think of ourselves as a free and democratic country. We do not like to think that we are like those Europeans of the Old World, with their formal, bureaucratic, and legalistic ways; and certainly we do not want to be considered in the same terms and categories as Latin America, Asia, or other "developing" areas.

No, Americans prefer to think of their country as *sui generis,* as different from (and superior to) other nations. The United States was founded on principles of individualism, laissez faire, and freedom—both in the economic and the political marketplaces. All of these characteristics are usually thought to be inimical to corporatism—and they are and have been *historically.* So we do not like to hear about corporatism; that is for other countries. A quick survey of the textbooks on American government and politics reveals that almost none of them mentions corporatism, let alone uses it as a framework at the heart of the analysis.

But it is the thesis of this chapter that the United States does practice corporatism—and does so increasingly. We are and have been experiencing a form of creeping corporatism. However, we seldom call it that, and most Americans are ill-equipped to recognize it when it appears. We lack the terminology; we also lack the comparative perspective from other nations that would enable us to use their experiences with corporatism to cast light upon our own. Nevertheless, whenever we talk about private groups (such as business, labor, teachers) being *incorporated* into the political system; whenever we have government-sponsored group entitlements, set-asides, quotas, or group favoritism; whenever we discuss health care reform, industrial policy, reforming Medicare or Medicaid, welfare or Social Security reform—then corporatism, or elements of corporatism, or partial corporatism, are almost always involved. Especially since Americans are unused to and may be uncomfortable in dealing with corporatism, let us look at the issue in detail.

Historical or Natural Corporatism: The Absence of an American Political Tradition of Corporatism

The United States had almost no experience with natural, historical, or traditional corporatism. That is because the United States is such a new society; it was, in a sense, "born free." In contrast, most of the other societies we have been discussing—Asia, Europe, the Middle East, Africa—have recorded histories and cultures that go back some two, three, or four thousand years. The hand of history—including of traditional corporatist institutions like the family, the clan, the caste, or the tribe—still weighs heavily upon them. But the United States—if we exclude for now our indigenous populations—has a history that goes back only two hundred years—only three hundred fifty, if we count the colonial period. As a country or as a civilization, the United States is a mere "youngster" as compared with most other countries and civilizations, and it does not have the legacy of special privilege and entrenched social hierarchy that other, older societies usually have.

An interesting comparison would be Latin America. Both the United States and Latin America share the Western Hemisphere; both are products of Columbus's discovery of the Americas. But Latin America was founded a full century before the colonies in North

America; and, as products of Spanish and Portuguese colonialism, it was founded on a basis that was feudal and medieval. Hence, with these feudal origins, natural or historical corporatism in Latin America has always been stronger and more entrenched than in the United States.

The United States lacks a feudal and medieval past.[2] The United States never had a system of feudal estates, which was one of the main sources of historic European corporatism. Nor did the United States have a system of guilds growing out of the Middle Ages, nor an established church, nor powerful and entrenched military orders—all of which constituted important parts of the base of European corporatism. Nor was U.S. society—except in the slaveholding South—ever based so strongly on considerations of hierarchy and "place" as was the case in Europe, which provides another basis for corporatism. In fact, that is precisely why people came to the United States: to get away from the rigidities and social restrictions of the Old World and to begin again unfettered by the chains of hierarchy and an established social order in the New World of America.

The United States was founded on a basis that was free and individualistic, unencumbered by the obligations of such premodern, corporative institutions as clans, tribes, estates, or feudal orders. It is a product of the Enlightenment, the Protestant Reformation, capitalism, the Industrial Revolution, the revolution in scientific thinking ushered in with Galileo and Newton, and the revolution leading to limited government and democracy that was consolidated in England and Holland in the seventeenth century. All of these profound changes may be identified with the modern world, not with the medieval one of historic corporatism.

The United States highly values its liberties, but it should be recalled what freedom meant at the time of the United States' founding in the eighteenth century. It mainly meant personal or individual freedom from feudal and corporate obligations. All men are born free, said Jefferson, and they have inalienable rights as *individuals,* not just as members of some corporate groups. Voting and representation in the United States have always been on an individualistic basis—one person, one vote—and not on the basis of functional representation or corporate group rights. In the American tradition we value the yeoman farmer, the individual entrepreneur, the private risk taker who by dint of his own skill and hard work succeeds in our free economy. The U.S.

economy is based on laissez faire, the freedom of both producers and consumers to enter the marketplace of their own volition, without excessive government restrictions or interference.

The United States stresses rights, but they are individual rights, not corporate or group rights. And while we have lots of interest groups operating in our political system, these are free and independent interest groups. Unlike in corporatist systems, these groups were not created by the state, nor are they licensed, controlled, and dominated by it. The autonomy that such groups enjoy is part of the larger picture we have painted—now changing—of an economy and polity dominated by freedom and individualism, unfettered by historic corporatism. Without a feudal past, with seemingly boundless resources, with an apparently endless frontier that always enabled one to start anew, and heavily influenced by the modern notions of freedom and individualism, the United States began life as a nation in a singularly advantageous position. It had no past to overcome, no strong medieval roots, none of the entrenched corporative ties, obligations, and barriers that other nations had to struggle to break free of before freedom and democracy could be established.

One can easily see, therefore, why the few advocates historically of corporatism in the United States have had a hard time of it, and why even now such programs as corporate group quotas, set-asides, and ethnic favoritism are so controversial. Or why national economic planning or an industrial policy under which the government selects and favors certain industries have never gained much public support. These policies run contrary to very long American traditions. They seem to violate the ethic of individualism, to run counter to the entire American tradition. These are programs that Europeans advocate but not Americans, with their fierce sense of personal freedom and individualism. They seem, in this sense, to be somehow un-American. If Europeans and other countries want to engage in such practices, that is up to them; but it was exactly to escape the class and caste barriers and the obligations of such statist and corporatist features that many Americans came to this country.

In the entire experience of the United States, there has only been a handful of advocates of an American corporatism. John Quincy Adams, the sixth president, advocated some corporatist ideas and, in his notions of "concurrent majorities," nineteenth-century political philosopher John Calhoun put forth a corporatist message. Calhoun's ideas were based on geographic rather than functional or occupational representation, however; as a pre–Civil War Southerner, he believed that each region of the country should have veto power over the others, and that a "concurrent majority" in each region would have to give its approval before a bill could become a law. Calhoun presented a sophisticated argument, but in the American tradition he has been dismissed as a minority voice for slavery and states' rights.

America is a "liberal" polity. By that we mean almost everyone in the American tradition—Ronald Reagan as well as Bill Clinton—believes in the classic nineteenth-century freedoms: freedom of speech, religion, press—the Bill of Rights. Recall also that this hallowed addendum also includes freedom of assembly, of petition, and of association. These provisions stand in the way of a corporate ordering of society where, recall, group rights take precedence over individual rights and a group's juridical personality must be recognized by the state before that group can participate in the political process—i.e., can assemble, petition, and associate. No such restrictions stand in the way of an American's exercise of his political freedoms. This liberal tradition— the belief in democratic, individualistic, free, and representative government—is so strong in the United States that almost everyone believes in and accepts it. No other alternative political system (communism, authoritarianism, fascism, corporatism) is acceptable. So if corporatism is ever to find a foothold in the United States, it has to come in through the back door, disguised and by stealth, and be called "liberalism" rather than "corporatism."

But it is not just the absence and unacceptability of corporatism in America's cultural and historical traditions that account for the weakness of corporatism in the United States—although these are very important factors. Institutional factors are also extremely important. First, U.S. trade unions are very weak as compared with most European countries. Only about 8 to 10 percent of American workers are unionized, and the percentage is falling rapidly. But remember that it was in response to the "social question"—the rise and potential threat of organized labor—that manifest corporatism arose in Europe in the late nineteenth and early twentieth centuries. If organized labor in the United States is so weak, however, and certainly does not constitute a revolutionary threat, then why have corporatism at all?

A second institutional debility historically impeding the growth of corporatism is America's weak state—even antistate—tradition. The

U.S. Constitution is based on notions of limited government, checked-and-balanced government. Again, it was precisely to get away from statism and authoritarianism that so many immigrants came to the United States. And without a strong and powerful state in either an economic or a political sense, there can be only limited kinds of corporatism. This antistatist sentiment in the United States is expressed in various ways. For example, it is and has been the practice in the United States for the marketplace to set prices, wages, and production, not the government. Moreover, the government's share of GNP in the United States is *by far* the lowest of all the industrialized countries. The United States has a weak and a limited state, not a *dirigiste* (directing) or a mercantilist state. Again as compared with Europe, the United States' regulatory apparatus that manages and regulates the economy is similarly weak. How can we have corporatism with its tripartite arrangements (labor, employers, and the state) if at least two of those ingredients (labor and the state) have such limited influence?

The United States has a weak state not just in an economic sense but in a political one as well. Americans do not believe in Big Government— unless, as we shall see, their own entitlement is affected. Most politicians run *against* Washington and the Big Government that it symbolizes. As a country, the United States tends to be antibureaucracy and "anti" all the regulation, paperwork, and restraints on unchecked individualism that it implies. The United States, in fact, seems now in the process of dismantling its state even further through budget reductions, privatization, and the turnover of many federal programs to the states. But if the central government in the United States is comparatively weak in both an economic and a political sense, wherein lie the possibilities for an American, state-directed corporatism?

Although the discussion thus far has emphasized the absence of either a cultural or an institutional basis for American-style corporatism, it also contains tantalizing hints about how such corporatism might emerge. For example, although the U.S. political system has always stressed limited government, in the 1930s and thereafter the regulatory apparatus of the state began to grow. And although the United States remains a basically laissez faire economy, since World War I the government's role as a participant and "partner" in economic development has grown significantly. Dating from approximately the same period (the interwar years), certain American interest groups began to enjoy privileged positions before the state. We began to talk about group rights as distinct from the historic emphasis on individual rights. The government bureaucracy has similarly grown enormously from this same period (the 1930s), and with that growth has come the incorporation of more and more interest groups into the state system, as consultants, regular participants, and with veto power. The system of state-sponsored entitlements has also grown enormously, with many of these now organized on a group or corporate basis. And, while organized labor in the United States is currently quite weak, there was a time when labor was not only strong but also quite radical, prompting the rise in America of the "social question" and the by-now familiar corporatist co-optation/repression mechanisms for dealing with it.

Hence, while corporatism in the United States had few firm historical or institutional foundations, there came a time in the twentieth century when both the conditions for and the practices of corporatism began to grow there. But we seldom called it corporatism. Instead, we practiced pluralism or, as Theodore Lowi calls it, "interest group liberalism," which became the widely accepted American ideology. Hidden within interest group liberalism, however, as Lowi's own analysis makes clear, were the seeds of a U.S.-style corporatism.[3]

The Origins of Corporatism in the United States

In the United States, the early rise of corporatism had little to do with history, tradition, or cultural factors. Instead, corporatism arose primarily out of institutional and political factors and from the conditions and circumstances prevailing in the United States in the early twentieth century. During the pre–World War I decades, capitalism in the United States was achieving unprecedented wealth and power. But this era was also known as the Progressive Era; the Progressives sought to rein in and regulate the largely unchecked capitalism of the time. Labor unions were also becoming stronger; the social question was coming to the fore. Some labor leaders, like their European counterparts, were attracted to syndicalist or anarcho-syndicalist ideas; others put forth quasi-corporatist schemes that they called "vector pluralism" or "welfare capitalism." Some clergy and intellectuals were similarly attracted to the corporative idea of class collaboration between labor and capital, and there were also businessmen who came to believe in a form of corporate liberalism. At the same time these decades marked the beginning of the Good Government Movement, with the founding of the

League of Women Voters, the National Civic Federation, and such Washington-based think tanks as the Brookings Institution and the Carnegie Endowment. These diverse interests and organizations provided a climate in which corporatist ideas could begin to take root.[4]

World War I provided an added impetus to the growth of American corporatism and brought the U.S. government in for the first time. During the war President Woodrow Wilson established the War Industries Board as a mechanism to facilitate industrial production for the war effort and to ensure the adequate supply of raw materials and manufactured goods. But the board also sought to maintain labor peace during the war by incorporating both capital and labor under government guidance. Such prominent businessmen as Gerald Swope and Bernard Baruch served on the board, but Wilson also brought in labor leader Samuel Gompers as part of this essentially corporatist, tripartite (business, labor, the state) arrangement to protect against strikes during the war and to ensure the necessary massive and uninterrupted production.

During the next twelve years, under the successive Republican administrations of Warren Harding, Calvin Coolidge, and Herbert Hoover, the United States returned to "normalcy." We usually think of normalcy as meaning demobilization of the military forces and a return to peacetime pursuits, but it also included a dismantling of the wartime economic controls and of such quasi-corporative institutions as the War Industries Board. Nevertheless there continued to be businessmen, labor leaders, and others in the 1920s who advocated corporatist-like solutions to rising social and economic problems, and it was President Hoover who set forth the vision of a corporate-style "associative" state.[5]

But it was not until President Franklin Roosevelt's New Deal in the 1930s that a peacetime form of corporatism became a part of U.S. government institutions and policy. A number of factors were involved. First, some of Roosevelt's key advisers, his "brain trust," such as Adolph A. Berle Jr. were committed to corporatist solutions to the social and economic problems of the depression. Second, quite a number of businessmen, despite their commitments to a laissez faire economy, saw the value of heading off a radical challenge from organized labor by bringing labor into the political process and giving it certain benefits—the familiar co-optive strategy of corporatism. Third, Roosevelt himself saw the value of expanding his political base by moving toward greater pluralism and incorporating organized labor into the Democratic Party coalition. Fourth, even in an era of isolationism,

European ideas of corporatism—then widespread—were seeping into the United States and finding receptive audiences. And fifth, such moderate labor leaders as Matthew Woll of the PhotoEngravers Union, Sidney Hillman of the Amalgamated Clothing Workers, and David Dubinsky of the International Ladies Garment Workers Union argued that a Marxist-like confrontation with business was unproductive for labor; far better, they concluded, to enter into a "social partnership" with capital for the good of all. But that is precisely the formula for corporatism.[6]

The main piece of corporatist legislation passed by the New Deal was the National Recovery Administration (NRA) of 1933. The NRA was part of Roosevelt's and his advisers' efforts to steer the United States out of the depression. It was of a piece with the Works Projects Administration, the Social Security Administration, and the National Labor Relations Board (NLRB)—all products of the torrent of legislation during Roosevelt's "First Hundred Days." While the NRA and its companion legislation are usually lauded as part of the effort to lift the country out of its deepest economic crisis ever, its manifestly corporatist aspects are often forgotten.[7]

The National Industrial Recovery Act, which was the enabling legislation for the NRA and constituted the cornerstone of the New Deal, provided for direct state support for business. In addition, the state or government was authorized to assist employers in the organization of business associations that would help set prices and production. But the legislation also affirmed the right of labor to organize and set standards of employment. Roosevelt and his advisers recognized that without the incorporation of labor as a balance to the power of capital, the contradictions in the U.S. economy—already in crisis because of the depression—would only deepen. So both employer groups and labor—along with government representatives—were incorporated on the various boards that were to develop codes of conduct for each industrial sector. Only by such a corporatist mechanism, the Roosevelt administration reasoned, could it both get the country out of the depression and avoid class conflict—and, not coincidentally, gain the political support of labor.

But in the early 1930s the U.S. labor movement was still badly split among communist, socialist, and less radical unions. The radical unions, perhaps still dreaming of a workers' revolution, rejected the NRA as a sell-out to employers and capitalism. But more pragmatic unionists, like Sidney Hillman, recognized that a workers' revolution in the United States was unlikely. Further, Hillman and his allies reasoned, the confrontational and strike tactics of the radicals would only prolong the depression and leave workers worse off. In the early 1930s, therefore, Hillman became the principal labor advocate of corporatism. He called for an Economic Council for Industry (similar to the old War Industries Board of 1917–18), which would have "representatives of all the parts that make up industry including management, capital, labor, and government representing the public." Such a council would be empowered to make recommendations to both industrial leaders and Congress.

This was a formula for out-and-out corporatism—except for the fact the council's recommendations were advisory, not binding. And with the NRA, Hillman's corporative vision, along with that of the Roosevelt administration, became the law of the land. Hillman recognized full well that by accepting labor incorporation into the state structure, he was also accepting capitalism as well as certain restraints on his union's autonomy. But that is the price of the corporatist contract that we analyzed in the previous chapter. Under corporatism, labor gives up something in order to get something back: higher wages, social security, a seat at the political table. That is the compromise that Hillman and his allies, thinking pragmatically, were willing to accept. The more radical union leadership, thinking ideologically, rejected the Roosevelt plan as embodied in the NRA, and thus were isolated and eventually slid downhill.

The NRA was the most manifestly corporatist legislation ever enacted in the United States. Like the War Industries Board of World War I, it was a product of crisis: the depression. But in 1935 in the famous Schecter Poultry Case, the Supreme Court struck down the NRA as unconstitutional. Interestingly, the Court voided the NRA not because its corporatist aspects were seen as unconstitutional but purely on technical and procedural matters. The Court's objection to the NRA was not that the legislation delegated public authority to private institutions, but that it unconstitutionally delegated power from the Congress to the executive branch. Presumably that meant that some future legislation *could* provide for a corporatist granting of state power to private groups for self-regulation and the planning and implementation of public policy, *and* that such delegation could be constitutional.

And that is precisely what happened. Although by the end of his second term Roosevelt had lost interest in corporatism and had shunted such corporatist brain trusters as Berle aside, corporatist practices had become widespread in the government. These practices were reinforced, solidified, and made quasi-permanent by the requirements of World War II, which demanded central (emergency) planning, labor peace, industrial mobilization, and controls on prices and wages. The economic regulatory mechanisms of the New Deal state, first instituted in the 1930s, were now vastly enlarged. By 1944 economist Neil Chamberlain was noting a pattern of industrial organization that resembled a loose, American-style system of corporatism: "industry-wide self-government with labor and management cooperatively establishing the rules, presumably under the surveillance but not the thumb of the state."[8]

And with the Wagner Act of 1946, many of the corporative provisions of the NRA governing labor-employer relations now received legislative approval, but this time without the objectionable provisions that had caused the Supreme Court to throw out the NRA. The form of U.S. corporatism was thus gradual, incremental, societal corporatism, not the abrupt, authoritarian state corporatism of so many of the interwar European countries. And it was "loose": pragmatic, piecemeal, nonideological, pluralist, with few sanctions or tight controls, and very American. It tended to be advisory rather than compulsory, but that changed over time. Moreover, the form of corporatism had also changed over time: instead of the ad hoc syndicalism or vector pluralism of earlier decades, the model now came close to the corporatist ideal of functional representation.

Although there were some early Republican corporatists like Herbert Hoover, and though some businessmen supported a corporatist-like reordering of society, most of the corporatist plans we have seen so far came from Democrats and labor leaders, and with a concrete political agenda as well: to lock the vote of organized labor into the Democratic Party. Republicans for the most part, with their stronger beliefs in individualism, free enterprise, and open markets, had not often been pro-corporatism. But after World War II this began to change as many Republicans accepted one or another of the New Deal's, and corporatism's, reforms. In this sense, the post–World War II period would be very different from the post–World War I period, when Republicans viewed Wilson's wartime economic regulations and the corporately structured War Industries Board as strictly temporary and emergency measures, and moved after the war to roll back and repudiate the Wilsonian programs.

Modern Republicanism in the 1950s was most closely associated with the presidency of Dwight Eisenhower, 1952–60. Some Republicans still wished to repeal all the New Deal legislation, including even Social Security, but not Eisenhower nor the Republican mainstream from the 1950s through the 1970s (Nixon, Ford). Eisenhower, as a political pragmatist, not only accepted Social Security but he also left in place most of the New Deal/Fair Deal regulatory apparatus that had grown up over the previous two decades. Moreover, recent scholarship has indicated that Eisenhower had strong corporatist sympathies.[9]

The touchstone of Eisenhower's political philosophy was a vision of a corporate commonwealth. The concept of a corporate commonwealth meant to Eisenhower a noncoercive but self-disciplined, well-ordered, and harmonious society; an active but limited state; cooperative relations between business and labor; an emphasis on national consensus and serving the public good rather than narrower private interests; and a stable and Western-oriented international order. Eisenhower believed that the inevitable conflicts of short-sighted and self-interested classes and interest groups could be resolved only through the leadership of public-spirited and professionally skilled managers such as himself. At the heart of his thinking and policies was the effort to reconcile and resolve the most fundamental conflicts of modern society, including income disparities, vast gaps between the classes, and the constant struggle between interest groups.

Eisenhower opposed what he called a "regimented statism," yet he favored the government playing a role as coordinator and harmonizer of interests. And whereas the New Deal had sought consciously to bring organized labor into its governing coalition while sacrificing the support of business, Eisenhower tipped the pendulum back the other way toward a pro-business stance, seeing business as the engine of economic growth. However, in keeping with his ideas of social harmony, Eisenhower also saw his administration as a reconciler of labor conflicts and worked to achieve cooperation among business, labor, and government. His administration similarly expanded the interpenetration of the public and private sectors. The Eisenhower presidency was thus shaped by the self-conscious quest for a corporate commonwealth in which the problems of a modern economy and society would be resolved through self-restraint, discipline, disinterested public service, an active but still limited government, and cooperation between classes and social groups.

Note that the Eisenhower system was labeled a "corporate commonwealth" and not a "corporate state." Moreover, the idea of a corporate commonwealth was really Eisenhower's *vision* for society; only in limited ways was this vision reflected in actual legislation. The result is that Eisenhower's corporatism was much like that of Roosevelt's: still limited, evolutionary, voluntary, pragmatic, incremental, never really contemplating a complete corporate state as in Europe, often mixed in with U.S.-style liberalism and pluralism, hidden or disguised rather than explicit, with greater emphasis on the societal forms of corporatism than on the statist, still only partial, a vision (including social harmony, class collaboration) rather than a set of concrete proposals or a legislative agenda. We also noted that the Roosevelt/Democratic brand of corporatism tilted somewhat toward the labor and the liberal side of the corporatist conception, while the Eisenhower/Republican brand tilted toward the business and conservative side—a division that would become more pronounced in the future.

Over the fifty-year period from about World War I through the 1950s, therefore, we can see the gradual growth of a U.S.-style corporatism (creeping corporatism). In more recent decades, however, the creep of corporatism has accelerated to a full gallop.

Galloping Corporatism

Through the 1950s, despite some corporatist influences, the dominant theory of American politics was still interest-group liberalism and pluralism. Political scientist J. Leiper Freeman portrayed the system as one of "iron triangles" involving congressional committees, interest groups, and executive branch agencies.[10] Other political scientists focused on the play of interest groups as lying at the heart of the U.S. political system; public policy was largely seen as a reflection of the interest-group struggle.[11] Another political scientist, Theodore Lowi, elevated "interest group liberalism" into the official ideology of the U.S. polity.[12]

But by the 1960s it was clear that something more than traditional interest-group liberalism and pluralism—among the glories of the U.S. political system—was at work. The United States was going beyond pluralism toward corporatism. For example, in the Department of Agriculture, not only did the main farmer interest groups, the Farm Bureau and the Farmers' Union, have political influence as outside interest groups; they also had actually moved *into* the department, taken over the running of many public programs, and were using the department's resources mainly to benefit themselves through subsidies and price supports. At the Department of Commerce the story was similar, except that here the main interest (now corporate—operating from *inside* the bureaucratic system) group was big business, which had moved into some of Commerce's bureaus, "colonized" them for itself, and essentially used a public agency for private purposes. Much the same happened at the Department of Labor where, in effect, organized labor, in return for moderating its demands, was "bought off" by being given programs and cushy patronage positions within the federal bureaucracy.

Note how far beyond interest-group pluralism the United States had come. This was no longer just interest groups vying for political influence. This was interest groups operating *within* the system, operating from inside, being incorporated *into* the state system of Cabinet ministries and other agencies. Note also that, as under corporatism, *all* the main economic groups were so incorporated: farm groups, big business, big labor. Soon other groups of smaller businessmen would similarly "hive off" for themselves other federal agencies, such as the Small Business Administration. This merging and blurring of private groups and public agencies is what corporatism, as analyzed in chapter 1, is all about. Moreover, such a blurring of the private and the public tends to produce corruption, special favoritism, and the serving of private interests over the public weal. As political scientist Grant McConnell wrote about this era, the line between public and private interests in America had been "hopelessly lost."[13]

The trends toward the increased corporatization of American society and politics were greatly accelerated by the Great Society programs of President Lyndon Johnson in the 1960s. These comments are not meant to imply political criticism of Johnson's social programs per se, only to suggest that the way they were structured and administered represented further steps toward European-style neo-corporatism—although without calling it that. For example, Johnson introduced Medicare and Medicaid and greatly expanded the Social Security program—all, arguably, admirable programs. But then the Johnson administration brought in the lobbyists, the private advocates, and the associations of retired persons to help run and administer these programs, bringing them *into* the government and all but turning these programs over to the private groups. This is corporatism by any other name.

Similarly with welfare: Johnson greatly expanded welfare programs—all arguably good—but then largely turned the running of these programs to the welfare groups and their advocates, again blurring the line between public and private and providing for a certain "corporatization" of welfare. The same comments apply to his education reform: Johnson expanded the federal government's role in education and created the Department of Education, but then he allowed, even encouraged, the National Education Association (NEA—part of Johnson's political constituency) basically to take over and run this new department. Similarly, a greater federal government role in health care opened the door for health care advocates, health maintenance organizations, nurses' and doctors' associations to dominate the health care field—once more for their own private interests and not necessarily to serve the broader public good. Meanwhile, under both John F. Kennedy and Johnson, tripartite boards, incorporating business, government, and labor, were established to supervise wage and price controls—another step on the road to corporatism.

It is striking that the succeeding, Republican, Nixon and Ford administrations did little to roll back this corporatist tide; indeed, under them and President Jimmy Carter these entitlement programs continued to expand to cover new policy areas. Price and wage controls were reintroduced by Nixon—to renewed cries of "fascism." But it was in entitlements where explosive growth occurred, covering many new sectors. American scholars and universities were closely tied in quasi-corporatist fashion into the Departments of Education and Defense as well as the National Science Foundation and the National Institute of Health; artists and performers not only came to rely on the National Endowment for the Arts but also to try to control its grant-making processes; oil companies "moved into" the newly created Department of Energy as inside "consultants" on energy resources; while conservation groups successfully "colonized" the Environmental Protection Agency. The military-industrial complex provided perhaps the richest, in a budgetary sense, domain of corporatist-like government—private-sector collaboration.

Over the course of two or three decades it seemed as if every interest group and every sector of U.S. society, in one form or another, had their "hooks" into the system. These ostensibly private groups not only placed their own personnel in many public agencies but also then often moved to take over these agencies for themselves, using their inside access and influence to channel grants, contracts, and patronage back to their own groups. This is more than the symbiosis of corporatism; it verges on incest and is rife with conflict of interest. For example, in some of the agencies that the author knows best, such as the Agency for International Development (AID—the main U.S. foreign aid and development agency), various private population-control groups had largely taken over the family planning program, the women's groups had a virtual monopoly on the Women and Development Program, environmental groups had moved in on the Sustainable Development program, and other groups had hived off other parts of AID's activities.

Now, no one denies that these private groups should be able to lobby on behalf of their own agendas; that is what interest-group liberalism is all about. But being incorporated into public agencies, taking them over in some cases, siphoning off grants and contracts, and using public funds and facilities to pursue a private agenda—that goes beyond interest-group liberalism. That is corporatism. And with so many private groups now dependent on and having inside access to the money and patronage of ostensibly public agencies, the corporatization of U.S. public policymaking went forward inexorably.

Given this penetration of U.S. public agencies by so many private groups, it is easy to see why reforming this system would be difficult. Too many groups have too big a stake in the public bureaucracy to allow change to go forward. For example, when Vice President Albert Gore in his Reinventing Government campaign sought to merge AID with the Department of State, a howl of protest went up. The public argument was expressed in terms of which structure of organization would be most efficient. But the real inside argument was about corporatism, or the threat of its dismantling. For the private groups that had stealthily insinuated themselves into AID's programs and bureaucracy recognized that merging AID into State would mean a loss of their special access and funding. So they fought like tigers to kill the proposed reform. And since these groups were part of the Clinton-Gore political constituency whose votes the Clinton administration did not want to lose, they won. The result of this battle royal was that greater governmental efficiency lost, corporatism won. Reform of the Department of Education is similarly difficult because of opposition from the NEA; of the health and welfare systems because of opposition from their constituency groups; and of the Department of Defense budget because of the powerful military-industrial complex.

We have been portraying this corporatization process in the United States as if it were the private groups that were seeking, often sneakily, to insinuate themselves into the public domain. But often the process works in just the opposite way: it is the state or government that creates and/or encourages private groups to join forces and incorporate themselves into public policymaking. Recall that under Roosevelt's National Recovery Act, for instance, the government encouraged and facilitated business associations to organize in economic sectors where they had not been organized before, and then incorporated them into its evolving corporative regulatory structure. Routinely, now, the state helps create associations to lobby on behalf of particular government programs, meanwhile also helping these groups financially and bringing them into its official activities. It was striking, for example, that when the Democratic Clinton administration passed a major educational reform called "Goals 2000," the legislation actually told each state what groups (NEA, business, minorities, others) it *had* to consult in implementing the reform at the state level and, where the preferred groups were weak or nonexistent, the state should *create* an interest-group constituency for the reform even if none had existed before. Later, a Republican Congress moved to amend some of these blatantly corporatist features, allowing states to determine who sits on the policy-making committees instead of legislating which groups were represented.

Another type of corporatist development took place in the area of industrial policy. Many Clinton administration officials had been early backers of a European-like, or perhaps Japan-like, system of targeting certain industries for government assistance in order either to keep them from failing or to make them competitive with similarly state-assisted industries in other countries. Labor Secretary Robert Reich was a particular advocate both of an expanded industrial policy and of closer labor-management relations.[14] To these ends, the Clinton administration created both a corporately organized National Partnership Council aimed at improving the often-strained labor-management relations between the federal government and its public-sector unions; and a new, again corporatist, structure for private business. In return for paying higher taxes and accepting more regulation, U.S. business would receive assistance from the government in selling and competing abroad, federal subsidies for research and development, and protection from Japanese and other competition. But many economists outside the administration remained opposed to this kind of industrial policy, arguing that the government had a poor record in picking leading industries of the future, that the selection process would inevitably be politicized and biased, and that greater government regulation, taxes, and protectionism are not good, long-term, economic strategies for the country.[15]

Clinton's industrial policy was never called corporatism; that is a loaded term in U.S. political discourse. By whatever name, however, his industrial policy involved a social pact that included not just the usual corporatist partners of labor, business, and government, but also involved women, blacks, environmentalists, and other member groups of the Clinton political coalition. The Clinton program, in other words, combined a corporatist system of functional or group representation with the needs of political patronage and coalition building—not unlike what Roosevelt, Eisenhower, Johnson, or Nixon had done before. It brought together both corporatism and politics. But Republicans in the Congress opposed these measures, both on ideological grounds (anti-industrial policy) and because they sensed the political advantages that the Clinton administration was seeking to build through this form of state-subsidized coalition-building.

By the 1980s and 1990s, as other calls began to be heard to slow, halt, or even dismantle this mushrooming corporatist system, it became clear that corporatism was so deeply entrenched that the reform or reversal of it would prove nearly impossible. In the language of the time, the United States had become a nation of entitlements. So many groups had so many mitts into so many public programs and were so incorporated into the governmental system that, in effect, the political culture had changed. As contrasted with the earlier values and even ideology of American individualism, laissez faire, and individual initiative and responsibility, the United States had—at least at some levels—incorporated an ideology of groupism, of collective entitlements, of quotas: economic, ethnic, social, racial, and geographic. The corporatized group system had become so strong that it embodied huge sectors of the population, several of which (labor, business, teachers, women, military, African Americans) were sufficiently strong that they had effective veto power over reform. Teachers' unions could block educational reforms, for example, while the military-industrial complex could block Department of Defense budget reductions. It was the actions of these powerful, vested, corporatized interests, along with the partisan split between Congress and the executive branch, that accounted for the frequent paralysis and gridlock of American policymaking in the 1980s and 1990s.[16] Political philosopher Ernest Barker called this a change from individual individualism to *corporate* individualism.

These divisions, the arguments over creeping corporatism, and the lineup of different corporatized interests behind both major political parties were also at the heart of the political debate in the United States during this same time period, as we see in more detail in the next chapter. On the one hand, the Democratic Party became known as the party of entitlements, quotas, and special interests, including in its coalition labor, women, blacks, environmentalists, the NEA, and other groups—just about enough support to win a presidential election. On the other hand, the Republican Party—opposed to these particular entitlements and claiming to be against quotas, industrial policy, and special interests in general—nevertheless had its own corporatized groups (big business, military interests, and the like) who came into office or favor when the Republicans were in power.

Hence, the United States was treated at the ideological and policy level to a debate for and against corporatism, while at the level of practical politics both parties had their own sets of supportive corporatized interests ("strap hangers," we will call them) who rode the Washington Metro into and out of administrative positions depending on which party was in power at any particular time. In other words, the Democrats had a whole raft of corporate interests that came into government when they won elections, and the Republicans had their own (though smaller) raft of interest groups that accompanied them into office. And when the United States had situations of divided government, with the Congress in charge of one party and the White House controlled by the other, both sets of partisan/corporate interests jockeyed for positions, influence, and programs. The famous "gridlock" or "logjam" that engulfs Washington, in other words, is not just a result of the clash between the parties or between the White House and Congress but of the even larger, cultural, ideological, and interest-based conflict that characterizes the competition of the two parties' respective corporatized hangers-on as well.

The United States: What Kind of Corporatism?

The United States has a form of corporatism very different from that of the European and other countries. The reasons for this are several.

First, because of its short history and the absence of a feudal past, the United States has never had a strong corporatist tradition, corporatist political culture, or historical or "natural" corporatism. Second, the United States, unlike Europe, never had a history of corporatist ideology in the nineteenth century that might serve as a basis for modern, twentieth-century corporatism. Third, the United States never had a system of manifest authoritarian corporatism as Europe had in the interwar period and Latin America had in the 1960s and 1970s. And fourth, even as the United States moved belatedly toward neo-corporatism in the 1960s and 1970s, it never called it that—preferring the terms "pluralism" or "interest-group liberalism." Europe openly practices neo-corporatism and calls it that, but the United States has never publicly acknowledged its corporatist practices.

When corporatism came to the United States, nevertheless, it emerged out of many of the same conditions and in response to many of the same socioeconomic and political circumstances and crises as did corporatism in Europe. First came World War I and Wilson's need to coordinate production for the war effort, then came the depression and Roosevelt's efforts to preserve capitalism by corporatizing it. Meanwhile, organized labor loomed as a potential threat that needed to be "civilized," while business had to learn to accept its "social responsibilities" as well. Later came the rise of the welfare state in the form of Johnson's Great Society, pressures from diverse quarters for centralized economic planning in the form of an industrial policy, entitlements, and eventually quotas. U.S. corporatism, thus, emerged not out of any historic or cultural traditions but out of crises and concrete political and gradually evolving socioeconomic needs—although at this stage it appears that corporate-like groupism and entitlements have become embedded in at least some elements of the political culture.

A U.S.-style corporate state has arrived unsung, unheralded, and almost never mentioned. The emergence of corporatism has to do with the parallel emergence of Big Labor, Big Agriculture, Big Business, Big Universities, Big Defense, Big Welfare, and Big Government, all operating in a symbiotic relationship. It also has to do with the growth of modern social policy, with the government assuming a great role in the management of the economy, with the greater emphasis on group rights and group entitlements over individual rights, and with the growth of a large administrative-state regulatory apparatus. Among its implications are the merging of the public and private sectors, the delegation of public power to private-interest associations, and the increased central government consolidation of economic and political power. The United States has at various levels been "corporatized" as Japan, many European, and various other countries have been, but without this implying, as in the 1930s, repression, a corporatist ideology, or fascist authoritarianism. U.S.-style corporatism seems to have arrived mainly as a pragmatic way to manage complex group relations in modern society and as a system of political/power brokerage and compromise.

American corporatism, in addition, has always been partial, incomplete. The United States never developed a fully institutionalized system of formal corporatism—unlike Portugal, Austria, or Italy, for example, in the interwar period. American corporatism has always sat beside, and was always a minority current within, the dominant system of liberalism and interest-group pluralism. The United States has *elements* of corporatism, but it has never adopted the whole structure and accoutrements of corporatism. So the U.S. system is one of limited corporatism, of partial corporatism, of mixed liberal and corporatist influences. Moreover, because the individualistic and laissez faire ethos is still so strong, and because corporatism was for so long associated with fascism and Nazism, the United States has never called what it practices "corporatism." Not even the innocuous "neo-corporatism" is permissible politically in the United States.

Because U.S. corporatism is still limited and partial, it is important to know where it is located. U.S. corporatism is present in part in the political parties, now organized more on a corporate group or functional basis, which bear similarities to the Venezuelan and several European party situations. Both main parties are divided functionally and sectorally: labor, women, blacks, business, gays, and on and on. Corporatism is also located in the U.S. system of labor/industrial relations, particularly in the regulatory legislation that governs both business and union activity, and in a growing system of compulsory processes for dispute negotiations. It is ensconced in the U.S.-style welfare state and particularly in the system of entitlements that has grown up over the last four decades and that now encompass a large number of groups and persons. It lies in industrial policy and in the on-and-off debates over price and wage controls. It lies in the military-industrial complex and in a variety of social programs including education, welfare, health care, and Social Security. It also lies in the hiving off by diverse groups of whole sectors and policy areas of the federal government for themselves, and in the emerging system of ethnic or group quotas, preferences, and set-asides that have grown up in recent years. And increasingly corporatism seems, in the United States, to be present at the level of state and local policymaking as well as at the federal.

The United States may prove to be fertile ground for increased corporatism in the future. As the disparities widen between rich and poor and as ethnic/racial tensions grow, the central government or state will likely seek ways to co-opt more of these interest groups so as to avoid conflict and maintain stability. Market-based solutions to such social problems as education, health care, and poverty often fail to deal with the larger systemic issues that cause inequalities of opportunity and attainment, which also suggest a strong state role. Additionally, the disruptions caused by the newly emerging world economic order (or disorder) suggest increasing economic dislocations for many American workers. The inadequacy of the current political and economic system to deal with these larger issues will likely precipitate a search for political alternatives that offer avenues for stability. For the United States as well as for other countries, this probably means an increase in corporatist practices and institutions.

While the practice and institutions of corporatism have clearly been expanding in the United States, there are severe limits on American-style corporatism as well. The United States lacks the strong trade unions necessary for full-fledged corporatism that some European countries have. It lacks a strong, guiding, directing state, a *dirigiste* or mercantilist state, with vast economic and social power as in Europe. It also lacks what we will call a "bureaucratic tradition"—that is, the tradition of settling labor disputes and other conflicts through bureaucratic, state intervention as distinct from direct bargaining by the concerned parties. And, in addition, the traditional U.S. ethos of individualism, free enterprise, and pluralism is still sufficiently strong that it often impedes the development of even stronger corporatism.

To date, the United States has never had a full-blown debate about corporatism—in part because America refuses to call it that and it is hard to debate something that has no name and officially doesn't exist. Occasionally, in discussing industrial policy, one will see reference to what is called "friendly fascism," but that both misses the point (corporatism is not fascism) and trivializes what is, in fact, a serious development in U.S. society with major implications for democracy and various areas of public policy.

But there are signs that may be about to change—and in this, as in other matters concerning neo-corporatism, the United States is following Europe's lead. For implicit (and often more than implicit) in British Prime Minister Margaret Thatcher's, German Chancellor Helmut Kohl's, as well as Ronald Reagan's championing of free trade, open markets, and laissez faire capitalism is a direct challenge to neo-corporatism as well. This revolution of neo-liberalism, as it is often called, has now spread beyond European and U.S. borders to encompass much of the world. For if the United States stands for democracy in the political marketplace and free enterprise in the economic marketplace, then there is little room for either economic or political statism, authoritarianism, or corporatism. And, in fact, the debate over corporatism has recently waxed hot and heavy—particularly in Europe, less so in the United States—and, in the meantime, a number of widespread, even global economic and sociological forces are also beginning to undermine corporatism. Hence, in chapter 7 we turn to both the criticisms that have recently been launched against corporatism *and* the broad-scale socioeconomic and political trends that are already subverting it.

Notes

1. Graham K. Wilson, "Why Is There No Corporatism in the United States?" in Gerhard Lehmbruch and Philippe C. Schmitter (eds.), *Patterns of Corporatist Policy-Making* (Beverly Hills: Sage, 1982), 219–36; and Robert H. Salisbury, "Why No Corporatism in America," in Philippe C. Schmitter and Gerhard Lehmbruch (eds.), *Trends Toward Corporatist Interest Intermediation* (Beverly Hills: Sage, 1979).

2. The best study is that of Louis Hartz, *The Liberal Tradition in America* (New York: Harcourt, Brace and World, 1955).

3. Theodore Lowi, "The Public Philosophy: Interest Group Liberalism," *American Political Science Review* 61 (March 1967): 5–24, and *The End of Liberalism* (New York: Norton, 1969).

4. James Weinstein, *The Corporate Ideal in the Liberal State, 1900–1918* (Boston: Beacon Press, 1968).

5. Ellis W. Hawley, "Herbert Hoover, the Commerce Secretariat, and the Vision of an 'Associative State'," *Journal of American History* 61 (June 1974): 110–40.

6. Ronald Radosh, "Corporate Ideology of American Labor Leaders from Gompers to Hillman," *Studies on the Left* 6 (1966): 66–68.

7. Richard R. Weiner, "Pluralism and Neo-Corporatism: The Legacy of the New Deal and the 'Social Contract'," paper delivered at the 13th Congress of the International Political Science Association, Paris, 1985.

8. Neil Chamberlain, "The Organized Business of America," *Journal of Political Economy* 52 (2) (1944): 97–110.

9. Robert Griffith, "Dwight D. Eisenhower and the Corporate Commonwealth," *The American Historical Review* 87 (February 1982): 87–122.

10. J. Leiper Freeman, *The Political Process: Executive Bureau—Legislative Committee Relations* (Garden City, NY: Doubleday, 1955).

11. David Truman, *The Governmental Process* (New York: Knopf, 1951); and Earl Latham, *The Group Basis of Politics* (Ithaca, NY: Cornell University Press, 1952).

12. Lowi, "The Public Philosophy."

13. Grant McConnell, *Private Power and American Democracy* (New York: Vintage, 1966).

14. Robert Reich, *The Work of Nation: Preparing Ourselves for 21st Century Capitalism* (New York: Vintage, 1992).

15. For the opposition see Chalmers Johnson (ed.), *The Industrial Policy Debate* (San Francisco: Institute for Contemporary Studies, 1984).

16. An excellent political-legal survey is Arthur Selwyn Miller, *The Modern Corporate State: Private Governments and the American Constitution* (Westport, CT: Greenwood Press, 1976).

7

Critiques of the Corporatist Approach

The corporatism phenomenon sped like a meteor across the landscape of study and analysis in the 1970s and during most of the 1980s. Here was a new way of thinking, seeing, and conceptualizing comparative political systems and even the United States. For the corporatist approach not only offered a new subject area for study, it also provided a new framework for analysis. It represented a paradigm shift. It challenged old (liberal, pluralist, Marxist) ways of thinking and offered a dynamic, exciting, and controversial alternative. It opened new panoramas, whole new subject areas of inquiry. It fundamentally challenged several social science disciplines and asked new questions and offered innovative interpretations of major policy and developmental issues.

For those early pioneers in exploring the comparative sociology and politics of corporatism, these were heady days. They were lauded—and occasionally vilified—for all but single-handedly introducing a whole new approach and field of study into the discipline. There were dozens of international conferences, often in exotic locations, on the corporatism theme. A cottage industry of papers, articles, and books followed, several translated into diverse foreign languages. A new international network of scholars—no longer just Americans, as with most other paradigm breakthroughs in the past—sprang up, devoted to this subject area. A host of lectures, panels, study projects, and special seminars was organized around the new approach. It was little short of a revolution in the social sciences and an illuminating example of how major paradigm shifts occur.

But along with the plaudits came the critiques. Right from the beginning the corporatist approach was subjected to sometimes withering criticism. This is natural and often the case when a new conceptual paradigm is introduced and attracts such widespread attention, because it means the old paradigms—and all the grants, international conferences, publication possibilities, and fame that attended *them*—now get pushed to the sidelines. At least by academic standards, the stakes in these scholarly disputes are large; and the debate over corporatism waged—and continues to wage—hot and heavy. The attacks on the corporatist approach came mainly from advocates of both the Marxist and the liberal-pluralist models—those whose paradigms were precisely the ones being gored or supplanted—as well as from neutral scholars. We analyze the scholarly criticisms in the first part of this chapter.

Meanwhile, on the ground, at the level of *real* politics and society, something else was happening to corporatism. In the late 1970s, with Margaret Thatcher's election as prime minister of Great Britain, followed by Ronald Reagan's election as president of the United States, and eventually becoming a global revolution, corporatism was coming under political—as distinct from scholarly—attack. Corporatism and its attendant features—big government, big unions, big bureaucracy, big entitlements, what were often seen as inefficient and corporatized public policies, entrenched interests that had burrowed into the state system and were ripping it off—became the subjects of political attack. What had begun as a scholarly approach to analyzing new social and political phenomena—the corporatization of the state, of interest groups, and of state–society relations—now became a matter of major *public* controversy. Neo-corporatism was challenged by neo-liberalism and, in the wake of the Cold War, the battle lines were drawn both at the national and global levels. Some called for a revolution, the total dismantling of corporatist structures through privatization, downsizing, and decentralization; others, less ambitious, wanted to reduce, reform, and make more efficient the state and corporatist institutions that already existed.

So the conflict raged, at both the scholarly and the political and public policy levels. Hence, in this chapter we need to analyze both the scholarly and intellectual criticisms of corporatism, *and* the concrete and real-life attacks on it and the social and political forces pushing to supplant it. If modern neo-corporatism is dismantled, however, we also need to ask—and we return to this theme in the last chapter—what will replace it as the main sociopolitical form of the modern state?

Scholarly Criticisms of the Corporatist Approach

Corporatism is both a descriptive term used to describe a particular configuration of sociopolitical and institutional forces, *and* an alternative model (alternative to liberalism and Marxism-Leninism) of the policy process and particularly of state–society relations. In the following section of this chapter we will be concerned with the criticisms of corporatism as actual practice; here we focus on the criticisms leveled against corporatism as a conceptual model.

The corporatist model has right from the start been subjected to some harsh examinations and criticism. Most of the criticism has come from advocates of the alternative approaches, persons who have an axe to grind. But some of it has also been careful and objective. While some corporatism scholars have wilted under the barrage, my own view is that the criticism has, in general, been healthy for the concept and for the scholarly fields where corporatism has had its major impact. For it is in this interplay between those who advocate a new conceptual framework and those who see flaws in it or do further empirical or theoretical work to refine it that the process of theory building in the social sciences takes place and goes forward.

Definitional Problems

The first problem pointed out by the critics is that corporatism is not a unified concept and that there are different definitions of the term. This is a problem, but one that need not bother us overly. Although it would be *nice* if writers on the concept all used the same definition, that may not be realistic or possible. We do not all agree on the definitions of other key descriptive terms like "liberalism" or "democracy"; why should we expect the level of agreement on a precise definition of corporatism to be any greater? Although the absence of a single definition is sometimes upsetting to students, my own view is that, especially in the early stages of a new approach, definitional preciseness is not only unlikely but it may even be unhealthy—that is, if our interest is to allow the new concept to flower and stimulate new thinking and new research.

Corporatism has, in fact, been used in several different ways. There is, first, an economic meaning of corporatism: the restructuring of economic activity and industry along sectoral or industry-wide lines, such as fishing, wheat, steel, which are overseen by a bureaucratic set of "corporations" that bring together workers and employers usually under state control; but this idea largely died in the 1930s. Second, there is a sociological meaning of corporatism: the organization of society in terms of "natural" functional groups (neighborhoods, parishes, families, clan groups, associations, guilds, farmers, labor, business, and so on); this meaning is closer to our usage here. And third, there is a political-ideological meaning of corporatism, one tied to the ideology of corporatism earlier in this century and the political movements (e.g., Workers' Circles, Catholic political parties) associated with it. But almost no one proclaims himself or herself an ideological corporatist anymore; this meaning of corporatism died in Europe during World War II along with the economic one—although in many recent Third World authoritarian regimes a lingering admiration and adhesion to ideological corporatism still exists.

There is corporatism in the old-fashioned, largely 1930s style, and then there is modern neo-corporatism in which groups are incorporated into government policymaking in such areas as social welfare and industrial policy. There are state corporatism (authoritarian, top-down; largely gone in Western Europe, fading in Latin America, still present in East Asia and in many developing nations) and societal corporatism (democratic, participatory, akin to neo-corporatism).

In this book we have distinguished between four different definitions and historical time periods of corporatism: (1) traditional, natural, or historic corporatism; (2) ideological corporatism of the nineteenth and early twentieth centuries; (3) manifest corporatism of Europe between the world wars, Latin America at a somewhat later date, and many developing nations even today; and (4) modern neo-corporatism. We have added a fifth definition: corporatism as a model or analytical framework.

As long as corporatism was mainly a descriptive term, as in the first four definitions above, it was not very controversial. Scholars might disagree somewhat over the facts and interpretations of different corporatist systems, but these disagreements were relatively mild. However, as an alternative *model* of interpretation of national development and of state–society relations in the modern world, corporatism has been put under a great deal of scrutiny and criticism since its arrival as a concept during the 1970s.

The most prominent—and controversial—formulation was offered by Philippe C. Schmitter. His oft-cited definition was quoted earlier in the book but it is useful to recall it here.

> Corporatism can be defined as a system of interest representation in which the constituent units are organized into a limited number of singular, compulsory, noncompetitive, hierarchically ordered and functionally differentiated categories, recognized or licensed (if not created) by the state and granted a deliberate representational monopoly within their respective categories in exchange for observing certain controls on their selection of leaders and articulation of demands and supports.[1]

Remember also that Schmitter sharply contrasted corporatism with other major systems: pluralism, monism (totalitarianism), and syndicalism.

The Schmitter definition, while influential in some quarters, has also been roundly criticized. First, in its emphasis on the "singular," "compulsory," "noncompetitive," "hierarchically ordered," and "monopolistic" features of corporatism, it is both too rigid and too tied to the statist, bureaucratic, and authoritarian forms of corporatism (Brazil, Portugal) that Schmitter originally studied. It is not an adequate definition for democratic, participatory, pluralist, societal, or neo-corporatism. Second, the Schmitter definition focuses almost exclusively on such economic groups as organized labor and business as corporate actors, thus ignoring such noneconomic corporate actors as military and religious institutions, universities and cultural forces, as well as women's groups, indigenous movements, and others. Moreover and related, Schmitter's definition was too closely tied to a particular political agenda—quasi-Marxist and social-democratic—of the 1960s and 1970s, which is both inappropriate in a serious scholarly analysis *and* has since faded from the scene, unfortunately dragging the focus on corporatism down with it. Finally, this formulation was too static; it had almost nothing to say about corporatist political dynamics and thus could not account for the transformation of one form of corporatism to another. So, for example, when the neo-corporatism phenomenon began to fade in the late 1980s (see below), the Schmitter approach and definition seemed to have little left to offer.

It is far better, therefore, to have a definition that emphasizes corporatism's permanent features rather than one that is tied to a particular time and place. Moreover, our definition must be relevant to all societies in distinct culture areas that practice different forms of corporatism, not just the Western form. We require in addition a definition that provides a handle for understanding how corporatism changes over time and evolves into new forms. A useful starting point in this regard is to define corporatism (as we did in the Preface) as a system of social and political organization in which various associations (such as tribes, clans) and interests are sectorally or functionally organized (military, economic, religious, and the like) and are integrated or incorporated into the structure and decision making of the state and of public policy. Often these groups are structured on a monopolistic basis or under the guidance, direction, tutelage, and control of the state so as to achieve coordinated, integral, peaceful national development. Recall also the related markers by which we can usually tell if corporatism is present: (1) a strong state, (2) controlled or limited numbers of interest groups, and (3) interests that become interlocked with or are part of the state (review chapter 1, if necessary).

The Causes of Corporatism

A second reason for corporatism being so controversial is that leading corporatism scholars themselves have vigorously disagreed as to its causes. Is corporatism caused by historic, religious, and political-cultural causes; is it a product of economic and institutional forces; or does it emerge out of circumstances of crises?[2] These issues have vexed and divided scholars of corporatism from the beginning of the debate until today.

The answer is so obvious as to raise questions as to why the debate over corporatism's causes has been so heated for so long. *All three causes are involved.* First, corporatism is clearly related to crises—the war industries boards of World Wars I and II, the depression of the 1930s, the perceived Bolshevik threat, and the political challenge of lower class and/or guerrilla groups in Latin America and elsewhere in the 1960s. Crises and challenges tend to force governments to tighten up, to look for control mechanisms—such as corporatism—by which they can manage potentially threatening groups. But while crises and a corporatist response are related, focus on the crisis cause alone begs the question of why it is corporatism to which states and regimes turn when they are challenged and not to some other form.

The answer to that question leads to the other two main causes of corporatism: cultural factors and institutional ones. There can be little doubt that cultural factors—history, tradition, religion, values, and beliefs—are important in shaping both the traditional, historic forms of corporatism and the corporatist ideology of the nineteenth century, particularly its Catholic expression. Continuing today, these cultural factors underlying corporatism remain important in influencing the Asian/Confucian pattern of group and community solidarity, Indian corporatism as manifested in part through its caste associations, African tribalism and ethnicity, as well as the organic and functional conceptions that undergird Latin American corporatism. Even later, manifest corporatism in Spain, Portugal, Austria, and other countries was influenced by the cultural traditions of earlier Catholicism—although other, structural factors were also involved. There are even aspects of modern, social-welfare–oriented neo-corporatism that owe *part* of their inspiration to religious/cultural notions of group solidarity, mutual obligation, and the social obligations of capital. One cannot understand corporatism and its appeal without coming to grips with these political-cultural factors.

In the twentieth century, however, the structural or institutional causes of corporatism—both political and economic—came to outweigh the cultural ones. For example, in the 1930s, the causes of Italian, Spanish, Portuguese, and other European forms of corporatism were due more to institutional factors than to cultural ones. These included fear of Bolshevik revolution, fear of an organized and revolutionary trade union movement, the threat of economic collapse occasioned by the depression, the desire to control spiraling economic and political challenges, and so on. These are all institutional and structural factors, not cultural ones. Historic and cultural factors often provided a setting in which corporatism in these countries could grow and flourish, and corporatism was probably stronger in those countries that had compatible cultural (for example, organicism, communalism) traditions. But by the 1930s the main causes for corporatism, in Europe at least, were no longer cultural and religious; they were mainly political, economic, and bureaucratic—all structural and institutional factors.

Similarly with modern neo-corporatism. While in some European countries (Holland, Belgium, Germany) notions of both Protestant and Catholic religious obligations partially shaped the ideas of social solidarity and class harmony that went into their newer systems of corporatism, the main factors were economic, political, and institutional.

Modern social-welfare programs as well as central economic planning, while perhaps owing something to cultural and religious factors, are mainly secular activities of the modern postindustrial state. They are the product of economic demands, pressures from organized business and labor, as well as political and bureaucratic requirements, not cultural factors. And surely the case of the United States, as we saw in chapter 6, which has almost none of the cultural conditions that have led elsewhere to corporatism, nevertheless has developed a nascent corporatist system due almost exclusively to the institutional/structural factors of twentieth-century capitalism, war, bureaucracy, and politics.

During the twentieth century, in fact, a shift occurred in the modern industrial nations, away from cultural causes of corporatism and toward institutional/structural causes. This shift is related both to growing secularism in modern societies as well as to the demands of a modern economy, a modern welfare system, and modern social and political organization. The cultural underpinnings of corporatism in these societies have not disappeared but they have been superseded by structural factors. However, in the less developed countries of Asia, Africa, the Middle East, and Latin America, the cultural and historical causes of corporatism are still often important. The lesson, therefore, is: In the early stages of a country's development, when traditional institutions and practices are still powerful, the historical and cultural causes of corporatism are often influential. As a country moves toward greater secularism and modernity, however, institutional/structural factors become more important.

One other consideration deserves mention in this context, and that relates to the various definitions of corporatism and how those influence one's view of this debate over causes. Schmitter and his fellow students of modern neo-corporatism have defined corporatism almost exclusively in terms of the relations between labor, business, and the state. They associate corporatism almost exclusively with the needs and dynamics of modern capitalism. But these are, *by definition,* structural factors; small wonder, therefore, that the Schmitter school has emphasized structural factors as causative. But if one holds an ampler definition of corporatism that leaves room for noneconomic corporations such as military institutions, religious bodies, women's groups, and ethnic groups, then one can see why cultural factors would play a greater role. Obviously *both* sets of factors, cultural and institutional, are influential in shaping corporatism in its various forms and incarnations; but the causative agents may also vary in importance over time and in distinct settings.

Corporatism and Pluralism

A third criticism of the corporatist approach is that it is not really different from pluralism, only a new and extended version. These waters are muddied by the fact that scholars often use the term corporate pluralism and, under the category of societal corporatism, refer to the democratic and pluralist characteristics of modern neo-corporatism.

But corporatism and pluralism, first of all, are very different. Under pluralism, corporate groups are free and unfettered; but under corporatism the groups are integrated into, and sometimes even created by, the state. It is one thing, as under pluralism, to consult with the nation's interest groups, but it is quite another, as in corporatism, for the state to fabricate and absorb its own interest associations and thus to erase the line, necessary for democracy, between state and society. This is a fundamental difference that helps explain the free associability of a liberal pluralist society as opposed to the controlled, fettered, often co-opted character of interest groups under a corporatist regime. These are differences of *kind* and *type,* not just of degrees.

At the same time, we must recognize that there is also a fundamental difference between the authoritarian corporatism in Europe of the 1930s (and continuing in many developing countries) and the democratic or societal corporatism of today. The former suppressed all forms of pluralism, while modern neo-corporatism is quite compatible with democracy and pluralism. Under the older corporatism, interest groups were based on coercion or snuffed out; but neo-corporatism is based on consent, on a democratically negotiated social contract between the state and its participatory groups. These groups voluntarily give up some degree of autonomy in return for certain benefits, such as pay raises or greater social programs, that they receive from the state. So, at one level the free associability of pluralism is very different from the system of group controls of the older authoritarian corporatism; but in the case of modern neo-corporatism, while the differences remain, they are blurred somewhat by the existence of pluralism within corporatism and by the group's ability voluntarily—at least in theory— to opt out of the corporatist contract.

Underdeveloped Corporatist Theory

A fourth criticism of the corporatist approach is that its theory is incomplete and undeveloped. Particularly as compared with such other grand theories as liberal-pluralism and Marxism, corporatism does not have a clear, consistent body of agreed-upon theory.

The responses to these criticisms are several. First, as with any new approach in the social sciences, it takes time for a clear body of theory to appear. Nor is the absence of such theory at first so critical since we want, in these early stages, for a variety of perspectives to be set forth and tested, for a thousand flowers to bloom. Second, we need to ask if the critics want a *formal* corporatist theory or if something less grandiose would be satisfactory. As for a formal corporatist theory, there is a body of such theory beginning to be built up—for example, in Peter Williamson's book *Varieties of Corporatism.*[3] But most of us who write in this area are content with something less pretentious. We think of the corporatist approach as a set of suggestions, a way of thinking and looking, an heuristic (teaching and learning) device and not a formal model. It tells us what to look for, what patterns to observe and test, what questions to ask. It gives us suggestions as to important societal relationships and public policy processes; to most of us, this is utility enough—without the added requirement of a formal model.

Three other, fairly modest notions should be introduced at this point. First, although corporatism is an intriguing and important concept, one must remember that it is not the only explanation of modern society and the directions of political and institutional trends. Corporatism is often a *necessary* explanation for understanding modern sociopolitical development, but it is not a *sufficient* one. Second and related, we should not, therefore, elevate corporatism to the status of being a complete and all-encompassing cause of current trends in state–society relations; again, it is a useful explanation but not a final one, and we should not give it an importance it does not have. Third and once more related, we need, therefore, to consider corporatism along with other competing paradigms—liberal, Marxist, others—for all of them have something to say about modern society, but no one of them is sufficient unto itself. Hence, some unaccustomed modesty needs to be introduced into the claims for corporatism as an approach and explanatory device; and we also need to recognize that while corporatism helps shed light on *some* important political processes—labor relations, social welfare, industrial policy, and others—other approaches can be simultaneously used, or used in combination with the corporatist one, to provide insights into areas in which the corporatist explanation is silent or only partial.

The corporatist approach should be viewed as offering important insights into state–society relations as well as helping to fill the gaps in comparative analysis for which other explanations are inadequate. Its utility in my view is purely pragmatic: where it is useful in helping us understand certain political phenomena and public policy issues, let us by all means use it; where other paradigms are needed, let us use them—or various combinations. This is not an ideological issue but a pragmatic and sensible one; at the same time we need to avoid reifying the corporatism concept. If the corporatist approach helps us understand trends in modern and developing societies, then that is all to the good; but if and when it runs out of explanatory steam, then we need to utilize other concepts to get at different or related issues.

There are, accepting these limits, a number of steps that need to be taken to develop better corporatist theory. First, we need more case studies of corporatism at the individual country level. There are many corporatist regimes or governments, often with partially corporatist structures, that remain wholly unstudied, and these unique features need to be factored into our overall understanding of corporatism. Second, we need studies at the culture-area level (such as Asia, Africa, Latin America, Eastern Europe) to see the patterns of corporatism—differences as well as similarities—within and across different culture areas. This is called theory building at the middle-range level. Related, third, and also at the middle-range level, is the need for studies that look at particular policies or aspects of corporatism—the role of the state, military or religious groups, labor groups, industrial policy, welfare policy, and so forth—across countries, culture areas, and time frames. Fourth, we need work at the level of grand theory. For up to this point, most of the research in the field has been on (1) Europe, and (2) the particular form known as neo-corporatism.

But there is much more to corporatism than this. For a further elaboration of grand theory, we need (1) to examine many other areas besides Europe; (2) to build, as we did in chapter 5, a further development-related dynamic into the general static picture we currently have of corporatism; and (3) to be able to predict the newer forms of corporatism now that the "neo" kind is fading and under attack.

An Underdeveloped Empirical Base?

The corporatist approach has also been attacked by critics for building a large, architectural, theoretical edifice on top of a weak empirical base. This criticism has validity.

We do need, as indicated above, more empirical case studies of corporatism in individual countries, in distinct regional areas, and cross-culturally on specific issues, political groups, and policies. In particular, we need many more studies of non-Western forms of corporatism as distinct from the earlier studies that focused mainly on Western Europe and Latin America. For that focus not only limited our knowledge base but it also skewed the process of theory building that was mainly derived from the European experience and concentrated on one particular form of corporatism: neo-corporatism.

More case studies in distinct regions and of different issues not only would build up our knowledge base and understanding of corporatism but would enable us to go beyond the ethnocentric concentration on Europe and would also enable us to begin reformulating a genuinely cross-cultural and global theory of corporatism that is broader, more truly universal, and explores many (including non-Western) forms and facets of corporatism besides the neo-corporatist kind.

A Descriptive Term or Full-Fledged Theory?

Our answer to this issue has already been given: corporatism is *both* a descriptive term *and* a full-fledged theory.

As a descriptive term, corporatism expresses a set of characteristics, such as the integration of societal interest groups into the state, that are unique to corporatist systems. But we have argued that corporatism is more than just a descriptive term. And it is this "more" that has made corporatism so controversial. For as long as the term "corporatist" was used only to describe a particular type of sociopolitical system, it was relatively noncontroversial; but when corporatism was presented as an alternative social science model, that is when the controversy began.

We go beyond those scholars like Wyn Grant[4] and Martin Heisler,[5] who believe corporatism is just a new form of pluralism. And we go beyond those Marxist scholars like Leo Panitch,[6] who believe that corporatism is just a new way by which capitalism exploits the working class. Corporatism may be those things, but it is also more than that. Something else, in both old and new forms, is involved. For corporatism, as we have insisted throughout, is both an alternative viewpoint to the other major "isms" out there of liberal-pluralism and Marxism, and another way of organizing state–society or sociopolitical relations. That "way," which involved organic, integral, communitarian, and/or corporatist/functional modes of organizing political society, has a long but often neglected history in political theory, sociology, and political economy. Now we find it strongly present, although in diverse forms, in both developing and already developed nations and in diverse areas of the globe. Clearly the corporatist approach to understanding these phenomena represents a new and innovative approach and offers insights into certain (not all, recall) issues and political phenomena that other approaches have not addressed or provide inadequate understanding.

Too Narrowly Conceived?

On a number of fronts the corporatist approach *has* been too narrowly conceived. First, as argued earlier, it was too narrowly concentrated on and in the Western European area. Second, it was too narrowly limited by several prominent scholars of corporatism to socioeconomic interests (business, labor) and should have been more broadly conceived to include other, noneconomic corporate bodies such as military institutions, religious institutions, universities, bureaucracies, professional associations, ethnic groups, clans, tribes, and the like. Third, it was too narrowly limited to examining neo-Keynesian economic policies (incomes policy, social welfare, industrial policy) and thus was also tied too closely to a specific party and policy (largely social-democratic) agenda. When this agenda went by the boards or the parties that championed it lost favor, the corporatist approach also lost favor.

Our orientation here is to correct these and other faults in some earlier corporatist literature. First, we insist that the corporatism concept be expanded to include non-Western as well as Western societies. Second, we insist on a broader conception of corporatism that encompasses not just socioeconomic but also bureaucratic, professional, ethnic, and even gender-based groups. And third, in order to retain its status as a neutral and social-scientific term, corporatism needs to be divorced from any specific partisan, political, or ideological agenda. Only in these ways can corporatism's value and utility as a social-scientific approach be maintained, and only in this way can the corporatist approach survive what is, in fact, the decline (see below) of a certain, related partisan agenda that has been under attack.

The Political Decline of Corporatism?

Corporatism as a social science approach and model has often been criticized and attacked; in the preceding pages we have presented the main scholarly criticisms as well as provided answers that help clarify the issues raised. But corporatism has also been attacked "on the ground," in terms of its actual practice. Hence, in this section we deal with the criticisms of corporatism as practice, and also discuss the long-term societal trends that may be undermining corporatism or, alternatively, leading to its being practiced in new ways.

The criticisms of the older (Mussolini, Franco, Salazar) forms of manifest, statist, or top-down corporatism have been familiar to us at least since the 1930s. They are: that this form of corporatism is authoritarian; that it is anti-democratic; that it often violates the rights of workers and is repressive; that it is inefficient economically; that it is static and makes no provision for social change; that it is fascistic.[7] Most scholars and policymakers now recognize these criticisms. Set against the negatives, however—particularly as articulated by more recent developing nations in Asia, Latin America, and other areas—is the argument that corporatism provides discipline, stability, order, social peace, and a set of political institutions capable of presiding over the difficult transition from underdeveloped to modern. It is said by the proponents of this position that only a strong, disciplined, usually corporatist state can provide the stability and order in which economic growth can begin and become self-sustaining; only later, once a certain level of development has occurred, can the country move toward a more open, pluralist, and democratic system.

These are complex issues; they cannot all be resolved here. In the developed nations, it is clear, this kind of authoritarian corporatism has been largely discarded, overcome, superseded; it has been replaced in most countries by neo-corporatism. But in the developing nations—Indonesia, Mexico, Singapore, Malaysia, for example—the arguments for corporatism and its stabilizing, ordering, controlling mechanisms are still strong. Even among developing nations, however, and certainly in those in Latin America and increasingly those in Asia, the arguments are now at least equally powerful that democracy, pluralism, and open markets are more conducive of stability, social peace, and political continuity—particularly in the long term—than is corporatism. Although the debate between these two positions will doubtless continue, global trends in recent years tend to point toward this latter, pro-democratic position.

So the real question today is over neo-corporatism. The neo-corporatism issue is more interesting at present because (1) the older form of manifest or authoritarian corporatism has largely been superseded; (2) it is in the advanced countries that the arguments over neo-corporatism have been strongest; (3) these countries often provide a model for the less-developed countries to follow; and (4) it is in the developed countries where the leading trends away from neo-corporatism have recently been occurring. Hence, it is to these broad-scale social and political trends, and their implications for modern neo-corporatism, that the discussion now turns.

The Decline of Trade Unions

All over the world trade unions seem to be in decline, often precipitously. In the United States the percentage of unionized workers has been falling for decades and is now down to 8–10 percent; in Great Britain, Germany, and other highly unionized countries the percentages have also been falling—although not to such a low percentage as in the United States. Japan has relatively few unionized workers; it practices what one writer has called "corporatism without unions."

The reasons for organized labor's decline in so many countries are several. They included infighting among the unions, political differences and rivalries, and the bad image (corrupt, violent) that some union leaders present. Conservative politicians such as Margaret Thatcher and Ronald Reagan have been hostile to unions and their practices, and the public similarly has become less favorably inclined toward unions. Perhaps the biggest problem, however, is that while the economies of most modern nations have changed dramatically in recent years, the unions haven't changed apace. Labor organizations, we know, do better in one big plant or industry than in many small ones;

they do better in traditional "heavy" industries (steel, coal, manufacturing) than in modern service industries; they do better in countries with centralized wage systems than in those with decentralized bargaining; and they do better among older workers than younger ones. But it is precisely the former characteristics in each of these four sets of traits that are fading in modern societies and the latter ones—which point toward fewer and weaker unions—that are ascendant.

Labor has long been one of the three key actors (the others being business and government) in any modern corporatist arrangement—and even more so under neo-corporatism. But if labor is so necessary in these tripartite corporative systems, and if organized labor is fading in modern society, then what happens to corporatism in systems where labor's voice has become so weak?

The Attacks on the Welfare State

One of the key factors accounting for modern neo-corporatism, we have seen, is the rise of the modern welfare state. As the welfare state emerged, expanded ("cradle-to-grave welfare"), and enjoyed great popularity from the 1960s on, corporatist and neo-corporatist structures were progressively used to incorporate the recipients of these programs (workers, farmers, welfare recipients generally) into the planning, decision making, and implementation of social programs.

But many of these programs over time became bloated, inefficient, and corrupt. They came under strong attack worldwide; *all* the modern nations began to discuss reforming their welfare systems. In Great Britain, France, Germany, Italy, the United States, and other industrialized nations there was a great deal of talk and even some action to reduce the size and costs of social welfare. Most nations decided they could not afford such plush, cradle-to-grave welfare programs; even the Scandinavian countries, who had pioneered social programs in many of these areas, began reducing their financial commitment to welfarism, looking for ways to reorganize their programs, or even electing conservative governments that halted their growth.

The argument here is similar to that regarding organized labor: if the development of the modern social-welfare state went hand-in-hand with the emergence of corporatism, and if the welfare state is presently being attacked and weakened, then will not corporatism be weakened as well?

In most countries, however, the welfare state has remained ubiquitous despite recent efforts to reduce it. Changing or reducing welfare benefits has proved to be far harder than most politicians had imagined—as the U.S. efforts to change or reduce welfare, Medicare and Medicaid, or the health care system have demonstrated. So far in Europe and America there has been some tampering around the edges of welfarism but no wholesale assault on its benefits. Instead what we are sometimes seeing is a redefinition of the role of citizen and state, workers and owner, but little real reduction so far in the welfare state. And the reason of course is that the manifold interest and corporate groups that benefit from welfare or see it as part of their entitlement are so large, strong, and deeply entrenched within the system that politicians are reluctant to go against their wishes.

The Internationalization of Business

A third factor accounting for the decline of neo-corporatism is the internationalization of business (and of labor too, although that has received less attention). The facts are that at least 30 percent of America's gross national product, for example, is now generated through international trade; worldwide, more and more businesses are becoming multinational as distinct from national. Are General Motors, Ford, and Chrysler really U.S. companies anymore when they produce whole cars, or major components, in Europe, Asia, and Latin America? Is Honda strictly a Japanese company when it builds factories in the United States? And so on. Increasingly, business has become international, without real borders, without being identified with any single sovereignty.

But almost all the corporatist schemes examined so far have been national in scope. There is some corporatism at the international level (the EEC, NAFTA) but still few corporatist rules that are enforceable internationally. Hence, if business is becoming more international, but corporatism is still largely national in its regulatory scope and reach, then business is increasingly going beyond the reach of corporatist control mechanisms. This is another factor in the decline of neo-corporatism.

Political Attacks

During the 1960s and 1970s, recall, the rise of neo-corporatism was closely associated with the rise of socialist and social-democratic parties in Western Europe and with their expansive, pro-labor, welfare-state ideologies. But it was unwise for neo-corporatism to become so closely identified with a particular partisan or political agenda. For if that party or ideological position lost influence or was defeated at the polls, then corporatism would suffer a political loss as well.

That is precisely what happened in the 1980s and 1990s. The "revolution" (it was nothing short of that) against corporatism began with Margaret Thatcher, prime minister of Great Britain (1979–90), and, in a somewhat different way, with President Ronald Reagan of the United States (1980–88). Both Thatcher and Reagan campaigned against big government, against bloated social programs, against political cronyism and special favoritism, and in favor of freeing up the private sector. But Mrs. Thatcher also directed her attacks specifically against corporatism, actually using that term, and criticizing the corrupt influence of such corporatist groups as labor unions, teachers, and welfare recipients in infiltrating the public sector, taking it over for themselves, and using their inside access to carve out whole sectors of public policy (and public funds!) for themselves.[8] Mrs. Thatcher, as head of the Conservative Party, saw the agent of this hiving off as the Labor Party; hence, the further politicization of the corporatism issue. She vowed to carry out—and took active measures once in office to implement—a program that would not only reduce the size of the state but also reduce "corporatist" (by which she meant special interests) influence on public policy. Hence, corporatism was transformed from being a neutral term and a social science construct into a highly politically charged term with strongly negative connotations.

Since in the American political tradition corporatism is seldom if ever mentioned, Ronald Reagan approached this issue on terms different from Thatcher's. He never used the term "corporatism," only "big government" and "special interests" (Bill Clinton, a Democrat, would later use many of the same terms). But it was clear that what Reagan had in mind was the same incestuous relationship between interest groups and the state as did Thatcher. Moreover, as the Thatcher–Reagan revolution of reducing the state and freeing the private sector began to produce impressive economic results, other leaders followed suit. Not only did conservative leaders like Helmut Kohl in Germany, Carlson in Denmark, and Anibal Cavaco Silva in Portugal embrace the new free-market message, but soon even Socialists like François Mitterrand in France, Felipe González in Spain, and the Scandinavian

Socialists and Social Democrats had acknowledged the benefits of capitalism and the marketplace. Within a few years this revolution of what was called "neo-liberalism" (based on nineteenth-century free-market ideas) had a major impact on the rest of the world as well.

In Latin America, the other main area where corporatism has been concentrated, the critique of corporatism, reflecting that area's own traditions and level of development, was different from that in Europe.[9] Latin America, as a less-developed area, had not yet experienced much neo-corporatism; it still had leftovers from the earlier traditional (military, Church) corporatism, as well as an entrenched system of patrimonialism and special favoritism to such groups as labor unions, business elites, government bureaucrats, and the like. Hence, in Latin America, criticisms of corporatism did not concentrate so much on the system of tripartite relations among business, government, and the state as on the entrenched, privileged groups who had earlier gained legal recognition (juridical personality) from the state and then used that advantage as well as political patronage and payoffs to insinuate themselves deep within the vast Latin American state bureaucracy and to use their positions inside the system to gain wealth, perks, and special privileges for themselves. In Argentina, for example, scores of people would be "employed" on every train in the state-owned railway network when it only took two to three to run the train; many government workers held two, three, even four jobs simultaneously in the public sector and would show up for "work" only to collect their paychecks; artists, journalists, and much of the middle class collected government salaries and/or subsidies while at the same time holding down private-sector jobs; businessmen received contracts and entire monopolies from the state not on the basis of merit or competitive bidding but through special favoritism and inside politics; the armed forces similarly received special privileges from the state. And so on for virtually all groups.

In Latin America, therefore, the critique of corporatism was focused on this kind of generalized, corrupt, patronage-based, special favoritism and not so much on the neo-corporative relations among labor, management, and the state, as in Europe.

The Shrinking of the State

Whereas in the late 1970s political scientists and others were "rediscovering" the state and focusing on state–society relations (which was closely associated with the study of corporatism), by the late 1980s there was a different focus. Now the effort was to reduce the size of the state, deregulate, privatize, eliminate waste and bureaucracy, and reemphasize good, effective, streamlined government. This "revolution" in thinking had begun with Margaret Thatcher, Ronald Reagan, and the neo-conservative critique of Big Government, but by the late 1980s the trend had become a global movement. Almost everywhere the clarion call was to downsize the state and make it more efficient.

But with this downsizing, a further pillar was removed from the foundation of corporatism. For under corporatism, the state, along with business and labor, was one of the three main pillars on which corporatism rested. Now all three of these bases—Big Labor, Big Business, Big Government—were under attack, discredited, or (in the case of business) becoming so international as to be all but beyond the reach of any single country's corporative control regulations. So what would be left of corporatism if its three main institutional props were undermined?

Democratization

Beginning in the mid-1970s, and then accelerating with the collapse of the Warsaw Pact and the disintegration of the Soviet Union, the world experienced a great wave of democratizations. Starting in Southern Europe with Portugal, Greece, and Spain; then reaching into Latin America; next extending to East Asia (Taiwan, South Korea, the Philippines); growing and even *exploding* in Eastern Europe; and eventually reaching some parts of Africa and the Islamic world; this wave became a global phenomenon. With both authoritarianism and Marxism-Leninism now discredited, democracy emerged triumphant as the only viable government, the only legitimate alternative, what nearly everyone favored. With the decline and demise in many cases of authoritarianism, the state corporatism often associated with it went by the boards as well.

At first this revolution of democracy was limited to the political sphere: reestablishing the rule of law, writing new constitutions, holding elections, and upholding human rights. But soon this democratic revolution spilled over into the socioeconomic sphere as well. If democracy means freedom in the political sphere, it was reasoned, then it should also mean democracy in the social and economic arenas. That meant that, along with the classic political freedoms, all the corporative controls on social and interest-group activities, as well as the corporative regulations governing economic life (such as corporatively organized wage and price boards, production boards) would have to go. If the free and democratic exchange of ideas was to govern in the political realm, then the social and economic realms would have to be granted greater freedom as well. So the democratic wave from the mid-1970s to today resulted in a triple whammy delivered at corporatism: the decline or overthrow of authoritarianism and its accompanying corporatist controls, fewer controls and regimentation of interest-group life, and economically free markets that reduced heavy-handed corporatist regulations.

The Triumph of Neo-Liberalism

By the end of the 1980s the neo-liberal (free-market) ideology had triumphed virtually everywhere. Autarchy was inefficient and nonproductive, communism had collapsed, and capitalism had emerged victorious and virtually alone. And not just in Thatcher's England and Reagan's America. Along with democracy, neo-liberalism had become a global movement. In the United States and Western Europe these trends were most important, but in Latin America; East, South, and Southeast Asia; and Russia and Eastern Europe the march of private enterprise, free trade, and open markets was also impressive. Even socialist governments were forced to acknowledge—often reluctantly—the benefits of capital investments and free markets; so did the World Bank and other international lending agencies—historically the bastions of state-led development ideas. Neo-liberalism emerged as the new orthodoxy.

This trend is related to others already discussed. For clearly the triumph of neo-liberalism and its free-market ideology runs counter to the system of controls, both political and economic, associated with corporatism. The difference is that, by the late 1980s and on into the 1990s, neo-liberalism had become a truly global movement; and no other set of economic or political arrangements had sufficient legitimacy or the proven track record to serve as an alternative. In Mexico, for example, President Carlos Salinas (1988–94)—educated in the United States (Ph.D., Harvard, economics)—put into practice a neo-liberal program to privatize the Mexican economy and reduce the size of the public sector, which produced upward of 75 percent of GNP. As he proceeded with his economic reform program, the Mexican political system, organized on an authoritarian and corporatist basis, also began to open up to political movements that were liberal and independent from the state. In Mexico and virtually everywhere, the triumph of neo-liberalism economically also had major implications for the undermining of corporatism politically. In many countries (including Mexico and many parts of Asia), however, these changes were partial and incomplete, so corporatist and liberal institutions, statism and free markets, continued to coexist, often uncomfortably, side by side.

Austerity and Budget Cuts

The final factor accounting for the decline of corporatism is austerity and budget cuts. If neo-liberalism and its triumph were the main themes of the 1980s, then austerity, budget cuts, and downsizing have become the *leitmotif* of the 1990s. It is not just Newt Gingrich and the American congressional Republicans that have been forced to cut back the size of government in the 1990s; virtually everywhere, heavily taxed electorates demand that the state practice an unaccustomed budgetary prudence. Such cuts, everywhere, are controversial; electorates favor downsizing only until it is their entitlement that goes on the chopping block.

Austerity and budget cuts are also damaging to corporatism. Corporatism demands not just a big state and bureaucratic structure but also a vast array of social and welfare programs. Moreover, in the model of corporatist dynamics presented in chapter 5, corporatism demands an ever-expanding economic and social-welfare pie so there will always be new "pieces" to hand out to the clamoring new groups demanding a greater say in decision making and bigger pieces of the pie for themselves. But under austerity, neither a big state to deliver them nor such a vast array of social services can be afforded. Electorates everywhere are telling the state to rein in big spending, to provide greater efficiencies, to streamline and downsize. But as they do that, they may also be sounding the death knell for an expansive corporatism. Or are they?

Is Corporatism Dead?

In addition to the scholarly challenges analyzed in the first part of this chapter, corporatism has suffered some severe blows politically, "on the ground," over the course of the 1980s and 1990s. The broad political, economic, and social forces outlined above—away from authoritarianism, statism, socialism, and bigness and toward democracy, freedom, and open markets—undoubtedly have made the climate for corporatism more difficult. But it is much too early to sound corporatism's death knell. Several things need to be said.

First, although manifest, authoritarian-corporatism was formally repudiated in much of Latin America in favor of democracy in the last two decades, corporatism continues to be practiced there often below the surface and without calling it that. The power of such major corporative interests as the armed forces, the Church, the business elites, and other groups is still powerful. In addition, corporatism and liberalism now coexist in a variety of mixed, overlapping, crazy-quilt patterns. So while the official ideologies and political systems are democratic, pluralist, and republican, in practice corporatist structures and ways of doing things still abound.

Second, despite the pressures for democratization, the older form of authoritarian corporatism continues to exist in many important areas of Africa, the Middle East, and Asia. Indonesia's regime remains an authoritarian-corporatist one as yet almost completely untouched by the newer liberalizing currents; while South Korea, Taiwan, Singapore, Thailand, and the Philippines, although making progress toward democracy, still have important vestiges of their earlier corporatist-authoritarian pasts. As giant China moves toward capitalism and away from Marxism-Leninism, we should be entirely surprised if increased corporatist control mechanisms emerge there. Indeed, since corporatism in its manifest and statist form seems, as we saw in chapter 5, to be a product of the drive to modernization and of the transition between underdeveloped and developed, as Africa, the Middle East, and Asia move along this path toward greater development we can expect to see *more* corporatism there, rather than less.

Third, what about the already developed countries like the United States and Western Europe, where both the intellectual and the political critiques of corporatism have been strongest? Here the going gets trickier; several trends must be pointed out. The first is that while such figures as Margaret Thatcher and Ronald Reagan were severely critical of corporatism's entrenched interests and took some, largely rhetorical steps against them, *not much has happened yet.* Perhaps some groups have been weakened in some limited particulars, but the facts are that

the interest-group battle still goes on, these groups continue to insinuate themselves or to be incorporated into the bowels of the state, these
groups are still involved in policy decision making, and corporatism is
still regularly practiced at various government levels.

A second factor in Europe and the United States is that while the
focus of corporatist interest intermediation is changing, the practice of
corporatism has hardly changed at all. Thus while it is true that labor
unions and some other groups identified with one particular, perhaps
early form of corporatism are in decline, other groups and newer issues
are emerging—and the policy process is still corporatist. Here we have
in mind teachers' groups and the debate over education policy; various
health care groups (doctors, nurses, health maintenance organizations,
organizations of retired persons) and the debate over health policy;
welfare proponents and the debate over welfare reform; environmental
groups and the debate over the environment; and so on. These examples illustrate that it is not so much corporatism that is under attack or
disappearing, just one particular arena (labor–management relations)
that is now being restructured and taking new directions. Indeed we
might speculate that while an early, *industrial* phase of corporatist
tripartite relations is fading, new *postindustrial* issues (education,
health care, welfare, the environment, others) are coming to the fore.
And most of these continue to be dominated by corporatist or mixed
corporatist-liberal relations between societal groups and the state.

A third consideration is that perhaps the Thatcher–Reagan neo-liberal
revolution will prove to be only a passing phase. These leaders have
now been out of power for some time. In the United States the presidency of Bill Clinton with its focus on industrial policy, education
reform, health care restructuring, welfare reform, and the environment
brought corporatism back into vogue (even though continuing a long
tradition of not calling it that); in Great Britain the prospect is that
Tony Blair and the Labor Party will bring the notion of corporatist constit-
uencies and policymaking back into power. Indeed by the late 1990s the
neo-liberal wave in Europe, in both the West and the East (including
Russia), seemed to have passed, and in many countries socialist and
social-democratic parties, with their corporately organized bases, policies,
and decision making were enjoying new electoral triumphs. In Latin
America, too, after several years of practicing neo-liberalism, a large
amount of disillusionment had set in and there was considerable backslid-
ing toward statist, mercantilist, and corporatist forms.

So the critiques and political attacks on corporatism had less impact than originally thought—and their impact may have been only temporary. Moreover, it was only corporatism of one particular type (labor and industrial relations) and in one particular area (Western Europe) that was attacked; elsewhere, corporatism in its several varieties continued to be practiced, or to stage a comeback, or to be practiced in mixed forms. Even in Western Europe and the United States, where the criticisms and political attacks were strongest, the main results were (1) only a temporary glitch in the march of neo-corporatism and (2) a shift in the issues away from those identified with an earlier industrialism to those of a postindustrial society. In the Conclusion, therefore, we need to sum up all these arguments about corporatism and see what its influence is in the present circumstances and what it will be in the future.

Notes

1. Philippe C. Schmitter, "Still the Century of Corporatism?" *The Review of Politics* 36 (January 1974): 93–94.

2. The relationship of corporatism to culture is often associated—far too simplistically—to the writings of the present author; see, for example, Howard J. Wiarda (ed.), *Politics and Social Change in Latin America,* 3d ed. (Boulder, CO: Westview Press, 1992). The economic-structural approach is associated with Schmitter as in the essay cited above, while the corporatism-as-a-result-of-crisis argument comes from Alfred Stepan, *The State and Society: Peru in Comparative Perspective* (Princeton, NJ: Princeton University Press, 1978).

3. Peter Williamson, *Varieties of Corporatism: A Conceptual Discussion* (Cambridge: Cambridge University Press, 1985).

4. Wyn Grant (ed.), "Introduction," in *The Political Economy of Corporatism* (London: Macmillan, 1985).

5. Martin Heisler (ed.), "Introduction," in *Politics in Europe* (New York: McKay, 1974); also Heisler, "Corporate Pluralism Revisited: Where Is the Theory?" *Scandinavian Political Studies* 2 (1979): part 3.

6. Leo Panitch, "Recent Theorization of Corporatism: Reflections on a Growth Industry," *British Journal of Sociology* 31 (1980): 161–87.

7. See Howard J. Wiarda, *Corporatism and Development: The Portuguese Experience* (Amherst: University of Massachusetts Press, 1977).

8. Margaret Thatcher, *The Path to Power* (New York: HarperCollins, 1995).

9. Jorge E. Bustamante, *La Republica Corporativa* (Buenos Aires: EMECE Editores, 1988). For an English-language summary and explanation see Howard J. Wiarda, "Dismantling Corporatism: The Problem of Modernization in Latin America," *World Affairs* 156 (Spring 1994): 199–203.

Conclusion

The Universe of Corporatism

Corporatism is one of those ideas—like democracy, tyranny, and organicism—that has had a long history in Western political thought and practice. Its history is now over two thousand years old and it reaches back to the ancient Greeks, Romans, and the Bible. The notions of organic unity in society, of harmony between groups and classes, of community, solidarity, and working together, are all concepts with long pedigrees in Western theory and sociology. The corporatist organization of society is similarly a part of this hallowed tradition and is closely related to the solidarist and communitarian principles noted above.

But we now know better than previously that corporatism is and has been strongly present in other, non-Western societies as well. In African and Middle Eastern clanism, tribalism, and ethnic solidarity; in Indian notions of community and caste associations; and in East Asian Confucianism, family and group loyalty, and mutual community obligation— traditions that are parallel and remarkably close to the Western organicist and corporatist tradition—are strongly present. Latin America provides another interesting case because, while the area is a part of the Western tradition, it also has strong indigenous traditions that are often similarly corporatist; at the same time, Latin America represents a fragment of the Western, particularly Hispanic, tradition of the early sixteenth century that was feudal and medieval and whose corporatism reflected this earlier time period as well as the area's underdevelopment.

In all these societies, Western and non-Western alike, corporatist-like organizations stand as intermediaries between the individual and state, as transmission belts, constituting a web of associability that helps hold society together and gives it coherence and meaning. The forms of corporatism may vary greatly from country to country depending on history, culture, institutions, and level of development; but of corporatism's presence, ubiquitousness, and usefulness in a great variety of regimes there can be no doubt. It once was thought—in the writings of the great German sociologist Max Weber, for example, and in much of the 1960s literature on political development—that such "traditional institutions" as Confucianism, caste associations, or tribal organizations had to be eliminated or swept aside before a country could modernize. These institutions, including various forms of organic unity, solidarity, and corporatism, were thought to stand in the way of national development. But we now know that these institutions can serve as the glue that holds society together particularly in times of wrenching transitions; furthermore, that many of these so-called traditional institutions can become modernizing agencies taking on the roles assigned in other countries to interest groups, political parties, and deliverers of public policies. Newer interpretations thus point to the *positive* roles these groups can perform and the fact they may be more or less permanent rather than necessarily being swept away by the forces of modernization. At the same time, many of these agencies are similar or comparable to corporatist institutions in the West. So we now have to deal with both Western and non-Western traditions and varieties of corporatism, as well as with societies at different levels of corporatist development.

Corporatism is present in so many forms in so many countries, in fact, that we need to guard against the danger of it becoming too broad a concept. We have "discovered" or rediscovered corporatism not just in the developed Western countries, where the actual term was first used, but also, in different forms and incarnations, in a large number of developing and non-Western countries. Hence, our effort in this book to try to expand the universe of countries where corporatism is practiced while at the same time keeping in mind a clear definition and set of characteristics of corporatism (interest groups and associations integrated into the state system) as well as doing justice to the great variety of corporatist forms present in the world. It is and will continue to be a difficult juggling act to incorporate all these countries and the seemingly ubiquitous presence of corporatism into the necessity of being clear and coherent about the corporatism phenomenon.

Corporatism in Practice

In our analysis we detected four stages of corporatist development— keeping in mind that these are "ideal types" and that there are various mixed and fused forms as well as subtypes. *Traditional, historical, or "natural" corporatism* was characteristic of Europe in the Middle Ages, with its religious bodies, military orders, guilds, and estates; and of many Third World nations, with their tribes, clan groups, castes, and the like, in more recent times. Then, in the Western tradition following the French Revolution, a full-fledged *corporatist ideology* began to emerge that sought to recapture the solidarity and group harmony of the past, that was at first conservative and reactionary and later became more progressive as it wrestled with the realities (the rise of organized labor) of modern times. The non-Western Third World seldom developed a full corporatist ideology, but in the blends of traditional institutions with modernizing functions many of the same features were present.

The third stage we called *manifest corporatism;* it was most often bureaucratic, statist, and authoritarian. It was characteristic of many European countries in the 1920s and 1930s; of Latin America, off and on, from then until the 1970s; of much of East Asia in the 1960s, 1970s, and often beyond; and of many African and Middle Eastern countries even today. The fourth stage was modern, postindustrial, *neo-corporatism,* often referred to as societal corporatism, characteristic of many of the advanced, industrialized nations in recent decades and beginning to be present in the more successful of the developing nations (Argentina, Chile, Taiwan, Singapore) today.

Note that there is an implied progression in these four stages that gives our discussion of corporatism a dynamic, change-oriented quality. Traditional corporatism is related to feudalism, but, of course, that can take many different forms in different parts of the world. Then as societies begin to modernize, new groups (such as labor) and new, often disruptive social and political movements are set loose that force either a new political philosophy ("corporatism") or an adaptation (in much of the Third World) of traditional corporative institutions to new pressures. Manifest or state corporatism often emerges at this developmental stage in authoritarian forms to help control these forces (like organized labor or peasants) if they threaten to get out of hand or to instigate revolution, or in times of crisis (depression, war). Finally, once this authoritarian stage is superseded and its problems of early industrialism overcome, a country can often afford to move on to democratic, pluralist, socially just neo-corporatism. Neo-corporatism in turn can be democratic, pluralist, and functional, or it can slide off into corrupt, quasi-anarchic, semi-syndicalist forms.

Our main concern in this book has been with the two most recent forms of corporatism: the state or authoritarian variety and the societal or neo-corporatist forms. State corporatism disappeared from Western Europe (with the fall of communism it may reemerge in the transitional Eastern European countries) with the fall of the Franco and Salazar regimes in the mid-1970s and the departure of the Greek colonels. It has also faded in the more developed, better institutionalized countries of Latin America (Argentina, Chile, Brazil, Colombia, Mexico, Venezuela); but beneath the facade of elections and newly democratic constitutions in the less developed, less institutionalized countries (for example, in Central America) it is still strongly present. Similarly in East Asia: the more successful countries (Japan, South Korea, Singapore, Taiwan) have utilized corporatism for a time as a way to hold newly mobilized groups in check until they reach a certain threshold of economic development; but now, having crossed that threshold, they are relaxing their corporative controls, moving toward democracy, and instigating new, neo-corporative programs. But in Africa, the Middle East, and some other countries of Asia, which are both less developed and less confident about controlling the forces that modernization sets loose, either a form of traditional corporatism or corporatism in its statist, often dictatorial modes, remains in power.

Neo-corporatism is the most recent form, growing out of modern economic planning and the welfare state. In its early years neo-corporatism was mainly concerned with the tripartite relations among labor, business, and the state. It dealt with such issues as wages, production, social programs, labor benefits, and the like; it was associated with the early or intermediary stages of industrialism. That remains the main focus and situation in some developed and newly emergent countries. But recall that neo-corporatism was often closely associated with a pro-labor, socialist, and social-democratic agenda. As such it was subjected to strong political attack by conservatives such as Margaret Thatcher and Ronald Reagan; it was also undermined by the decline of unions, antistate sentiment, democratization, government austerity, and the neo-liberal agenda. The result was in some countries a certain decline in this older neo-corporatism and, at the same time, the emergence of neo-corporatist intermediation and decision making in such postindustrial policy arenas as education, health care, welfare, and environmentalism. These were not just newer issues than came up under the older neo-corporatism, but they also involved different corporatized groups as well: teachers' unions, organizations of retired persons, doctors, environmental groups, and so on.

Many, especially transitional or newly emergent countries, exhibit mixes of the older forms of statist corporatism with the newer forms of neo-corporatism. Japan, South Korea, and Taiwan have retained some of the strict controls of state corporatism while also moving toward the advanced social legislation of neo-corporatism. In Latin America many countries have made the transition to democracy in the political sphere while still keeping in place many of the controls of earlier state corporatism. In Argentina, Brazil, Mexico, Venezuela and other countries, state-controlled or tightly regulated interest groups exist side by side and often compete vigorously with liberal, independent interest groups organized on the basis of free associability. Similarly, many countries in that area call themselves free and democratic but still retain the club of corporatist controls—just in case things get out of hand and social unraveling begins. The debate over corporatism at this level also has become politicized (as it has in the advanced nations): the public is generally opposed to corporatist special privilege—until it is their favorite program or entitlement that is threatened.

It is hard to see how modern society can get around neo-corporatism, since economic planning and intensive interest-group consultation over social issues are now regularly and almost inevitably built into decision making. Both conservative and progressive groups and parties may advocate corporatist solutions—although often in different forms and on different issues. The precise forms and interest groups involved may change and the popularity of big bureaucracy and bureaucratic decision making will rise and fall, but it is likely that corporatism in one variety or another is here to stay. Similarly in developing nations: while one's personal values may lead one to prefer a democratic system, one can understand, given the disruptive forces that modernization ushers in, why it would be tempting for leaders in these countries to try to harness these currents through corporatism. It is only a fortunate few developing countries (such as Costa Rica) that have been able to achieve modernization while also holding fast to democratic values and practices. These comments suggest that in both developed and developing countries, corporatism will be with us for a long time to come.

These comments also suggest a research agenda: more case studies in individual country practices, more studies of corporatism in different policy issues, more comparative studies of corporatism, and more studies of how countries move from one form of corporatism to the next. Recall also that we suggested as a future frontier the study of corporatism at the international level and the interrelations between a country's domestic forms of corporatism and its role and representation in international bodies.

The Corporatist Model

Corporatism is not just a descriptive term used to picture certain institutions and practices; it is also a model of change and of society. Recall, that was the fifth definition of corporatism offered in chapter 1: corporatism as a social science paradigm comparable to (and often competitive with) the other great paradigms in the social sciences, liberal-pluralism and Marxism. To a considerable extent, corporatism has superseded and replaced these other models, which often describe older systems of politics and class or social relations; at the same time, the corporatist approach often needs to be used in conjunction with these other paradigms.

Most students in the fields of comparative politics or comparative development studies think of corporatism not as a model in any formal, mathematical sense, but more informally as an approach, a way of thinking and looking. Corporatism and its practice will never be so neat and precise that we can strictly quantify all its aspects for all countries, but it does provide a new and systematic way of looking at and understanding certain new and interesting social and political phenomena. In this sense, corporatism is an heuristic tool, a teaching device, a means to conceptualize certain social and political trends that other approaches are either silent on or provide inadequate insights to. It tells us what to be alert to, what to look for, what patterns and what markers to try to observe. No more than that—and no less either. So let us get away from this notion that corporatism has to be a model with formal, logical, testable propositions; instead—at least for now—let us think of it less formally, less pretentiously as a set of suggestions that alert us to new areas of study. In this we want to be as rigorous and systematic as possible, but such modeling in the social sciences need not be like a mathematical proof, a natural sciences lab experiment, or a philosophical "proof" to be useful. Our expectations for the corporatism model are considerably more modest than that.

The corporatist model alerts us to look for strong and bureaucratic states, strong interest and other groups, and the integration or incorporation of these into the state. Historically, such corporatist groups included religious organizations, guilds, military orders, clans, tribes, caste associations, estates, and other traditional associations. In modern times, the main focus of corporatism—and the foundation on which much of the structure of the modern state and society was built—was on industrial relations and the tripartite interconnections between organized labor, business, and the state. More recently we have seen a host of other associations—including teachers, retired persons, doctors, nurses, welfare recipients, environmentalists—enter into a similar symbiotic, corporatist-like relationship with the state on a host of new policy issues.

It is not corporatism if these groups simply organize to lobby to defend their own interests; that is liberal-pluralism. Instead—and the distinguishing mark of corporatism—it is the *integration* and *incorporation* (hence, the term *corporatism*) of these groups into the state structure, into actual policy decision making and, frequently, policy implementation too.

That means, for example, that not everything in the state or in policymaking is corporatism. Not all issues are dealt with through corporatist bargaining. For example, in the United States, the Supreme Court is relatively free from corporatist interest-group influences; and much of U.S. foreign and strategic policy is comparatively free of corporatist intermediation—although with the end of the Cold War and the greater influence of domestic politics on foreign policy, that is changing too. Similarly, if legislation in the Congress or policy in the executive branch is the result simply of competing interest groups, that does not make it necessarily corporatist. Rather, corporatism refers to a *structural* or *institutional* feature: the incorporation of these groups into the state system and thus into the actual government process.

With both labor and business thus incorporated into the state structure of many modern nations, the corporatist approach is particularly useful in studying such issues as labor legislation, social security, industrial policy, wage policy, and social welfare. Now, with teachers' unions deeply entrenched in the U.S. Department of Education, the corporatist approach is also useful for studying American education policy. With farmers controlling parts of the Department of Agriculture, the corporatist model also offers insights into farm policy. With

the powerful military-industrial complex so influential on defense ac-
quisitions (but not on actual policy), corporatism is useful there too.
And with the antinuclear and environmental groups moving into the
Department of Energy and the Environmental Protection Agency, one
can appreciate the utility of the corporatist model in understanding
policy emanating from there, too. Other agencies and government institutions could be listed, but these are sufficient to demonstrate the
patterns of new and rising ("creeping") corporatism.

One needs to be appropriately modest in making claims for the
corporatist approach. Not all policies nor all interest-group bargaining
reflect or are the expressions of corporatism. Some policies may
emerge more out of class conflict. Some result from electoral decisions. Some are the products of bureaucratic behavior. Others come
out of genuinely competitive interest-group pluralism. Where these
factors are dominant, other explanations and models beside the corporatist one need to be used. If that is the case, let us, by all means, use
other models. Another complication comes when policy is the result of
both bureaucratic behavior and corporatism, or both interest-group pluralism and corporatism. In these cases we may need to use both sets of
models depending on exactly what it is we are seeking to demonstrate.

The choice of which model or models to use is thus a pragmatic
one, in my view, not an ideological one. If a model derived from class
analysis, from bureaucratic behavior, or from an electoral decision is
useful and tells us what we want to know, then by all means let us use
it. But if a corporatist approach helps shed light on the issue we wish to
explore, then let us use that. Or some combination of models. These
need to be pragmatic, reasoned choices on the part of students and
scholars, not choices derived from ideological language or by those
with personal or methodological axes to grind. Having said all this,
however, we also should recognize that in the modern, complex,
postindustrial society, the arenas of policy decisions amenable to corporatist analyses have been expanding while the power of some other
explanatory models has been shrinking. The march of neo-liberalism
may change this situation in the future, but so far both corporatism and
the corporatist approach have exhibited remarkable staying power.

It is often tempting for advocates of the corporatist approach to elevate
a useful but still partial approach into a single and all-encompassing one,
to the exclusion of all others. Both modesty and the recognition that
the corporatist approach has its limits lead us to conclude that other

explanatory paradigms are also useful. Most of us who are not down-right ideologues or true believers about it think of corporatism as an often necessary approach but not a sufficient one. We find corporatism to be a useful explanatory device, but we do not seek to reify the concept. The corporatist framework often gives us new and fresh insights into the workings of the political process on some issues and in some countries, but not necessarily in all. It provides us with a handle, a perspective to understand some recent and probably expanding range of issues, but not all. The corporatist approach is helpful for the light it shines on certain issues, but it is not a full and complete explanation and no claim should be made that it is.

Corporatism has by now been widely accepted as an explanatory device in the comparative politics and comparative political development fields, particularly with regard to welfare policy, labor policy, social security, and the like. The present author has also profitably used it recently in a study of American *foreign* policymaking to examine the influence of corporatist groups on foreign affairs.[1] Unlike some other recent approaches in these fields, such as dependency theory or bureaucratic-authoritarianism, the corporatist approach is seen as less ideological, more pragmatic, and, therefore, more useful.[2] It has been decoupled from the earlier ideological corporatism and also, in this book, released from its sometimes too-close ties with particular regimes or political movements. Corporatism has, by now, been incorporated as one of the main approaches in the comparative politics field, but quietly and no longer with great controversy. The approach and concept have been widely accepted in most textbooks and studies in the field, no longer as a subject of great controversy and curiosity but simply (and more modestly) as a useful, pragmatic approach that offers insights into the workings of the political system on some issues—but not all.

We need, at the same time, to remain mindful of the criticisms, the traps, and the partisan usages to which the concept is still sometimes subjected. We need also to be aware of the larger social and political forces in modern society—such as recent antigovernment attitudes—that may in long-range terms shrink the domain and influence of corporatism. So far, although the rhetoric and political posturing have been strong, for the most part that has not happened. It is the case, however, that one form of corporatism—the neo-corporatism of the 1960s and 1970s that concentrated on business, labor, and the state—is being transfigured in the advanced nations into new forms of corporatism that focus on new issue areas and also bring new interest groups to the fore. Meanwhile, other countries, mainly in Latin America and East Asia, are just entering the neo-corporatist stage; and still others are yet practicing statist, authoritarian, and various mixed forms of corporatism.

Corporatism is widespread in both developed and developing nations; the next question is: Is it democratic? Can it be made both responsive to public policy needs and responsible to the electorate? These are large and difficult questions. The author's position is that he is not a corporatism ideologue or advocate, but as a social scientist he sees corporatism continuing to be present in a variety of regimes—perhaps increasingly more so. It cannot be wished away, and therefore we need both to recognize it and to deal with it realistically. Moreover, since corporatism is associated with big government, large-scale interest groups, big bureaucracy, and modern social and economic policy, it is likely that in the future, as many countries move in these directions, we will see more corporatism rather than less.

Such corporatist development is not inherently evil—unless we allow the changes ushered in to lead to greater separation between bureaucratic/corporatist decision making and active citizen participation and oversight. Some developing nations (and probably some former communist states) will doubtless continue to use the older forms of authoritarian corporatism. But the main trends in Europe, Asia, and Latin America are toward a more democratic, participatory, and socially just form of corporatism, here called neo-corporatism. In any corporatist regime, however, the temptation is often strong, and the bureaucratic pressures such, to separate decision making on important social and economic issues from democratic participation and responsibility. If corporatism is not only here to stay but often expanding in modern and modernizing states, then we as citizens need to make sure that it remains a democratic, pluralist, and responsible form of corporatism, and not an authoritarian, irresponsible form divorced from citizen participation and oversight.

All these comments point to the conclusion that corporatism in its several manifestations and forms will be with us for a long time to come. And since there also seem to be many new policy arenas in which corporatism is present, and many new transmutations of older into newer forms of corporatism, the corporatist approach offers seemingly endless opportunities for new areas of study and research. It also raises a host of important moral, political, and citizenship issues. Corporatism is an exciting concept and it helps open many doors; we commend it to a whole new generation of students and scholars who can use it profitably to look at a host of new and exciting issues and political changes.

Notes

1. For an application of corporatism to foreign policy see Howard J. Wiarda, *American Foreign Policy: Actors and Processes* (New York: HarperCollins, 1996).

2. For elaboration on these themes see the author's *Introduction to Comparative Politics* (Belmont, CA: Wadsworth, 1992).

Suggested Readings

Almond, Gabriel. "Corporatism, Pluralism and Professional Memory." *World Politics* 35 (1983): 245–60.

Azpiazu y Zulaice, José Joaquím. *The Corporative State.* St. Louis: Herder, 1951.

Beer, Samuel. *Modern British Politics.* London: Faber, 1969.

Berger, Suzanne (ed.). *Organizing Interests in Western Europe.* Cambridge: Cambridge University Press, 1981.

Bianchi, Robert. *Unruly Corporatism: Associational Life in Twentieth-Century Egypt.* New York: Oxford University Press, 1989.

Black, Antony. *Guilds and Civil Society in European Political Thought from the Twelfth Century to the Present.* Ithaca, NY: Cornell University Press, 1984.

Bowen, Ralph H. *German Theories of the Corporate State.* New York: McGraw-Hill, 1947.

Bustamante, Jorge. *La República Corporativa.* Buenos Aires: EMECE Editores, 1988.

Cawson, Alan. *Corporatism and Political Theory.* Oxford: Blackwell, 1986.

———. *Corporatism and Welfare.* London: Heinemann, 1982.

Cawson, Alan (ed.). *Organized Interests and the State.* London: Sage, 1985.

Chalmers, Douglas. "Corporatism and Comparative Politics." In Howard J. Wiarda (ed.), *New Directions in Comparative Politics,* 59–81. Boulder, CO: Westview, 1991.

Collier, David. "Trajectory of a Concept: 'Corporatism' in the Study of Latin American Politics." In Peter H. Smith (ed.), *Latin America in Comparative Perspective: New Approaches to Methods and Analysis,* 135–62. Boulder, CO: Westview, 1995.

Collier, Ruth Berins, and David Collier. "Inducements Versus Constraints: Disaggregating 'Corporatism'." *American Political Science Review* 73 (December 1979): 967–87.

———. *Shaping the Political Arena: Critical Junctures, the Labor Movement, and Regime Dynamics in Latin America.* Princeton, NJ: Princeton University Press, 1991.

Cox, Andrew, and Noel O'Sullivan (eds.). *The Corporate State: Corporatism and the State Tradition in Western Europe.* Cambridge: Cambridge University Press, 1988.

Diamant, Alfred. *Austrian Catholics and the First Republic.* Princeton, NJ: Princeton University Press, 1960.

Elbow, Matthew H. *French Corporative Theory, 1789–1948.* New York: Columbia University Press, 1953.

Erickson, Kenneth P. *The Brazilian Corporative State and Working Class Politics.* Berkeley: University of California Press, 1977.

Field, G. Lowell. *The Syndical and Corporative Institutions of Italian Fascism.* New York: Columbia University Press, 1938.

Fogelsong, Richard E., and Joel D. Wolfe (eds.). *The Politics of Economic Adjustment: Pluralism, Corporatism, and Privatization.* Westport, CT: Greenwood Press, 1989.

Gobeyn, Mark James. *Corporatist Decline in Advanced Capitalism.* Westport, CT: Greenwood Press, 1993.

Grant, Wyn (ed.), *The Political Economy of Corporatism.* London: Macmillan, 1985.

Griffith, Robert. "Dwight D. Eisenhower and the Corporate Commonwealth." *The American Historical Review* 87 (February 1982): 87–122.

Harris, Nigel. *Competition and the Corporate Society.* London: Methuen, 1972.

Harrison, M. (ed.). *Corporatism and the Welfare State.* Aldershot, UK: Gower, 1984.

Harvey, Neil. "The Difficult Transition: Neoliberalism and Neocorporatism in Mexico." In Neil Harvey (ed.), *Mexico: Dilemmas of Transition,* 4–26. London: British Academy Press, 1993.

Heisler, Martin. "Corporate Pluralism Revisited; Where Is the Theory?" *Scandinavian Political Studies* 2 (1979): part 3.

——— (ed.). *Politics in Europe: Structures and Processes in Some Postindustrial Democracies.* New York: McKay, 1974.

Johnson, Chalmers (ed.), *The Industrial Policy Debate.* San Francisco: Institute for Contemporary Studies, 1984.

Katzenstein, Peter. *Corporatism and Change: Austria, Switzerland, and the Politics of Industry.* Ithaca, NY: Cornell University Press, 1984.

Landauer, Carl. *Corporate State Ideologies: Historical Roots and Philosophical Origins.* Berkeley: University of California, Institute of International Studies, 1983.

La Palombara, Joseph. *Interest Groups in Italian Politics.* Princeton, NJ: Princeton University Press, 1964.

Lehmbruch, Gerhard, and Philippe C. Schmitter (eds.). *Patterns of Corporatist Policy-Making.* London: Sage, 1982.

Lowi, Theodore. *The End of Liberalism: Ideology, Policy, and the Crisis of Public Authority.* New York: Norton, 1969.

Maier, Charles. *Recasting Bourgeois Europe: Stabilization in France, Germany, and Italy in the Decade After World War I.* Princeton, NJ: Princeton University Press, 1988.

Malloy, James (ed.), *Authoritarianism and Corporatism in Latin America.* Pittsburgh: University of Pittsburgh Press, 1977.

Manoilesco, Mihail. *Le Siècle du corporatisme.* Paris: Felix Alcan, 1934.

Miller, Arthur Selwyn. *The Modern Corporate State: Private Governments and the American Constitution.* Westport, CT: Greenwood Press, 1976.

Mozaffar, Shaheen. "Clarifying Some Analytic Issues in Corporatism." In Julius E. Nyang'oro and Timothy M. Shaw (eds.). *Corporatism in Africa: Compara-*

tive Analysis and Practice, 45–66. Boulder, CO: Westview, 1989.

Nyang'oro, Julius E., and Timothy M. Shaw (eds.). *Corporatism in Africa: Comparative Analysis and Practice.* Boulder, CO: Westview Press, 1989.

Offe, Claus. "The Attribution of Public Status to Interest Groups: Some Observations on the West German Case." In Suzanne Berger (ed.), *Organizing Interests in Western Europe.* Cambridge: Cambridge University Press, 1981.

Pahl, R.E., and J.T. Winkler. "The Coming Corporatism." *Challenge* (March–April 1975): 28–35.

Palmer, David Scott, and Kevin Middlebrook. *Military Government and Corporatist Political Development: Lessons from Peru.* Beverly Hills, CA: Sage Professional Papers, Comparative Politics Series, 1975.

Pike, Frederick B., and Thomas Stritch (eds.). *The New Corporatism: Social and Political Structures in the Iberian World.* Notre Dame, IN: Notre Dame University Press, 1974.

Roberts, David D. *The Syndicalist Tradition and Italian Fascism.* Chapel Hill: University of North Carolina Press, 1979.

Robinson, Pearl. "Niger: Anatomy of a Neotraditional Corporatist State." *Comparative Politics* 24 (October 1991): 1–20.

Schmitter, Philippe C. "Corporatism Is Dead! Long Live Corporatism!" *Government and Opposition* 24 (Winter 1989): 54–73.

———. *Interest Conflict and Political Change in Brazil.* Stanford, CA: Stanford University Press, 1971.

———. "Still the Century of Corporatism?" *The Review of Politics* 36 (January 1974): 85–131.

Schmitter, Philippe C., and Gerhard Lehmbruch (eds.). *Trends Toward Corporatist Intermediation.* Beverly Hills, CA: Sage, 1979.

Scholten, Ilja (ed.). *Political Stability and Neo-Corporatism: Corporatist Integration and Societal Cleavages in Western Europe.* Beverly Hills: Sage, 1987.

Shonfield, Andrew. *Modern Capitalism.* London: Oxford University Press, 1965.

Stepan, Alfred. *The State and Society: Peru in Comparative Perspective.* Princeton, NJ: Princeton University Press, 1978.

Weber, Max. *The Theory of Social and Economic Organization.* New York: Free Press, 1964.

Wiarda, Howard J. *Corporatism and Development: The Portuguese Experience.* Amherst: University of Massachusetts Press, 1977.

———. *Corporatism and National Development in Latin America.* Boulder, CO: Westview Press, 1981.

———. *The Corporative Origins of the Iberian and Latin American Labor Relations Systems.* Amherst: University of Massachusetts, Labor Relations and Research Center, 1976.

———. *Democracy and Its Discontents: Development, Interdependence, and U.S. Policy in Latin America.* Lanham, MD: Rowman and Littlefield, 1995. Part 3.

———. "Dismantling Corporatism: The Problem of Modernization in Latin America." *World Affairs* 156 (Spring 1994): 199–203.

———. *From Corporatism to Neo-Syndicalism: The State, Organized Labor, and the Changing Industrial Relations Systems of Southern Europe.* Cambridge: Harvard University, Center for European Studies, 1981.

————. *Introduction to Comparative Politics.* Belmont, CA: Wadsworth, 1992.

————. *Politics in Iberia.* New York: HarperCollins, 1992.

————. "Toward a Framework for the Study of Political Change in the Iberic-Latin Tradition: The Corporative Model." *World Politics* 25 (January 1973): 206–35.

Wiarda, Howard J. (ed.). *Politics and Social Change in Latin America.* 3d ed. Boulder, CO: Westview, 1992.

Wilensky, H.L. *The New Corporatism, Centralization and the Welfare State.* London: Sage, 1976.

Williamson, Peter J. *Corporatism in Perspective: An Introductory Guide to Corporatist Theory.* London: Sage, 1989.

————. *Varieties of Corporatism: A Conceptual Discussion.* Cambridge: Cambridge University Press, 1985.

Winkler, J.T. "Corporatism." *Archives Européennes de Sociologie* 17 (1976): 100–36.

Zeigler, Harmon. *Pluralism, Corporatism, and Confucianism: Political Association and Conflict Regulation in the United States, Europe, and Taiwan.* Philadelphia: Temple University Press, 1988.

Index

Howard J. Wiarda is Professor of Political Science and the Leonard J. Horwitz Professor of Latin American and Iberian Studies at the University of Massachusetts/Amherst. He is also Senior Associate at the Center for Strategic and International Studies (CSIS) in Washington, DC. He is the author of numerous books, among them *Politics in Iberia: The Political Systems of Spain and Portugal, An Introduction to Comparative Politics, Latin American Politics and Development, New Directions in Comparative Politics, American Foreign Policy, Corporatism and Development: The Portuguese Experiment, Democracy and Its Discontents,* and *Corporatism and National Development in Latin America.*